FILM AND TELEVISION AFTER 9/11

FILM AND TELEVISION AFTER 9/11

Edited by Wheeler Winston Dixon

Southern Illinois University Press • *Carbondale*

Library of Congress Cataloging-in-Publication Data
Film and television after 9/11 / edited by Wheeler Winston Dixon.
    p. cm.
    Includes bibliographical references and index.
    1. Motion pictures—United States. 2. September 11 Terrorist Attacks, 2001. I.
Dixon, Wheeler W., 1950–
PN1993.5.U6 F477 2004
791.43'0973'090511—dc21   2003010378
ISBN 0-8093-2555-1 (alk. paper) — ISBN 0-8093-2556-X (pbk. ; alk. paper)

Printed on recycled paper. ♻

Contents

FILM AND TELEVISION AFTER 9/11

Introduction
Something Lost—Film after 9/11

Wheeler Winston Dixon

This volume reflects the thoughts of many in the film and media community who sense a definite shift in modes of perception, production, and audience reception for films such as *Black Hawk Down* (2001), *Collateral Damage* (2002), *We Were Soldiers* (2002), and other films that demonstrate a renewed audience appetite for narratives of conflict, reminiscent of the wave of filmmaking that surrounded American involvement in World War II. Unlike the Vietnam war, which was hotly contested throughout the United States, the attacks on the World Trade Center in New York and the Pentagon in Washington have galvanized the American public into a call for action, although the enemy being fought is both illusory and highly mobile, spreading throughout the world in numerous clandestine cells. The Bush administration is attempting to divert the public's attention with a war on Iraq, but this move is increasingly unpopular both at home and abroad. The movies, then, reflect this variety of impulses; some films seem to encourage the warrior spirit, while still others question it, and others still avoid the issue altogether.

While some contemporary films offer escapism, the bulk of mainstream American cinema since 9/11, whether the films were in production before the events of that day or not, seems centered on a desire to replicate the idea of the "just war," in which military reprisals, and the concomitant escalation of warfare, seem simultaneously inevitable and justified. Yet how will this play out in the months and years to come? How will these films shape the perception of other nations, for whom the American cinema is now our dominant cultural export? What sort of dialogue do these films establish? What kind of a public do they construct as their ideal viewer?

Beyond these questions, how do we now review the films of our shared cinematic past in light of these recent events? What effect will the events of 9/11 have on filmic genres? Are we about to replay the events of the 1940s and 1950s, albeit in a hyperstylized, MTV edited format? What other questions arise as we consider the films of the past, and the present, in view of this violent and tragic introduction to the twenty-first century?

I write these words on September 11, 2002, exactly one year after the attacks on the World Trade Center and the Pentagon. It has been an uneasy year, one that has seen the chasm between the rich and the poor widen. Our rights as U.S. citizens have been seriously eroded by the Patriot Act, signed into law a mere six weeks after the attacks of September 11. As an anonymous writer for the Associated Press noted in an article on September 11, 2002, the Patriot Act "tipped laws in the government's favor in 350 subject areas involving 40 federal agencies," creating, at least for the foreseeable future, a number of "fundamental changes to Americans' legal rights," including

- Freedom of association: Government may monitor religious and political institutions without suspecting criminal activity to assist terror investigation.
- Freedom of information: Government has closed once-public immigration hearings, has secretly detained hundreds of people without charges, and has encouraged bureaucrats to resist public records requests.
- Freedom of speech: Government may prosecute librarians or keepers of any other records if they tell anyone that the government subpoenaed information related to a terror investigation.
- Right to legal representation: Government may monitor federal prison jailhouse conversations between attorneys and clients, and deny lawyers to Americans accused of crimes.

- Freedom from unreasonable searches: Government may search and seize Americans' papers and effects without probable cause to assist terror investigation.
- Right to a speedy and public trial: Government may jail Americans indefinitely without a trial.
- Right to liberty: Americans may be jailed without being charged or being able to confront witnesses against them. ("Terrorism")

In this bleak landscape of personal loss, paranoia, and political cynicism, American culture has been forever changed. We have been through a traumatic election in 2000, in which the victor assumed the office of the presidency under a cloud of doubt and dissension. Thus a deeply contested election and then genuine tragedy—2,931 confirmed deaths, 47 persons reported dead, 25 missing, for a total of 3,003 victims of the worst terrorist attack on U.S. soil, dwarfing even the attack on Pearl Harbor—can be manipulated as political and social capital. War with Iraq seems inevitable, the dot-com crash has cost billions of dollars and thrown thousands of people out of work, pension funds have been looted, the national debt grows at an alarming rate, global warming is melting the polar ice caps, and television "news" channels broadcast an unremitting stream of propaganda that makes *1984* seem tame in comparison. In short, there's only one thing to do. Let's go to the movies and forget all about it!

In the days and weeks after 9/11, Hollywood momentarily abandoned the hyperviolent spectacles that dominated mainstream late 1990s cinema. Films were temporarily shelved, sequences featuring the World Trade Center were recut, and "family" films were rushed into release or production, to offer the public escape from the horrors of 9/11. Predictably, however, this reversal of fortune did not last long, and soon Hollywood was back to work on a series of highly successful "crash and burn" movies. But despite this rapid retrenchment, one salient fact remains: the memory of 9/11 can never be obliterated from the American national consciousness, no matter how crassly it is exploited for personal, political, or corporate gain. With the events of 9/11, America truly entered the twenty-first century, an era marked by uncertainty and danger, in which wars are conducted not by nations but by terrorist cells. Indeed, even one year later, words inevitably fail to describe the horror of 9/11, the terror of the passengers on the two jets that crashed into the twin towers, the agony of the literally thousands of people who perished in a matter of hours in the World Trade Center attack. And yet, as Jean Baudrillard notes, it is an event we have anticipated and, in a sense, specifically constructed. Writes Baudrillard,

> The countless disaster movies bear witness to this fantasy, which they clearly attempt to exorcise with images, drowning out the whole thing with special effects. But the universal attraction they exert, which is on a par with pornography, shows that acting-out is never very far away, the impulse to reject any system growing all the stronger as it approaches perfection or omnipotence. (7)

Commodified and repackaged, cheapened by commemorative plates or hastily assembled "memorial" videos, the stark human tragedy of 9/11 obliterated all attempts to comprehend the scope of its impact. 9/11 now joins July 4 and Memorial Day as dates of national remembrance, even as the United States struggles uncertainly toward its new position in a radically altered political landscape.

Nevertheless, production of "memorial" films and television programs continues unabated both in mainstream and marginal projects. By one count, there were at least sixty "memorial" programs on television during the week of September 11, 2002, alone, all shown on national broadcast and cable television channels (Stasi 82). Some were merely a rehash of existing footage with new commentary, while others were more thoughtful projects. Perhaps one of the most unusual films about 9/11 is the collective enterprise *11'09"01—September 11* (2002), directed by Samira Makhmalbaf, Claude Lelouch, Youssef Chahine, Danis Tanovic, Idrissa Ouedraogo, Ken Loach, Alejandro Gonzalez Inarritu, Amos Gitaï, Mira Nair, Sean Penn, and Íhohei Imamura. Denounced by *Variety* as "stridently anti-American" (Godard 1), *11'09"01* is composed of eleven short films made by eleven directors, each lasting eleven minutes, nine seconds, and one frame. Youssef Chahine and Ken Loach present episodes that are directly critical of American policy overseas, while Samira Makhmalbaf and Sean Penn weave more delicately personal tales. Several of the episodes of the film are critical of current U.S. policy, it is true, but they bring a welcome breath of dissenting opinion to current cinematic discourse on the attacks of 9/11. Alan Riding described *11'09"01* as seeming reminiscent of the French collective film *Loin de Vietnam,* the 1967 collaborative effort created by Jean-Luc Godard, Joris Ivens, William Klein, Claude Lelouch, Chris Marker, Alain Resnais, and Agnès Varda as an act of conscience against the war in Vietnam. Lelouch, still active, has returned to the battlements in *11'09"01,* which far from being anti-American, is more accurately critical of American *policy* in the wake of 9/11, a very different matter. When Riding spoke to Alain Brigand, the producer of *11'09"01,* Brigand noted that

> Sept. 11 was an American tragedy, but also a universal catastrophe. . . . The entire world shook, but what was it thinking? The directors were given total freedom to respond. The only constraints were time, a maximum budget of $400,000 each and a commitment not to promote hate or violence or to attack peoples, religions or cultures.

Most episodes are personal reflections on the tragedy viewed through different prisms like mourning, love, poverty, war, and refugees. "I think that rather than 11 shorts, we have a feature film of 11 sequences, like a mosaic," Brigand said.

> Samira Makhmalbaf of Iran imagined news of the attack on the twin towers reaching an Afghan refugee camp inside Iran. A young teacher tells her young pupils that a terrible tragedy has occurred in New York, and she asks them to remember the victims in a minute of silence. When she realizes that they do not understand, she leads them outside and has them look up at a tall chimney giving off smoke.
>
> No less touching is the short by Danis Tanovic of Bosnia, whose *No Man's Land* won the Academy Award for best Foreign Language film this year. He sets his episode among widows of the 7,000 victims

of the Srebrenica massacre in Bosnia on July 11, 1995. On the 11th of every month, they remember their dead. When news of Sept. 11 reaches them, they walk in protest "for them and for us."

More critical of the United States is the short by the veteran British director Ken Loach, who films Vladimir Vega, a Chilean exile in London, as he writes to families of victims of Sept. 11. In it he recalls that on the same day in 1973, a U.S.-backed coup overthrew the elected government of President Salvador Allende. Amid film of the coup, Vega writes, "Friends, your leaders set out to destroy us." And he ends: "We will remember you. I hope you will remember us."

[In the episode directed by] Youssef Chahine of Egypt . . . the ghost of a U.S. Marine killed in a terrorist attack in Beirut in 1983 is led to visit a Palestinian family in the Israeli-occupied West Bank as a young man leaves to carry out a suicide bombing. The young man's father blames the United States for supporting Israel. "Bush lets them decide who the terrorists are," he complains.

Alejandro Gonzalez Inarritu of Mexico chose to present "11 minutes of visual silence," with a black screen interrupted by images of bodies falling from the towers and the sound of a prayer for the dead by Mexican Chamula Indians, interrupted by Sept. 11 radio reports and street sounds.

Sean Penn's short also dwells on mourning, this time by an aged widower, played by Ernest Borgnine, who sleeps beside a nightdress of his dead wife and chooses her clothes each morning. Dozing as his TV reports the terrorist attack, he does not even notice the greater tragedy when the collapse of the towers allows sunlight to flood into his room. (Riding)

Such a film would be a welcome addition to the literature of films on 9/11 in the United States, but don't look for it to be released here anytime soon. If it is distributed at all, it will probably be in film festivals and on DVDs from foreign distributors. As Riding comments,

while *11'09"01—September 11* has been acquired for distribution in several European countries, Japan and Israel, [producer Alain Brigand] believed it was "too soon" for it to be shown in the United States. "People are still in shock," he said. "But I think that in time people will be able to see that Sept. 11 was an American drama, but also a drama that affected all of humanity." (Riding)

Even in other European countries, *11'09"01—September 11* remains controversial. As Pamela Sampson reports, the film was not well received in the Italian press. "It's garbage," the Italian daily *Il Foglio* said of the movie. "The French financiers recruit 11 well-known and some unknown directors to explain to us how the United States deserved what happened" (Sampson). While this seems far from the film's actual intent, the fact remains that the film's divided opinions reflect much of what the European community feels about the events of 9/11. A recent survey noted that "55 percent of Europeans believe U.S. foreign policy is partly to blame for the September 11 attacks, [according to] Agence France Press" (Sampson). When *11'09"01* was screened at the Toronto International Film Festival, audience response was mixed. As one reporter put it,

> After *Variety* labeled *11'09"01* "stridently anti-American," many [festival patrons] were expecting the worst. Instead, members of the media and film industry were treated . . . to a collection of films that were sometimes insightful, at times bewildering and occasionally darkly humorous. . . . Piers Handling, director of the film festival, said he thought the collection is a "very thoughtful piece of work." He said festival planners were well aware of the programming requirements near the anniversary. Two films—*11'09"01* and *The Guys,* both with Sept. 11 themes—[were shown as part of the festival]. . . . Handling said the film was "certainly not" anti-American. "The review that came out of *Variety* was a snap opinion on a very complex film," he said. "It's very easy to label something and once the label is there, it's hard to remove. The films are really quite remarkable. . . . Obviously these directors were very aware of the sensitivities surrounding the day. . . . This is an attempt to open a dialogue" [Handling said]. Handling compared *11'09"01* to another controversial film at [the Toronto] festival,

Michael Moore's *Bowling for Columbine* (2002) which offers a scathing account of gun culture in the United States. "Certainly Michael Moore's film *Bowling for Columbine* has been called anti-American. But it's by an American director and he's been quoted as saying he loves his country, he just wants to make America better." (Wherry)

But what about more conventional, U.S.-produced films on the subject of 9/11? As Benjamin Nugent rhetorically asks, "where's the 9/11 film?" The answer is that the films are on the way, but no one wants to be in too big a hurry to rush such a controversial and painful subject to the screen of your local multiplex.

The Guys, an indie film about a journalist and a mourning fire fighter, is in the works, but big-time filmmakers and TV executives still seem cautious about bringing the tragedy to the screen, worried they will be accused of bad taste. "No one wants to seem like an ambulance chaser, so they do it on the down low," says director Spike Lee. CBS has announced a TV movie on Flight 93, the hijacked plane that crashed in Pennsylvania. But a network spokesman stresses that the movie is still in development and might not ever see the light of day. Meanwhile, an NBC biopic on former New York City Mayor Rudy Giuliani is also undergoing close scrutiny for its handling of the tragedy. Jeff Gaspin, an NBC executive vice president in charge of movies, says the network is trying to figure out how many script pages should be devoted to Sept. 11. . . . The risk, he says, is coming off as exploitative. (Nugent)

Which isn't to say that we still don't want to see things get blown up on screen, so long as the event is safely fictional. We are assured by the very act of entering a movie theatre, the public domain of visual fiction, that what we are about to see is entirely a construct. And despite the carnage of 9/11, the more violent films currently in release seem to be doing perfectly well at the box office. David Ansen astutely comments,

Hollywood was not wrong in thinking we didn't want to see a lot of buildings blowing up (unless it was Mythical) or watch cartoon depictions of Arab terrorists. But that didn't mean the audience's appetite for violence and warfare was depleted, as the seers first predicted. Au contraire. War movies such as *Behind Enemy Lines* [2001] (its ad campaign re-tooled in basic red, white and blue) and the ultragraphic *Black Hawk Down* [2001] seemed to benefit from the wartime rhetoric emanating from the White House. . . . Perhaps the best gauge that things had returned to business as usual was the success of *The Sum of All Fears,* which was released in May [of 2002]. Here was a movie in which the nuclear destruction of Baltimore by terrorists (albeit of the neo-Nazi, wine-drinking variety) seems to have been taken utterly in popcorn stride by the audience. (Ansen)

More recent films, such as *Daredevil, Cold Mountain, Gods and Generals,* and *The Core* (all 2003), offer equally unrelenting spectacles of contemporary, futuristic, or historical destruction and carnage. Indeed, many people have said that watching the World Trade Center collapse was like watching a movie, simply because they had no other referent to fall back on in the face of such apocalyptic destruction. As analyst Harry Wilmer of the Institute for the Humanities commented, the scenes of 9/11

are images that nobody has seen before. . . . It's an archetypal image of the destruction of a monument in our commercial civilization. Nobody's ever seen a monument or a temple destroyed by some supernatural power. You can't take your eyes off some tragic thing that's happening. It's an instinctual reaction to horror—an utter fascination with it. (qtd. in Garcia)

Even Hollywood professionals were astounded by the violent spectacle they witnessed on television, brought live to the entire world at the moment it was actually happening. Said Lawrence Wright, screenwriter for *The Siege* (1998), which presented the fictional tale of the abduction of a U.S. military leader by a group of Muslim militants, the events of 9/11 were "cinematic in a kind of super-real way. It was too Hollywood. We could have never used [the tower attacks] in *The Siege*. It would be too impossible" (qtd. in Garcia). Film critic David Thomson agreed: "There was a horrible way in which the ghastly imagery of September 11 was stuff we had already made for ourselves as entertainment first. We had been gloating over [such imagery], making merry with it for a long time" (qtd. in Garcia).

One film that has been screened on CBS to general acclaim is *9/11*, a documentary by two young French filmmakers, Jules and Gedeon Naudet, who were working in New York City on a film examining the life of probationary firemen in the New York Fire Department, when the events of 9/11 erupted in the midst of shooting. As the press kit for the film recounts,

> [a]round 8:30 A.M. on September 11, the company received a routine call to investigate a suspected gas leak at an intersection less than a mile north of the World Trade Center. Jules went on the call. While there, he heard a roar from above and turned his camera upward, and captured the only known video of the first plane striking Tower 1. The firefighters jumped in their truck and sped to the fire, arriving within minutes. They were among the first firefighters to arrive. Jules followed the firefighters into Tower 1, and filmed as Battalion Chief Joseph Pfeifer helped set up the command center that coordinated the rescue of thousands inside the buildings. Jules remained with Chief Pfeifer for 45 minutes inside Tower 1 until the unexpected collapse of Tower 2. His camera kept rolling, and for a time provided the only light, as Chief Pfeifer led other firefighters in a desperate race to save themselves before it, too, collapsed. ("*9/11:* A Documentary")

Yet not everyone was pleased with the documentary's content, nor did they wish to see the images that the Naudet brothers had captured. When *9/11* was screened on the BBC as part of their World Service, many of the members of the victim's families complained that the footage brought back too many painful memories or was too exploitative. William Schmidt, a public prosecutor in Bergen County, New Jersey, home to many of the victims of 9/11 who worked in the World Trade Center, told reporters,

> "We are particularly concerned about the potentially negative psychological effects that graphic details of death and destruction may have

on the thousands of individuals who have been traumatized by the events of 11 September." . . . Carie Lemack, 26, president of Families of September 11, also expressed deep concern. "They're going to show my mom exploding," she said. Her mother, Judy Larocque, died on American Airlines Flight 11. "We are a country in which we don't show public executions, and that's basically what this boils down to." ("BBC")

Television critic Linda Stasi put it more bluntly:

> I lived though Sept. 11—I don't need to see the whole nightmare treated like some disaster movie by every media outlet on earth. . . . I don't want to watch the live memorials and I don't want to watch the concerts. I saw it happen. I worked it and lived it. . . . [I]f you choose to watch, however, the choices of tragic entertainment are limitless. (Stasi)

As one example of how "limitless" the viewing choices are, in Belgium, a "black comedy" film entitled *Afterman 2* held an open audition for Osama bin Laden look-alikes on September 11, 2002, exactly one year after the attacks on the World Trade Center and the Pentagon. Not surprisingly, the event attracted considerable attention, all of it negative. But Belgian cult horror director Rob Van Eyck was entirely unapologetic about the project, telling a reporter that 9/11 is

> "the only day when you are going to get such media coverage. When I did the casting in May, no one came." Asked whether auditioning on the first anniversary of the deadly attacks on the United States was not in bad taste, Van Eyck shrugged: "It's not pleasant for the Americans, but every day people are killed in attacks." . . . Van Eyck, 63, said his comic book–style film would be a black comedy. "It's good to shock people sometimes with humor. Americans are incapable of laughing at themselves." (Nguyen)

And, as the reporter correctly pointed out, "controversial American rapper Eminem dressed up as the elusive al Qaeda leader in the music video, *Without Me*" (Nguyen). For every cheap shot that the cinema may offer in the wake of the tragedy of 9/11, it seems clear that sincerely sympathetic projects will easily outnumber the more cynical enterprises. Yoko Ono, widow of ex-Beatle John Lennon, created a special short film for 9/11, which ran globally on MTV. In the film, she pleaded with viewers around the world one more time to "give peace a chance." Said Ono,

> Let's create peace, unity and light. I think John's words are needed just as much now as when they were written —"Imagine all the people living in peace" and Give Peace A Chance. . . . Like all of us, I'd like to see the human race survive, living in health and in love with each other. ("Yoko")

On American television, *Frontline* offered a two-hour documentary, *Campaign Against Terror,* while MSNBC presented *Target Manhattan,* a title redolent of a 1950s science fiction invasion thriller. PBS aired *Heroes of Ground Zero,* while A&E created a minute-by-minute of 9/11 entitled *Anatomy of September 11. Dateline* on NBC presented *America Remembers* as a special segment of the long-running reality series, and the Discovery Channel allowed viewers to witness *Portraits of Grief,* which focused on the victims of the attack. ABC, CBS, NBC, and BBC World News presented nonstop coverage of various memorial events on September 11, 2002, and even the Travel Channel felt compelled to create their own tribute, *World Trade Center: Triumph and Tragedy.* This onslaught of programming and counterprogramming scarcely gives one time to reflect and meditate on the true magnitude of the events of 9/11, as images of the collapsing twin towers are ceaselessly recycled to create "new" programming. Is this catharsis or exploitation? Can one pay respect to the dead through silence alone? These are not questions that television pauses to answer, as it indefatigably manufactures video documentaries for viewer consumption. On the other side of the coin, television embraces a return to the past, revamping reliable formats and series concepts to create an alternative escapist universe. More *Law and Order* spin-offs, *The Bachelorette,* a new version of *Dragnet, Joe Millionaire, The Anna Nicole Show,* another season of *The Sopranos,* and other reliable retreads all compete for the public's viewing attention, with the current flavor of

the month being "reality shows," which are relatively cheap to produce and require no scripts. And what of the contemporary American cinema as a classical theatrical experience? Eminem appears as a
troubled working-class rapper in *8 Mile* (2002), while Madonna and
her husband Guy Ritchie create a risible (and instantly invisible) re-
make of Lina Wertmuller's *Swept Away* (1974; remade 2002) with
Madonna in the title role. Reese Witherspoon returns with a simplistic
star vehicle, *Sweet Home Alabama* (2002), while Tim Allen reprises
his role as an ersatz St. Nicholas in *The Santa Clause 2* (2002). James
Ivory continues his string of costume dramas with *Le Divorce* (2003),
and Antonio Banderas and Lucy Liu star in the effects-laden action
thriller *Ballistic: Ecks vs. Sever* (2002) directed by the aptly named Kaos
(a "nom de cinema" for director Wych Kaosayananda). Elvira, Mis-
tress of the Dark, returns to the screen in the modestly budgeted camp
thriller *Elvira's Haunted Hills* (2002), and Tom Green gets another shot
at fleeting stardom with *Stealing Harvard* (2002). *The Four Feathers*,
the ultimate colonialist epic, has been released yet again, in its fifth
filming, with Heath Ledger in the lead role of Harry Faversham, while
Jackie Chan offers audiences his typical brand of acrobatic comedy
in *The Tuxedo* (2002). Edgier films, such as Michael Moore's much
praised *Bowling for Columbine* (2002), will inevitably receive limited
distribution ("starts Friday in selected cities"), while more mainstream
films such as *Auto Focus* (2002), Paul Schrader's biopic of the late Bob
Crane, starring Greg Kinnear as the ill-fated actor, will receive mar-
ginally wider distribution. Brett Ratner's *Red Dragon* (2002) offers up
Anthony Hopkin's Hannibal Lector one more time as the ultimate
serial killer; *I Spy*, the 1960s television series that once was considered
groundbreaking for its black and white casting (Bill Cosby and Robert Culp) gets a big-screen revamp with Eddie Murphy and Owen
Wilson; *Harry Potter and the Chamber of Secrets* (2002) attempts to
continue the lucrative franchise; and *Harry Potter and the Prisoner of
Azkaban* is slated to go before the cameras in 2003 for a 2004 release
with direction by Alfonso Cuarón, whose *Y Tu Mamá También*
(Mexico, 2002) was a surprise independent hit and one of the rare

contemporary foreign films that is afforded the luxury of a general release in American theaters. *Barbershop* (2002) is an ensemble African American feel-good film; *Analyze That* (2002) follows on the heels of *Analyze This* (1999); *Star Trek: Nemesis* (2002) reunites the cast of the teleseries *Star Trek: The Next Generation* in yet another deep-space adventure; *The Lord of the Rings: The Two Towers* (2002) continues Frodo's quest for the Ring; and we can, in coming years, look forward to more installments of the James Bond series, *Spider-Man II* and *III* (perhaps more), as well as other characters from the Marvel Comics stable in their own films, plus new adventures of Batman, Superman, and other assorted superheroes and heroines. Even Godzilla is making a comeback, still portrayed by a man in a monster suit, decimating Tokyo for the umpteenth time. And, as ever, Godzilla's appeal resides in his unremitting dedication to destruction. As one Japanese fan of the long-running series puts it, "He [Godzilla] relieves me of my stress, because he does things you are not supposed to do. I feel joy when I see the Tokyo government office or Ginza, where I work, destroyed by Godzilla. Godzilla films show me images that I cannot normally experience" (Belson). While some viewers seek versions of these films with the violence edited out, either through a variety of video filters and reedited versions sold to a small segment of the public (Lyman, B1, B5), for most audience members, the lure is the assurance of annihilation.

As always, there will be quirky, interesting films from home and abroad that once would have traveled the length of the no-longer-extant art house circuit, such as Jean-Pierre and Luc Dardenne's *The Son* (2002), Alexander Sokurov's *Russian Ark* (2002), Manoel de Oliviera's *The Uncertainty Principle* (2002), Marco Bellocchio's *My Mother's Smile* (2002), Alexander Payne's newest slice of Midwest agony, *About Schmidt* (2002), Aki Kaurismäki's *The Man Without a Past* (2002), and numerous other adventurous and challenging films that most of America will never get to see, except on DVD or pay-per-view long after their initial release. In short, business as usual, with ever-widening release patterns to fight off global piracy, increased hyperconglomerization of production and distribution, and ever-increasing budgets for production and publicity. The cinema as we know it in the 1960s, or even as late as the 1980s, has utterly vanished, to be replaced with an assembly line of factory-tooled genre vehicles that deliver predictable thrills to increasingly unsophisticated audiences. The past of cinema, except for a few carefully chosen canonical classics, has vanished; what matters to Hollywood is what will sell now. Audience marketing and research have become increasingly sophisticated, to the point that the lifetime world gross of any given film can be extrapolated from its earnings in the first seventy-two hours of its release. Nothing *can* be left to chance, if only because the financial stakes are so high. A few directors, such as Martin Scorsese, can take their time producing overblown epics such as *Gangs of New York,* but most directors today are mere traffic cops in the tradition of Steven Spielberg, whose sole responsibility is to bring a film in on time and under budget. There is little room for creative freedom in the new cinema unless one wishes to exist only in the rarefied world of film festivals. For the international marketplace, Hollywood product still dominates the box office as it has since World War I. And with the concomitant decline of foreign films released theatrically in the United States (in the twenty-first century, it is so much easier to remake them with American stars, in English, as with *Insomnia* [2002]), other cinematic cultures are being marginalized both at home and abroad. Most viewers have no idea that *Insomnia* was originally a 1997 Norwegian thriller starring Stellan Skarsgård; for them, it is simply the latest Al Pacino–Robin Williams vehicle, with Williams determinedly reinventing himself as a villain after years of increasingly saccharine vehicles finally lost favor with audiences. The original version of *Insomnia,* one might say, has been obliterated—it has, for all intents and purposes, ceased to exist. And for the final vanishing act, film itself will cease to exist in favor of digital projection within the next ten years, leaving what we have known as a movie finally ensconced as an artifact of twentieth-century culture. What will happen in the twenty-first century is more of the same but larger, louder, more violent, and more schematic. As the essays in this volume make clear, there will be a number of approaches to film in the post-9/11 era, but for mainstream cinema, spectacle, sex, and violence will continue to be the predominant commodities. As the film *Final Fantasy: The Spirits Within* (2001) demonstrated, movies can now do away with the human element entirely, in favor of synthespians who are voiced by well-known actors phoning in their chores from a recording booth. As Mark Hamill presciently remarked after filming the original *Star Wars* for director George Lucas in 1977, "if there were a way to make movies without actors, George would do it" (qtd. in Sullivan 71). Lucas is already far along in such a project and is one of the chief proponents of doing away with film altogether in favor of digital video projection. Other acolytes include Robert Rodriguez, the writer-director of *Spy Kids 2: Island of Lost Dreams* (2002), who began his career so promisingly with the resounding low-tech *El Mariachi* (1992) but soon fell under the spell of high-tech effects without substance in such films as *The Faculty* (1998) and *From Dusk till Dawn* (1996).

But what other films will be made in the future? What can we say about them now, and what sorts of themes will they address? In his essay "Architectural Nostalgia and the New York City Skyline on Film," Steven Jay Schneider argues,

> While the state of cinema theory, production, and culture (in all its aspects) is still in flux in America after the events of September 11, 2001, one thing that definitely has changed—at least for those with a prior physical or emotional connection with New York City and its distinctive skyline—is audience reception when it comes to scenes in fiction films, whatever the genre, that depict lower Manhattan either prior to or after the destruction of the World Trade Center towers. . . . I consider a number of examples of post-9/11 production strategies and audience responses . . . with respect to images of the New York City skyline in various Hollywood feature films. . . . My aim is to better understand the highly particular sense of "architectural nostalgia" that such images—some with the World Trade Center intact, others with the twin towers already missing from view—can be said

to have evoked in many spectators, current or former New York residents in particular.

In an early draft of "The Shadow of the World Trade Center Is Climbing My Memory of Civilization," Murray Pomerance notes that

> September 11, 2002, has been widely considered in causative terms as what Kenneth Burke would have called the motive for both events and explanations in social and filmic worlds. My essay uses a modified version of Goffman's "biographical reconstruction" to examine the catastrophe as a pretext for redefinition in light of present experience of filmic material produced earlier; specifically, the trope of the uncivilized barbaric creature affiliated with the American—indeed, the New York—architectural triumph. A close analysis of the 1933 and 1976 films *King Kong* attends to the "invasive monster," the "crisis of civilization," the sociopolitical meaning of the skyscraper, and the air attack on the building—all newly interpretable in light of contemporary readings of September 11. Special attention is given to the use of the World Trade Center in the 1976 Guillermin film, and the fact that its presence has become ghostly: given their status within the narratives, were the skyscrapers of *Kong* not, perhaps, always more symbolic and ethereal than corporate and financial in status? My argument is not that *King Kong* was a foreshadowing but that seen in light of September 11, it must be understood as open to new interpretation.

David Sterritt's essay, "Representing Atrocity: From the Holocaust to September 11," argues that

> [t]he attacks of September 11 unleashed waves of media representation that both recall and contrast with representations of the Holocaust and its horrors. . . . Chronicles of the Holocaust necessarily contain little authentic moving-image documentation, while the occurrences of 9/11 became internationally visible when they were still taking place. Conversely, the physical tortures of the Holocaust have reached public awareness most vividly through images of atrocity captured after the Nazi camps were liberated, whereas the physical containment of the damage inflicted on September 11—facilitated

by the nature of the attacks and the fact that the World Trade Center towers imploded instead of scattering their wreckage outward—rendered the destruction of human life almost invisible to the eye. The popular media rushed to compensate for this invisibility with a blitz of belligerent journalism on related matters, hammering incessantly on aspects of the case that are readily turned into narrative (e.g., the hunt for Osama bin Laden) and seizing on a fitfully fought, nebulously defined "war against terrorism" as a durable support for commercially marketable "public affairs" coverage.

In this context, note the progression of Holocaust representation through several stages, beginning with the poetic evocations of Alain Resnais's *Night and Fog* (*Nuit et brouillard,* 1955), then moving through more conventional documentaries and such widely disseminated narrative movies as Otto Preminger's *Exodus* (1960) and Stanley Kramer's *Judgment at Nuremberg* (1961), and turning in more recent years to the intellectually sophisticated accounts of such cinematic historians as Marcel Ophuls and Claude Lanzmann, who have chosen to omit all "atrocity footage" from their works. Also interesting are the parallels among the avoidance of atrocity images in films by Ophuls and Lanzmann, the homemade tributes placed near the World Trade Center site by survivors and mourners, and the work of an artist like Christian Boltanski, who has skirted the twin pitfalls of sensationalism and sentimentality by exploring the Holocaust through ephemeral materials that achieve resonance through their very refusal of monumental form.

In an early draft of "'America under Attack': Pearl Harbor, 9/11, and History in Media," Marcia Landy examines

> films such as *Pearl Harbor* and *We Were Soldiers* to explore the "means and ends" of historicizing in relation to the aftermath of 9/11. Drawing on the writings of such critics as Giorgio Agamben and Carlo Ginzburg, and on Michael Hardt and Antonio Negri's *Empire*, I focus on the nature and stakes of historical parallels in recent cinema. These films draw shamelessly, disingenuously, and selectively on the past. My essay is an attempt to understand *(1)* what appears to rep-

resent a familiar commonsense phenomenon to account for 9/11 and for an already established cultural language for modern catastrophe and crisis and *(2)* where these films offer a different discursive mode in relation to their affective investments, a mode not necessarily reassuring but imperative to understand.

In his essay "City Films, Modern Spatiality, and the End of the World Trade Center," Juan A. Suárez argues that one must

> reconsider the city film, an important subgenre in the experimental tradition, in light of the events of 9/11 and, conversely, to relate the rise, demise, and mourning of the World Trade Center (WTC) to the modernist regimes of spatiality and representation that inform city films. The attack on the WTC indelibly linked the spectacle of modernity, of which the twin towers were a prominent emblem, with urban ruin and devastation. Skyscraper architecture and gridlike design, signifiers of modernist utopia, universal rationality, and technological control, could not stand the return of modernity's others. Ruins, fanatical fundamentalism, and impoverished peripheries came back to haunt a center that had at once created them and turned them into its absolute others. Inaugurated by Paul Strand and Charles Sheeler's *Manhatta* (1921), city films, also called city symphonies, dwelled extensively on the dialectics of center and margin, spectacle and counterspectacle, novelty and ruin. Their style and iconography embodied many of the tensions that have recently exploded in the face of the metropolis. For this reason, it seems urgent to reconsider the genre as an incisive meditation on the embattled spaces of modernity and on the imbalances and contingencies of an aesthetic and social project that seems, today more than ever, dangerously out of reach.

Turning to televisual spectacle, Ina Rae Hark examines the television show *24* in her essay "'Today Is the Longest Day of My Life': *24* as Mirror Narrative of 9/11." She notes in an early essay,

> The Fox television series *24* concentrates a multifront political conspiracy and the race to prevent its accomplishing its goals into a single

day, that of the California presidential primary. This day unfolds in hour installments over the nine months of a television season. *24* contains some eerie and mostly fortuitous (since the show was planned out and much of it filmed prior to the terrorist attacks) parallels to the events of September 11, a multifront attack on America that has become known by the date on which it occurred and whose ramifications are playing themselves out concurrently with the run of *24*. In comparing the two, we can see how, though the real terrorist attacks were orchestrated for media coverage, U.S. network television cannot cover 9/11 nor dramatize an analogous terrorist assault without allowing personal melodramatics to stand in for complex political analysis.

Addressing the issues of performativity and conformity to generic standards in her essay "The How-To Manual, the Prequel, and the Sequel in Post-9/11 Cinema," Rebecca Bell-Metereau notes,

> In the period leading up to and following September 11, 2001, a number of cultural critics have recognized what Umberto Eco calls "Ur-Fascism," a culture of paranoia that values sacrifice, obedience, the cult of the hero, and the doctrine of constant warfare. . . . Women figure importantly as iconic devices in films that demonstrate the kinds of roles they play in the ur-fascist drama. Examples include the scapegoat and cause of downfall in *Independence Day* (1996), the sexual prize for which young men lay down their lives in *Pearl Harbor* (2001), and finally, the doyenne of the domestic world in *Panic Room* (2002). One may look at the growing number of militaristic movies, temporarily upstaged by real-life events but waiting in the wings like prima ballerinas, to see that the media not only reported but helped create a siege mentality, followed by a reaction of panic and consequent thirst for revenge. Clear patterns appear in the roles women have played in some of the most popular box-office films from before and after 9/11. They are viewed variously as scapegoats for blunders, as excuses for mayhem, and finally as participants in "justified" revenge, both in the public and private spheres of film narratives.

In a different vein, Mikita Brottman's essay "The Fascination of the Abomination: The Censored Images of 9/11" explores the images we *didn't* want to see. As she notes,

> any discussion of the events of September 11 on American television is still characterized by highly overcharged rhetoric, including the widespread use of the word *horror*. . . . However, despite all the rhetoric, television coverage of the events of 9/11 brought us no visual images to endorse these recurrent assertions of "horror." We saw planes crashing into the World Trade Center, which was spectacular. We saw the towers collapse, which was incredible. We saw huge clouds of smoke and piles of rubble, buildings covered in dust and ashes, people running in alarm through the streets of lower Manhattan. Later, we saw sobbing widows grieving over their missing husbands; we saw firemen and police officers mourning their valiant colleagues—but horror? If horror is defined as visual representations of violence done to the human body, most NC-17–rated films contain more horror than any station's broadcast of the events of 9/11. If the American television coverage of the events of September 11 had been an Arnold Schwarzenegger movie, people would be asking for their money back.

In his essay "Mohsen Makhmalbaf's *Kandahar:* Lifting a Veil on Afghanistan," Philip Mosley examines this prescient work, released shortly after the events of 9/11. Mosley notes in an early draft,

> Set in 1999, *Kandahar* (2001), by Iranian director Mohsen Makhmalbaf, is based on the true story of an Afghan-born Canadian woman journalist who undertakes a perilous journey across Afghanistan in an attempt to reach her suicidal sister in Kandahar. Visually striking, the film addresses matters that have preoccupied the West before and after the events of September 11, such as the plight of land mine victims, the indoctrination of impressionable minds, and the systematic social repression (especially of women) practiced by the Taliban. The film yields further complex meanings from its positioning as a critique of Islamic fundamentalism from within that society's orbit of cultural production (specifically from within the parameters of Iranian cinema),

while its circulation to Western audiences raises questions about its role in mediating the events of September 2001.

In his essay "Reel Terror Post 9/11," Jonathan Markovitz examines the big-budget spectacle films that dominate the world market. He argues,

> The September 11 attacks threatened to disrupt virtually every form of American cultural production, as pundits hastened to mourn the death of irony and Hollywood studios frantically began to reshuffle their release schedules. *Collateral Damage* (2002) and *Big Trouble* (2002) were moved to later dates because of a concern that terrorism might have temporarily lost some of its entertainment value, while the releases of *Behind Enemy Lines* (2001) and *Black Hawk Down* (2001) were moved forward, reflecting the fact that highly militaristic displays of patriotism, never entirely out of vogue, suddenly had newfound cachet. (*Black Hawk Down* also benefited from what then seemed like a strong possibility that the Bush administration's "war on terror" would soon expand to Somalia.) Hollywood has a long history of turning widespread fears into cinematic spectacles, but never before has the source of those fears been so singular, so easily isolated, or so thoroughly disseminated to national and international audiences. The box-office receipts for *Behind Enemy Lines* and *Black Hawk Down* suggest that there is still a market for celluloid violence, but now the exploding buildings and dead bodies displayed on screen are likely to be understood in entirely new ways. For audience members comparing these images to those that flickered across their television screens on September 11, suspension of disbelief has become impossible, as the artifice of cinematic terror is now apparent in dramatically new ways. In this context, the popularity of special effects–laden blockbusters may have less to do with their correspondence to real-life events and more to do with playing to an audience desire for revenge. The stark rhetoric of the Bush administration's quest to eradicate "evil" finds a perfect correlate in films that cast A-list Hollywood stars in battles against the calculating and murderous violence of always highly racialized terrorist "others." At the same time, films such as *Panic Room* have

taken an introspective (and claustrophobic) turn, finding resonance with audiences whose concerns about personal security and anxieties about the everyday world have been intensified in the current political climate. This essay examines the nature and cultural resonance of cinematic fear and terror in a post-9/11 world and asks whose fears are reflected and reinforced on the silver screen, and at what cost.

And finally, in an early draft of her contribution to this volume, "*Survivors* in *The West Wing*: 9/11 and the United States of Emergency," Isabelle Freda discusses the manner in which

> [t]he attacks of September 11 seemed to effect a national unity that pivoted on the figure of the president. Surprisingly, for some political observers at least, the president emerged from Air Force One on September 11 as a newly depoliticized—and newly empowered—entity, expected to "lead" the nation in a time of extreme crisis. A broad passivity on the part of the press and the media as a whole contributed to this phenomenon. The visual and rhetorical lineaments of the President's new role are not without precedent, in either popular culture or political history and theory. Cinematic and televisual intertexts provide crucial interpretive paths for the analysis of the manner in which politics has been so quickly submerged beneath a discourse of survival, fear and national unity after September 11. Understanding the unfolding of events after 9/11 requires a reflection on the manner in which the president and civic society is conveyed in film and television: not only in shows such as *The West Wing* but also in *Big Brother* and *Survivor*. In this light, the sense of uncertainty that already haunted the American political and social landscape prior to 9/11 has only been exacerbated by the terrorist threat, and the declaration of unlimited war becomes a possible opening for the return (or exacerbation of) what Arthur Schlesinger has described as the "imperial presidency," that is, a president who takes extraordinary powers (of secrecy, surveillance, and military action) in a time of "emergency."

All of these essays share a common thread; a desire to understand how the images that we visually consume on a daily basis inform our understanding of both the world and the political and social systems that govern it. Something *has* been lost in the aftermath of 9/11; the reality of destruction and physical violence has been made concrete and immediate. The deaths we witnessed when the twin towers fell were staged, but they were *real*—real suffering, real pain, and real loss. And yet it seems that our appetite for destruction has remained intact. For a short while, viewers were acutely conscious of the actual human toll of the tragedy of 9/11, but now, the images that so horrified us on September 11, 2001, have entered the iconic lexicon of history, along with the Zapruder film, the Hindenberg disaster, and footage of Nazi atrocities. Endlessly repeated, they have lost much of their impact to shock and become abstract images, as in the Rodney King beatings, to be played and replayed at will. Indeed, images of the disaster have already found their way into veejay mixes for techno concerts, or "raves," where veejays (video jockeys) mix video images stored on a computer into a light show reminiscent of the happenings of the 1960s and throw them onto a huge screen to the accompaniment of a live performer or prerecorded music.[1] Certainly no disaster in history has been as well documented, with a variety of news cameras and amateur camcorders. Literally thousands of hours of footage exist of the events of 9/11. What will we do with them? How will we process them? What sort of films will they inspire commercial and noncommercial film- and videomakers to create? These are some of the questions this volume seeks to answer as a first interpretational gesture toward the cinema of the twenty-first century.

Note

1. See Glaser for a discussion of this new phenomenon of cinema as animated wallpaper.

Works Cited and Consulted

Annan, David. *Catastrophe: The End of the Cinema?* London: Bounty, 1975.
Ansen, David. "The Arts after 9-11: Movies—Hollywood Tweaked Films with Touchy Subjects, but the Audience's Appetite for Violence Remained

Unchanged." *MSNBC.com.* Sept. 11, 2002. <http://www.msnbc.com/news/800374.asp?cp1=1>.

Bataille, Georges. *Theory of Religion.* Trans. Robert Haryle. New York: Zone, 1992.

Baudrillard, Jean. *The Spirit of Terrorism and Requiem for the Twin Towers.* Trans. Chris Turner. London: Verso, 2002.

"BBC Defends Showing 9/11 Film." *BBC News Online.* July 22, 2002. Sept. 11, 2002. <http://news.bbc.co.uk/1/hi/entertainment/tv_and_radio/2142593.stm>.

Belson, Ken. "The Majestic Godzilla Stomps On." *International Herald Tribune* Sept. 12, 2002: 18.

Berlin, Joey. *Toxic Fame: Celebrities Speak on Stardom.* Detroit: Visible Ink, 1996.

Chomsky, Noam. *9-11.* New York: Seven Stories, 2001.

Clymer, Adam, and Janet Elder. "Poll Finds Unease on Terror Fight and Concerns about War on Iraq." *New York Times* Sept. 8, 2002: 1, 14.

Davies, Phillip John, and Paul Wells, eds. *American Film and Politics from Reagan to Bush Jr.* Manchester, UK: Manchester UP, 2002.

Debord, Guy. *Society of the Spectacle and Other Films.* London: Rebel, 1992.

Eco, Umberto, Richard Rorty, Jonathan Culler, and Christine Brooke-Rose. *Interpretation and Overinterpretation.* Ed. Stefan Collini. Cambridge, UK: Cambridge UP, 1992.

Edozien, Frankie, Robert Hardt Jr., and Kati Cornell Smith. "'Monumental' Mistake: Even Pal Pols Pooh Pooh Rudy's Memorial Idea." *New York Post* Sept. 3, 2002: 2.

Erlanger, Stephen. "The Triumph of the Aesthetic Will." *International Herald Tribune* Aug. 31–Sept. 1, 2002: 20.

Farouk-Sluglett, Marion, and Peter Sluglett. *Iraq since 1958: From Revolution to Dictatorship.* London: Tauris, 2001.

Foreman, Jonathan. "Baghdad Death Trap? Not Bloody Likely." *New York Post* Sept. 3, 2002: 25.

Fournier, Ron. "Nation on Alert." *Lincoln Journal Star* Sept. 11, 2002: 1A, 2A.

Garcia, Chris. "Images of 9/11 Seared into Collective Memory." *Cox News-*

papers Online. Sept. 11, 2002. <http://wwwcoxnews.com/newsservice/stories/2002/0911-IMAGES.html>.

Glaser, Mark. "Making Digital Images Dance to a Rock Beat." *New York Times* Sept. 19, 2002: E1, E5.

Godard, François. "Canal Plus 9/11 Pic Courts Controversy." *Daily Variety* Aug. 21, 2002: 1, 20.

Hentoff, Nat. "General Ashcroft's Detention Camps: Time to Call for His Resignation. *Village Voice* Sept. 4–10, 2002: 30.

Herman, Edward S., and Noam Chomsky. *Manufacturing Consent: The Political Economy of the Mass Media.* New York: Pantheon, 1988.

Hoge, James F. Jr., and Gideon Rose, eds. *How Did This Happen?: Terrorism and the New War.* New York: Public Affairs, 2001.

James, Caryn. "Television's Special Day of Pain and Comfort." *New York Times* Sept. 6, 2002: B1, B21.

Johnson, Christopher. *Derrida: The Scene of Writing.* London: Phoenix, 1997.

Keane, Stephen. *Disaster Movies: The Cinema of Catastrophe.* London: Wallflower, 2001.

King, Geoff. *Spectacular Narratives: Hollywood in the Age of the Blockbuster.* London: Tauris, 2000.

Lapham, Lewis H. "The Road to Babylon: Searching for Targets in Iraq." *Harper's Magazine* Oct. 2002: 35–41.

Leurs, Jon, ed. *The End of Cinema As We Know It: American Film in the Nineties.* New York: New York UP, 2001.

Lipkin, Steven N. *Real Emotional Logic: Film and Television Docudrama as Persuasive Practice.* Carbondale: Southern Illinois UP, 2002.

Lucanio, Patrick. *Them or Us: Archetypal Interpretations of Fifties Alien Invasion Films.* Bloomington: Indiana UP, 1987.

Lyman, Rick. "Hollywood Balks at High-Tech Sanitizers: Some Video Customers Want Tamer Films, and Entrepreneurs Rush to Comply." *New York Times* Sept. 19, 2002: B1, B5.

"Marketing Violent Entertainment to Children: FTC Releases Report on the Marketing of Violent Entertainment to Children." *Federal Trade Commission.* Sept. 11, 2002. <http://.www.ftc.gov/opa/2000/09/youthviol.htm>.

Menard, Louis. "Faith, Hope, and Clarity." *New Yorker* Sept. 16, 2002: 98–104.

"New Twin Towers Footage on Channel Five." *Guardian Unlimited Online.* Sept. 11, 2002. <http://media.guardian.co.uk/september11/story/9,11469,762574,00.html>.

Nguyen, Katie. "Belgian Bin Laden Lookalikes Audition on 9/11." *Reuters.com.* Sept. 11, 2002. <http://www.google.com/search?hl=ISO-8859-1&q=%F11+movies>.

"*9/11:* A Documentary by Jules and Gedeon Naudet." *frenchculture.org.* Cultural Services of the French Embassy in the U.S. Sept. 11, 2002. <http://www.frenchculture.org/tv/programs/naudet911.html>.

"9/11 Film Stirs Controversy." *CBSNews.com.* Sept. 5, 2002. Sept. 11, 2002. <http://www.cbsnews.com/stories/2002/09/05/entertainment/main520958.shtml>.

Nugent, Benjamin. "Where's the 9/11 Film?" *Time.com.* Sept. 11, 2002. <http://www.time.com/time/magazine/article/0,9717,1101020909-346250,00.html>.

Perlez, Jane. "Across the Arab World, Anger at U.S. Rises to an Unparalleled High." *International Herald Tribune* Sept. 12, 2002: 8.

Preston, Julia. "U.N. Spy Photos Show New Building at Iraqi Nuclear Sites." *New York Times* Sept. 6, 2002: A10.

Ridgeway, James. "Now Fear This." *Village Voice* Sept. 4–10, 2002: 32.

Riding, Alan. "A 'Mosaic' of Projections on '11'09.'" *International Herald Tribune Online.* Sept. 11, 2002. <http://www.iht.com/articles/70113.htm>.

Sampson, Pamela. "9/11 Film gets Negative Reviews." *Washington Times Online.* Sept. 11, 2002. <http://www.washtimes.com/world/20020905-2036119.htm>.

Sardar, Ziauddin, and Merryl Wyn Davies. *Why Do People Hate America?* Cambridge, UK: Icon, 2002.

Schaefer, Stephen. "In *Signs,* Gibson Sees Reflections of 9/11." *Boston Herald.com.* Sept. 11, 2002. <http://www2.bostonherald.com/entertainment/movies/gibs07302002.htm>.

Shermer, Michael. *Why People Believe Weird Things: Pseudo-Science, Superstition, and Bogus Notions of Our Time.* New York: MJF, 1997.

Silberstein, Sandra. *War of Words: Language, Politics and 9/11.* London: Routledge, 2002.

Stasi, Linda. "Why I Won't Watch These 9/11 Shows: If You Lived Through That Day, Do You Really Need to Rewind It?" *New York Post* Sept. 9, 2002: 82.

Sullivan, George. *Quotable Hollywood: The Lowdown from America's Film Capital.* New York: Barnes, 2001.

"Terrorism Prompts Changes in Legal Rights." Associated Press. *Lincoln Journal Star* Sept. 11, 2002: 8A.

Turan, Kenneth. *Sundance to Sarajevo: Film Festivals and the World They Made.* Berkeley: U of California P, 2002.

Tyler, Patrick F. "Feeling Secure, U.S. Failed to See Determined Enemy." *New York Times* Sept. 8, 2002: 1, 19.

Usai, Paolo Cherchi. *The Death of Cinema: History, Cultural Memory and the Digital Dark Age.* London: BFI, 2001.

Virilio, Paul. *Ground Zero.* Trans. Chris Turner. New York: Norton, 2002.

Wherry, Aaron. "Will *11'9"01* Enrage America?" *National Post Online.* Sept. 11, 2002. <http://www.nationalpost.com/artslife/story.html?id=(9F0930CF-15E1-4BEF-B17E-6499A10E2C08)>.

Wojcik, Daniel. *The End of the World As We Know It: Faith, Fatalism and Apocalypse in America.* New York: New York UP, 1997.

"Yoko Ono Pleads 'Give Peace a Chance' on 9/11." *Reuters.com.* Sept. 11, 2002. <http://reuters.com/news_article.jhtml;jsessionid=QBBHAR4CN JLLMCRBAEZSFFA?type=entertainmentnews&StoryID=1433621>.

Zinn, Howard. *Terrorism and War.* Ed. Anthony Arnove. New York: Seven Stories, 2002.

2

Architectural Nostalgia and the New York City Skyline on Film

Steven Jay Schneider

> The most striking presence in this meandering movie is the World
> Trade Center; its towers make two brief, haunting appearances.
> Unlike some directors, [Bart] Freundlich was smart enough not to
> cut them from *World Traveler* after Sept. 11.
> —*Lou Lumenick, "Been down This Road"*

> "I think it's like our memories of a loved one," said director Sam
> Raimi, who left images of the Trade Center in his upcoming ad-
> aptation of *Spider-Man*. "Probably right after the death of some-
> one we love, it's sometimes hard to look at their pictures. Then later,
> there's a need to look at them."
> —*Associated Press release, April 18, 2002*

While the state of cinema theory, production, and culture (in all
its aspects) is still in flux in America after the events of September 11, 2001, one thing that definitely has changed—at least for
those with a prior physical or emotional connection with New York
City and its distinctive skyline—is audience reception when it comes
to scenes in fiction films, whatever the genre, that depict lower Manhattan either prior to or after the destruction of the World Trade
Center towers. In what follows, I consider a number of examples of
post-9/11 production strategies and audience responses (as described
in newspaper articles and the popular press) with respect to images
of the New York City skyline in various Hollywood feature films,

including *Zoolander* (2001), *World Traveler* (2001), *Glitter* (2001), *Vanilla Sky* (2001), *Don't Say a Word* (2001), *Serendipity* (2001), *Crossroads* (2001), *Men in Black II* (2002), *Changing Lanes* (2002), *Spider-Man* (2002), *Sidewalks of New York* (2002), and *People I Know* (2002). My aim is to better understand the highly particular sense of "architectural nostalgia" that such images—some with the World Trade Center intact, others with the twin towers already missing from view—can be said to have evoked in many spectators, current or former New York residents in particular.

As one of those current residents, I will begin by sharing those aspects of my own experience on September 11 that reveal the self-conscious and perhaps overly analytical mind-set of a film scholar who found himself caught between a powerful urge to run outside and participate in the makeshift relief efforts—to *do* something, anything really, to be of assistance—and an equally strong desire to hole up indoors, eyes glued to the television set, where I could watch the "before," "during," and "after" of the attacks on the towers again and again, repeatedly, incessantly. Already familiar with the slow fading away of once-vivid memories that seems (for me at least) to inevitably accompany the loss of something or someone held dear, a part of me that day was immediately—resolutely—nostalgic for the sight of a massive structure of steel and concrete that I had always taken for granted as a permanent fixture in my local visual field, and whose collapse and sudden disappearance from view has become a reminder in absentia of a historic loss of civilian life and of a city once known that is now forever in the past. Whether cinematic portraits of the World Trade Center and the pre-9/11 New York City skyline are already capable of providing a measure of satisfaction (or is it just pacification?) for nostalgic residents-cum-spectators or whether such portraits function primarily to engender paranoia and sorrow, and to reopen wounds that are still very fresh and very painful, remains to be seen.

On the morning of September 11, I woke to sirens blaring outside my seventh-floor apartment on Fifth Avenue and Fourteenth Street—the outskirts of Manhattan's Greenwich Village, approximately two and a half miles from the World Trade Center. Not surprising, given the countless times over the roughly twenty years I've lived in this apartment that I have been so rudely roused from sleep, I didn't even bother to get out of bed. It took a concerned friend from Toronto who called just before nine A.M. to jolt me to life with the news that there had been a massive explosion at one of the twin towers several minutes earlier. Poking my head out the living room window and seeing the fast-gathering mass of people on the street below, I turned on the TV—a somewhat revealing first impulse, to choose to look at mediated images and listen to rushed analysis (really just guesses at this point) rather than immediately head outside to see for myself what all the commotion was about—and like most everyone during those surreal and scarcely believable first few moments, my anxiety and astonishment were registered not so much in my mind or my body as in the pale, drawn, and stunned look that I'm sure was evident on my face. After the attack on the second tower around 9:05 A.M., my girlfriend and I ran downstairs and looked straight down Fifth Avenue to see the World Trade Center on fire, one of the towers with a plane implausibly and precariously sticking halfway out the side some three-quarters of the way up. As I recall it now, the mood at the time was primarily one of surprise and confusion and worry. It wasn't really one of fear or sadness or anger just yet—though of course all of these emotions would come soon enough, and in massive supplies of each. At that point, the vision confronting us was just too weird and too inexplicable to assimilate, because there was no firm sense that what we were seeing was in fact a well-planned, horrifyingly successful attack on American lives by foreign terrorists, and because the scale of the damage, though obviously substantial, still seemed restricted to a relatively small area of the twin towers high in the sky above Manhattan proper. Neither the massive loss of human life nor the enormous and widespread global ramifications—psychological, social, cultural, military, religious, economic—could possibly have been guessed before the buildings imploded and before the first basic facts about what had happened were obtained and disseminated.

Besides the predictable emotions of terror, grief, and dread, I distinctly remember feeling confused and torn between disparate and conflicting impulses and desires on the days immediately after the attacks. Of course I was desperate for information about the source of the threat, the extent of the damage, and the U.S. government's response to what had happened. This need meant channel surfing with a vengeance, seeking out the very latest scraps of news coming live (or nearly live, sometimes just "pretend live") from Afghanistan; Ground Zero; Shankesville, Pennsylvania; or Washington, D.C. But beyond my craving for both "official intelligence" and unconfirmed rumor (it didn't much matter into which category the report in question fit), I wanted to watch—needed to watch—the planes hit the towers, over and over and over again. I obsessively sought out visual reconfirmation that what I was witnessing was *not* one of the most spectacular special effects ever conceived and recorded on camera but far and away the deadliest and most destructive terrorist attack on American soil in this country's long history. Was this obsession indicative of a guilty pleasure on my part, unacknowledged as such at the time? Or was it an understandable, if not wholly rational, response to events that had to be seen to be believed? I'm not sure of the answer to this, and in any case I don't know that these options are exclusive of one another.

In a recent essay, Robert C. Solomon argues that the only pleasure one might reasonably be said to obtain from watching real-life displays of horror—as opposed to their fictional counterparts—is of the *sadistic* variety:

> Regarding . . . [horror] movies (and theater and novels), it is all well and good to ask what pleasure people find in the fear or horror that otherwise would seem to be a most unpleasant emotion ("the paradox of horror pleasure"). But it makes no sense at all, or else it takes a very sick sense, to ask such a question of real-life horror. To be sure, the image of that second jetliner crashing into the tower is awesome, and one might argue that awe carries with it a certain horrified pleasure. But in this case, the overwhelming emotion is horror, not pleasure. (Solomon)

Of course this argument does not take into account the fact that *per-petrators* of such "real-life horror," as well as their supporters, will almost certainly not be overwhelmed with negative feelings upon observing the devastating results of their actions; if anything, quite the opposite. But Solomon has an immediate and obvious response to such an objection; namely that, for such parties, it is not accurate to describe the events in question as constituting real-life horror at all. He writes,

> One might imagine an al-Qaeda operative watching his brethren's handiwork from a safe distance and getting considerable pleasure out of it as he takes in the awesome power of the forces unleashed. But, of course, he is not horrified at all. He identifies with the antagonists (or are they, for him, the protagonists?) and their awesome display of power, and that may be a source of his pleasure. But it is not horror. (Solomon)

The most disturbing implication of this argument to my mind is that horror must therefore be understood in relative terms as a description of events and as an emotion that depend crucially on whose "side" you are on to begin with.

In my case, however, another possible motivation beyond that of perverse pleasure or irrational skepticism also suggests itself: maybe the confirmation I was hoping to obtain by watching the planes hit again and again was the impossible but wish-fulfilling one that these attacks *were* in fact mere special effects, that somehow repeated viewings would enable me to detect a flaw or a seam in the audiovisual presentation that would make clear that what I was seeing was only a clip from some new disaster movie, a cinematic nightmare that I could eventually wake up from (or at least walk out on) with no actual harm done to New York City or its populace. Describing his experience as a Vietnam combat photographer in Adam Simon's horror film documentary *The American Nightmare* (2000), make-up and effects expert Tom Savini recalls that

> looking through a camera at this stuff was a separation for me. I mean, there were arms laying on the ground that had exploded from gre-

nades off Vietcong. I almost stepped on an arm. But to me, looking
through the camera, it was a special effect. So that was a study for me.

Unlike Savini, however, neither I nor anyone I know has seemed capable of achieving that separation when it comes to photographic
images of 9/11. Perhaps it is because the act of shooting atrocity footage of whatever kind, where there is a tangible barrier (in the form of
the camera or video recorder) between the eye and the events taking
place live before the shooter, actually affords more opportunity for
psychological self-distancing than the act of watching that footage on-
screen at some later time. In the latter case, despite the lack of physical proximity to the events in question, one is in a position to observe—with both eyes open—what unfolds with all the immediacy
provided by the reproductive (documentary, realist) powers of the
cinematic medium.

More than anything else, I found the video footage of the towers
coming down on the morning of 9/11 simultaneously—and somewhat paradoxically—captivating and devastating. Frankly awesome
to behold, the footage was at the same time nearly unwatchable for
me, chiefly because of the sheer magnitude of the human death and
misery that I knew must be entailed by the falling buildings. I now
believe that it was precisely during the twenty-three-minute interval
between 10:05 A.M. and 10:28 A.M., the time of the south tower's
collapse through the time of the north tower's collapse, that the World
Trade Center first became wholly anthropomorphized in the hearts
and minds of American citizens, and that any preexisting symbolic
import it might have had underwent a radical change.

No longer thought of as standing (tall) for New York's unparalleled
financial might—what Slavoj Zizek has characterized as "*virtual* capitalism, of financial speculations disconnected from the sphere of
material production" (par. 10), as opposed to both the "old-fashioned
notion of the 'center of financial capitalism'" (par. 10) on the one hand
and the Third World's "desert of the real" on the other—the formerly
intact towers were retrospectively viewed as the architectural signifiers
of a city and of a country that until September 11 had little to fear

from outside its borders and believed personal safety, though never guaranteed, was at least assessable and a reasonable bet. As Benjamin Halligan, in "On the Interval Between Reality and Unreality," has suggested, the "Towers [can now] be considered as a kind of collective body armour." Halligan understands this simile in largely negative terms:

> The buildings seemed (or now seem to be) emblematic of a repository for that which was repressed: namely, a geopolitical perspective denied to North American consumers of news media. September 11 saw the unleashing of that denied perspective, specifically, that [*sic*] "information" that U.S. foreign policy could somehow bounce back onto U.S. soil.

However, while he sees the towers' symbolic import primarily in defensive and repressive terms as serving the sociopsychological purpose of keeping out the geopolitically un-American Other, I view them as retrospectively—that is to say, in their absence—enabling U.S. citizens to recall a post–Cold War fantasy in which not even the Other possesses the motives, means, or methods to cause us serious harm.

I take it that the near-instantaneous appearance after the attacks of street hawkers in downtown Manhattan selling hastily reproduced postcards, posters, and photos of the intact towers in all their glory, along with U.S. flags and other memorabilia of the World Trade Center and New York City emergency services (police department, fire department, port authority), constitutes a sort of evidence in support of the above assertion. In one sense, the twin towers have *already* been rebuilt as communal, if only virtual, objects of nostalgic sentiment, signaling America's former confidence and self-assurance while at the same time metonymically connoting the scores of innocent people whose lives were lost on September 11. This latter representational function has only been enhanced by the distressing fact that so many bodies were either partially destroyed or else completely annihilated in the attacks on the buildings and by Ground Zero's status as, in effect, a mass grave. As of June 2002, with the recovery mission finally coming to an end, more than 1,800 of the 2,814 reported victims of the World Trade Center attacks were still officially listed as missing (Brzezinski). It is the status and significance of the former twin towers as objects of nostalgia for post-9/11 cinema to which I shall now turn.

It is more than a little ironic that while the mind-boggling footage of the towers' collapse was constantly being replayed on the television news in the days immediately after September 11—thereby allowing viewers to satisfy a somewhat masochistic, if *not* sadistic, desire to reexperience our collective trauma—shots of the former World Trade Center were deleted from a number of Hollywood feature films made for the most part prior to the attacks and slated for late 2001 and early 2002 release dates across the United States. The irony here is that cinematic images of the twin towers as they used to appear—"healthy" and in all their unsuspecting and, now it seems, naïve glory—were for a time deemed more deleterious than images of those same buildings at the exact moment of their destruction.

When asked to justify the corporate decision to eliminate shots of the World Trade Center from films such as *Zoolander, Serendipity, Spider-Man, Men in Black II,* and *People I Know,* production company spokespeople tended to stress the serious concern of those in charge not to further depress or offend audiences, who would be understandably sensitive and possibly resistant to any visual reminders of the events of September 11 in their escapist movie entertainment. So, for example, producer Leslie Urdang told reporters that a surrealistic shot of the twin towers shown sideways in a scene from *People I Know*—intended to convey the state of mind of Al Pacino's character upon awakening from a nightlong drug binge—was removed from the film because the "abstract, highly stylised" image was now viewed as "completely inappropriate" (Fleming par. 3). And Miramax publicist Matthew Hiltzik, invited to explain why a shot of the twin towers in the romantic comedy *Serendipity* ended up being replaced by one (from the same shoot) in which the buildings could not be seen owing to the particular camera angle used, responded that "since we're still only a few weeks from the tragedy, we'd rather err on the side of sensitivity" (qtd. in Rice par. 4). Regarding the same film, Miramax co-chairman Harvey Weinstein was more frank and, not surprising, more presumptuous in a September 27, 2001, interview with Britain's *Guardian* newspaper: "What people are feeling is this: We don't want to be reminded in our entertainment of the disaster we went through" (qtd. in Rice par. 5).

Regardless of whether Weinstein was accurate in his estimation of what people in America were feeling shortly after 9/11, his more theoretical (rather than quasi-empirical) point about the possibility of a real-life disaster such as the World Trade Center attacks in some sense interfering with or detracting from the public's experience of fictional mass entertainments is worth considering in more depth. Instead of simply conferring an extra level or degree of authenticity to the particular diegesis, one achieved via an increase of contextual and iconographic (spatial, geographic, local) realism, the "serious concern" of Weinstein et al. might have been that cinematic images of the New York City skyline from before September 11 would now *rupture* the fictional world of the film in question, especially for residents of Manhattan and surrounding areas. Rather than assist viewers in suspending their disbelief that the specific world they are watching on-screen is in fact coextensive with the world in which they themselves actually live, work, and play, such images—which are not just depressing but also (to state the point baldly) *distracting*—could serve to take the audience "out" of the narrative altogether, at least for a while. In an important sense then, underlying the predictable production company rhetoric, there seemed to be a legitimate fear that images of the former World Trade Center in post-9/11 mainstream film releases would work *too* well; that instead of conferring an additional documentary or nonfictional quality upon the mise-en-scène of the fictional story, they might well *undermine* the story's narrative and powers of illusion, leading viewers to momentarily ignore the sensuous properties of the filmic medium and reflect instead on the all-too-real consequences of the recent terrorist attacks.

Somewhat surprising, however, was that the decision to remove images of the towers from the aforementioned films and several others resulted in a fairly broad, fairly vehement critical backlash, one that received a measure of support from audiences in Manhattan even if it did not have a noticeable (or at least a calculable) negative impact on box-office returns. New York–based reviewers such as *Variety's* Todd McCarthy, for example, railed against the practice of deleting images of the twin towers from post–September 11 releases. In his review of *Zoolander,* McCarthy wrote,

> Not so outstanding is the decision to matte out or otherwise obscure the late World Trade Center from shots that should have included the twin towers. Deletion of the towers from the picture is infinitely more disruptive, not to mention insulting, than leaving them in. (qtd. in Rice par. 8)

One can see how the removal of the towers might have been considered "insulting" by some viewers, if they concluded that the removal was neither an indication of sensitivity (the filmmakers or producers not wanting to rub 9/11 in the audience's collective face) nor an effort at achieving a more authentic and "up-to-date" geographic mise-en-scène (i.e., since the towers no longer exist in "reality," their presence in any film immediately dates that film's diegesis as existing prior to the events of September 11, 2001). This would leave their absence open to interpretation as a lame and uninspired attempt at repressing or denying some very recent, very painful history—a way of pretending that 9/11 never happened by removing all visual reminders of the attack's hardest hit target. This was precisely the view espoused by Katherine Heintzelman, executive editor of New York's *Premiere* magazine, who asserted in an October 2001 interview that "it's one thing if your movie features scenes of terrorism or destruction taking place at the towers. But to erase all traces of them, as if they never existed, seems a shame" (Schneller par. 10). Heintzelman then went on:

> [W]hy erase any trace of their existence from these films? The goal of terrorism is to disrupt people's lives, to get them to act in a man-

ner in which they would not react before. . . . The terrorists leveled the Twin Towers to strike fear into Americans (and, thus, in their allies), to destroy hope. Erasing the World Trade Center from *Zoolander* strikes me as the most inappropriate of responses. Where defiance is called for, instead we see capitulation. For New York—for the world— in real life, the towers are gone. Why, in the world of images, would [Ben] Stiller and co. want to finish the job the terrorists started?

The irony here, of course, is that the erasure of the World Trade Center from films like *Zoolander, Serendipity,* and *People I Know* is evidence of capitulation to the terrorists only if one believes that the true measure of defiance lies in denying the reality of the present and sentimentally holding on to the past, in this case by keeping images of the pre-9/11 New York City skyline in films released *after* September 11.

In general, moviegoers seemed to be in agreement, or at least in sympathy, with Heintzelman. As reported in numerous magazines and newspapers, some audiences went so far as to boo scenes of the New York City skyline absent the twin towers in *Zoolander,* whereas in *Glitter,* "skyline shots that included the towers elicited spontaneous applause" (Heintzelman qtd. in Schneller par. 7); this latter spectatorial behavior was all the more unexpected and impressive considering *Glitter'*s notoriously pitiful reception otherwise. (The producers of *Men in Black II,* who had a great deal more money to burn than their colleagues backing the lower-budget films mentioned above, were able to largely avoid controversy by not only digitally erasing the twin towers but by shifting the entire location of the climactic battle scene, which was originally supposed to take place with the World Trade Center in the background.)

Should we conclude from such examples that there was a profound emotional need on the part of a great many American, especially New York, moviegoers shortly after 9/11 to have their incipient nostalgia for the World Trade Center (and what it now symbolizes) stoked via cinematic images of the twin towers, and that this desire finally overrode their interest in fully engaging with—and therefore escaping into—the fictional world of the particular Manhattan-based film they were watching? For surely, and *contra* the implications of critics like McCarthy and Heintzelman, applauding the presence of such images reveals (and in fact constitutes) a disruption of the diegesis just as much as booing their absence does. Finally, should we conclude that the pragmatically motivated decision by certain producers and directors *not* to include images of the twin towers in their movies was roundly criticized precisely because this decision curtailed the potency of such "architectural nostalgia"?

All of this may well seem to be the case, but at least some measure of qualification is in order. For one thing, consider how hard it is to imagine any Manhattan-based film made, say, in the summer of 2002 or thereafter—and set in a fictional world contemporaneous with the real (i.e., post-9/11) world—being criticized for not having images of the towers in shots or scenes of the New York City skyline. It would appear that underlying the critical backlash directed toward films like *Serendipity, Zoolander, Spider-Man,* and (to a lesser extent, for the reason stated above) *Men in Black II* was anger not at the towers' mere *absence* from the skyline but at their postproduction *deletion* from the skyline; the true resentment was based not on perception but on epistemology. According to this line of thinking, the images of the towers should have been maintained in the final version of the film in question, since at the time of shooting, the towers really *were* there (in the skyline, in the film). To remove the towers from these pictures was in effect to state that they were never there to begin with. By digitally or otherwise deleting (e.g., via editorial or cinematographic trickery) the World Trade Center from pictures in which the World Trade Center once appeared, the inherent and automatic power of the cinematic medium to capture and re-present reality was rendered largely void—not unlike a negative version of those computer-generated graphics displays found in so many recent science-fiction and fantasy movies—and the mise-en-scène distinctly unrealistic. Since the originally intended audiences knew that the pictures under discussion were filmed prior to September 11, shots of the New York City skyline without the twin towers included therein were distracting and a source of anger because it forced them to contemplate the lie instead of allowing them to entertain the fiction.

In the end, and whatever the short-term differences and repercussions may be, I do not think it really matters for theorizing audience response whether the towers are present or not in popular film images of the New York City skyline, because the very notion of "architectural nostalgia" is one that cuts both ways, so to speak. Whether I see the twin towers in movies or not, one thing is a given: I will never be able to view my city's skyline, on-screen or in person, the same way again.

Works Cited

Brzezinski, Mika. "The End of the Recovery Effort." *CBS News.com*. May 26, 2002. Sept. 3, 2002. <http://www.cbsnews.com/stories/2002/05/28/eveningnews/main510349.shtml>.

Fleming, Michael. "Terrorism Projects Shelved." *Variety Online*. Sept. 18, 2001. Sept. 2, 2002. <http://velvet_peach.tripod.com/fpacpeopleiknow.html>.

Halligan, Benjamin. "On the Interval Between Reality and Unreality." Part of a virtual symposium entitled "Terror, Disaster, Cinema and Reality." Ed. Adrian Martin and Fiona Villella. *Senses of Cinema*. 17 (Nov.–Dec. 2001). Sept. 1, 2002. <http://www.sensesofcinema.com/contents/01/17/symposium/halligan.html>.

Rice, Jerry. "World Trade Center Images Cut from New Films." *San Bernadino County Sun*. Oct. 1, 2001. Sept. 3, 2002. <http://www.moviepie.com/wtc.html>.

Schneller, Johanna. "An Argument for Not Snipping the Twin Towers." *Globe and Mail Online*. Oct. 12, 2001. Sept. 2, 2002. <http://www.globeandmail.com/series/awards/2001/towers.html>.

Solomon, Robert C. "Real Horror." *Dark Thoughts: Philosophic Reflections on Cinematic Horror*. Ed. Steven Jay Schneider and Daniel Shaw (Lanham, MD: Scarecrow, forthcoming 2003).

Zizek, Slavoj. "Welcome to the Desert of the Real: Reflections on WTC." Lecture read November 7, 2001. *The Symptom: Online Journal for Lacan.com*. 2 (spring-summer 2002). <http://lacan.com/desertsymf.htm>.

This chapter is dedicated to the memory of Greg Richards.

3

The Shadow of the World Trade Center Is Climbing My Memory of Civilization

Murray Pomerance

> To name a sensibility, to draw its contours and to recount its history, requires a deep sympathy modified by revulsion.
>
> —*Susan Sontag, "Notes on Camp"*

New York is the most European place in America, if by European we can mean grounded upon the imperial principles of hierarchy, domination, and distinction; upon the belief in ascent and the Chain of Being and the systematic denial—in the spirit of achievement—of egalitarian simplicity and freedom. The rigorous, even calcified, class-consciousness America was founded to escape never escaped America. In New York it is made iconic by monuments to success, superiority, and the vertical organization of social life in which point of view is style, vista is vision, and height is strength. Light is for the very few who are very powerful and very high; the experience of the common man is a stifling, overpopulated darkness. "Those towers," writes James Sanders of the skyscrapers of New York in the 1930s, "so dramatic and gleaming from a distance, could block the sun and crowd the street with their bulk. Easily comprehended at arm's length, from close up they could be overwhelming or disorienting" (97). Haven of the tired and poor though it may be, New York is corporate megawealth that controls social space from pristine aeries where "the world opens up again, the air is clear, the place again seems manageable" (97).

Barry Sonnenfeld's goofy *Men in Black* (1997) is an homage to this topos and to the related theme of immigration and control.[1] At its conclusion, the Bug, an emphatically malevolent, ravenous, and desperate alien cockroach who has taken over the body of an exterminator (Vincent D'Onofrio), is climbing the port authority heliport at the 1964 New York World's Fair site in Flushing Meadow to reach his spaceship, which is secreted at the top. Under one arm he clutches Laurel Weaver, M.D. (Linda Fiorentino), the heroine of the piece, so that, in his own words, he'll have something "to snack on" during the long trip home. She manages to jump into a nearby tree, from which point of vantage she observes much of the ensuing battle as agents J (Will Smith) and K (Tommy Lee Jones) hiply arrive in pursuit, shoot the ship down, engage the monster in battle, and finally, with her invaluable assistance, blast it to smithereens. Why, however—to ask what may seem a preposterous question—if she is ultimately to be safe in a treetop witnessing most of this, must Laurel first find herself shrieking and squealing in the alien monster's grasp as he climbs the tower? What understanding is expected of, and achieved in, the audience through this trope; what images and memories does it summon; what view of the world does it suggest, beneath and beyond the strictures of the plot, for us to acknowledge as sensible?

I take this moment to be an homage to the conclusion of *King Kong* (1933, 1976), when another great alien beast climbs another monument to capital, technological achievement, progress, and dominion with yet another squealing female in tow. If Sonnenfeld's Bug has come from the countryside to the city to obtain treasure, however, and is now in flight with it, the pathetic Kong, for his part, is hardly trying to get out of New York so much as to escape the anxiety-ridden, volatile, cupidinous New Yorkers who persist in using him as capital. In 1933 the Empire State Building, and in 1976 the World Trade Center (WTC), was the highest, and therefore most tranquil, ground for his purposes.

The Empire State Building, described by Fatimah Tobing Rony as being, in 1933, "the ultimate U.S. symbol of progress, technology, and

Civilization" (186) and very like the other skyscrapers that had been climbing the skyline of New York since 1869, was possible, according to Burns and Sanders, because of two developments: steel frame construction and elevators (231). Both of these, interestingly, were dependent on iron, a resource the technology for producing which constituted a central development of the nineteenth century. David P. Billington writes that the new methods of producing iron

> involved replacing charcoal with coke in the smelting process. . . . Thus coal replaced wood in the process of iron making and in turn iron replaced wood for the products. . . . [A] far denser and stronger material supplanted the softer organic substance that had held together the technology of earlier civilizations. A nonrenewable resource replaced a renewable one; that is the primary ecological fact of the Industrial Revolution. Society thus began to mine its ecological capital rather than fell its agricultural income. (28–29)

The manufacture and use of iron and then steel thus constituted daring "economico-ecological" movements in themselves, exploitations of capital rather than income. And the skyscraper, epitomized by the skyscrapers of New York and especially—at the time of the first version of *King Kong,* the newest member of this family and the tallest building in the world—the Empire State Building, represented the apotheosis of this daring. (One of the earliest motion pictures was the American Mutoscope and Biograph Company's *Skyscrapers of New York* [1906], a drama set on high girders during the construction of one of these icons.)

The desperate and cocksure hopefulness that characterized American capitalism in the twentieth century was exemplified by the beginning of demolition and excavation for the Empire State Building at the same time as the October 1929 stock market collapse (Burns and Sanders 377). The builder, John Jacob Raskob, proclaimed to the *New York Times* with dramatic optimism that "he did not believe the effects [of Black Tuesday] would be other than temporary, lasting probably two or three months, and that he did not believe that the effects would be drastic in other than luxury industries" (qtd. in Burns and Sanders 376). The construction process itself, too, epitomized nothing if not ingenuity and daring: with more than three thousand men working on the "giant, three-dimensional jigsaw puzzle" from 3:30 in the morning until 4:30 in the afternoon, eating at one of the three canteens installed at different levels in the structure itself, preparing and driving eight hundred rivets a day for $1.92 an hour (379), the building could be completed at breakneck speed and was topped off March 18, 1931. The Empire State Building was the technological marvel of its age and a brand-new ladder for the ape to climb when *King Kong* was released less than two years later.

Skyscrapers depended upon elevators because clients of the many firms that could be agglomerated in them would not be persuaded to climb more than a few stories on foot. If Kong does not suffer from this human apathy, he is too large, too desperate, and too daring to use an elevator. The manner of his ascent and his size while he performs it confirm his superiority and his alienness from everyday human concerns, since his regard for the edifice is from outside a conventional perspective, such a view, perhaps, as would have entertained the architect himself, William Lamb, planning his answer to the challenge, "How high can you make it, so that it won't fall down?" (Burns and Sanders 377). For Kong, the building is constituted by its architectural essence, not its cultural cachet—rather than saying that he thinks like an architect, it can be said that an architect thinks like him. While, as an infrastructure of capitalism, the locale functioned daily for the fifty thousand employees who worked there as a vertical city, a multidimensional and dense Cartesian grid from which competitors and collaborators could control vast intercontinental empires in the closest proximity to one another's operations, Kong can treat it as a chain of footholds, a stairway to heaven. Even our view of him climbing to the top is something of a cultural architecture, founded upon a tacit understanding of masses, stresses, stabilization, and topography, not to say bestiality and military dominance, that puts value, power, and prestige in a stratum resting at the top of the New York skyline while consigning labor, vulgarity, and promise to the dark canyons below. The top is the topos of military advantage, the site of the unobstructed view, and the position that maximally exploits the investment of capital. The ape at the top of the tower is thus also a model capitalist, or at least—and I think this will help us understand the mechanism of the story—a pretender to that throne. In the sense that he is pretending, he is a child.

By 1973, when some 200,000 tons of steel, 425,000 cubic yards of concrete, 600,000 square feet of glass, and 12,000 miles of electrical cables had been assembled and lit with 23,000 fluorescent lights to form its twin towers, the WTC utterly eclipsed the Empire State Building as the world's tallest building and a wonder of engineering (Johnson). And soon thereafter—almost as soon as Schoedsack and Cooper produced his ancestor after the Empire State Building's opening to the public in 1932—came New York's new biggest immigrant in Dino De Laurentiis and John Guillermin's *King Kong* (Paramount—"a Gulf & Western Company," 1976). In it, an even more gigantic and surely more expressive ape, captured on an even mistier Skull Island by an even more insanely greedy magnate, oil executive Fred Wilson (Charles Grodin, playing Charles Bluhdorn or his factotum, Robert Evans?), is chloroformed and shipped to New York in an oil tanker (as so many creative spirits at Paramount may have been after 1974), where he is mawkishly put on exhibit at Shea Stadium as part of an oil company extravaganza (virtually a Paramount film himself) and finally flees to the city that never sleeps and the towers that newly reached above it to the sky. "What lonely grandeur will he achieve up there that he cannot find below" (Sanders 101)?

It goes without saying, I think, that until close of business on September 10, 2001, the twilight before another Black Tuesday, the De Laurentiis-Guillerman *Kong* was but a sluggish rivulet in the churning ocean of American popular culture. "The burning question at the fadeout is which is the bigger stiff, the corpse of Kong laid out in the plaza of the World Trade Center or the movie itself," wrote the *Washington Post* (Arnold); "It's something to make you cringe with embarrassment," declared the *New York Times* (Canby); and within a year, *Star Wars* had erased it from the public imagination. As a comparator to the classic 1933 film, which Susan Sontag had elevated to the rarefied precincts of "Camp" (277), it bore comment only because of the eccentric conceit of its having been made at all (for $24 million), for its Oscar-winning effects, and because of Jessica Lange, an unknown actress from Cloquet, Minnesota, whose distinctive screen career began with her portrayal of a shipwrecked ingenue who is rescued, thanks to the eagle eye of primate paleontologist Jack Prescott (Jeff Bridges); later captured by the natives of Skull Island and offered in sacrifice to their ape-god Kong; then abducted by the monster; and finally become the object of his overwhelming love. Surely no self-respecting cinéphile, no film scholar, no monster maniac could have esteemed so overproduced, derivative, and sententious a remake of what Thomas Doherty called "the only pre-Code Hollywood picture that lives universally in the American imagination" (289). In the wake of the destruction of the Trade Center on September 11, however, this film has taken on a new resonance. I would argue that as a cultural artifact, it is now the 1976 *Kong* that has universal presence in the American imagination—a presence, indeed, so profound we do not see it.

While its Depression-era antecedent was framed as the story of a group of hapless Westerners whose lives were changed when they captured and returned to "civilization" a monster ape, the 1976 *King Kong* essentially revolves around the creature himself, taunted by humans, abused by humans, ultimately executed by humans, yet in love with a human all the while. The skeleton of the plot is mostly a replication. On Skull Island, as part of Wilson's greedy oil-drilling expedition, the ingenue Dwan (Lange) finds herself kidnapped, drugged, outfitted as Kong's symbolic bride, and lashed to a scaffold from which the gorilla can seize her at will. He approaches, is stunned by her blonde radiance, carries her off. Prescott and company discover she is missing and rush after her. Alone with her in his jungle, meanwhile, Kong finds himself fascinated by the tiny golden figure in his hand. He stares at her, fingering her garments with curiosity. He gives her to bathe in a waterfall and then gently huffs and puffs her dry. She comes to trust him, and they try to express themselves to one another in moments that are at once embarrassing and distressing. He battles a giant serpent to save her, during which action Jack comes upon the scene and steals off with her through the jungle,

> the young man pulling on the woman to run even faster as she becomes progressively weaker, until she is so exhausted that she has to be carried to safety in the man's arms. This scene of the two running, running, forever running, is full of suspense—Will Kong catch up? Will they make it? Moreover, will they make it back to Civilization? Their running is a literal embodiment of the race of history, a race which is a locus of ethnographic cinema,

as Rony described the analogous scene in the 1933 film (170). Wilson and his team build a trap for the beast and bring him back to New York in the hold of one of their oil tankers, the rich oil deposit they had hoped to find on Skull Island being unready for tapping. If a living souvenir can be brought back for exploitation, the executive's seat at the board table can be saved!

At the public exhibition—set, like the finale of *Men in Black,* in Queens—Kong is displayed to his humiliation (since all along we have been taking him for a teenager inside a gorilla suit, not unlike the protagonist of Reisz's *Morgan* [1966]) in a cage that has been designed to resemble a giant gas pump. A company crown has been affixed to his head—screenwriter Lorenzo Semple Jr.'s snide updating of the nineteenth-century racial undertones appreciable in the original *Kong,* where in his shackles at the point of exhibition, as Noël Carroll noted, the ape "recalls the imagery of a slave being auctioned" (233). When he sees photographers advance on Lange (costumed and "bound" in a staged choreography of the jungle ritual in which he first saw her), the naïve Kong is outraged on her behalf and tears loose from his shackles in order to save her. The crowd flees in panic from his gallantry, many, including the slimy Wilson, getting trampled under his feet. Lange and Bridges make their way to—of all places—a midtown bar, where Kong finds them and carries Lange off. At the WTC, he climbs Tower 2 with her in hand, as Prescott attempts to catch up using the elevator. (Kong's giant legs permit him to move with such power and assurance that he beats Prescott—whose elevator is climbing at the rate of sixteen hundred feet per minute—to the top by only a few seconds.) Soldiers with flamethrowers are sent to attack Kong, but he incinerates them instead and then leaps with Lange to the north tower, where, Prescott observing helplessly, he is surrounded by military helicopters and gunned down. He tumbles from the roof, falling, as Sanders, disappointed with this film, has it, "to a final indignity. The huge plaza below swallows up Kong's body and again makes him seem almost puny. . . . Kong's body sits like the centerpiece of a party whose guests mill about aimlessly" (103). At film's end, we see his monstrous form—a colossal dead myth—surrounded by a sedate crowd of onlookers, Dwan shaken and weeping uncontrollably at his side, police vehicles with red and blue lights flashing in the night, and the silent silver towers in the background like a pair of ghosts.

While it has always been a worthwhile challenge to attempt to understand a filmic moment such as this in terms of its cultural setting, the WTC disaster brings a new imperative in this direction, encapsulating as it does—and as does *King Kong*—the image of massive destruction, the image of the weeping woman, the "attack" upon the monument to globalization by "alien" and "ethnic" force, and a huge emergency response by the feelingless forces of social order. It is the dead Kong who centers the final shot of the film, and the milling, thrilling, terrified crowd around him; while the buildings themselves hover in the background, already in 1976 shimmering but inactive forms of themselves, vitiated politicocultural advances, monumentalities emptied of purpose and life. They are not really so unlike the structures in that Flushing Meadow World's Fair site we see in *Men in Black*, nor do they fail to remind us of postwar capitalism itself, its pretty face being devoured from within like the icon in Bergman's *The Touch* (1971). Newly erected and shiny, they are already, with the dead Kong before them, the husks they would too soon become.

In a paper presented at the Society for Cinema Studies Annual Conference in 2002, Steven Alan Carr describes the leveling of the WTC as an "erasure":

> Built atop the remnants of turn-of-the-century ethnic immigrant urban neighborhoods and trade centers, urban revitalization projects such as the Towers—arguably the crown jewel of Lower Manhattan's gentrification—realized the Horatio Alger–like success of a melting-pot America by erasing the ethnic urban identities that once occupied its ground-level space. (n. pag.)

The impulse toward globalization that underlay the Center is thus seen as inherently a racist one, a schema for dominating, indeed replacing, urban ethnicity. The schema was symbolized demographically by the "seedy 'radio row'" (Johnson par. 2) electronics stores the WTC neatly covered over; and culturally and mythically by the notable un-Americanness of the al Qaeda fighters who took revenge through the agency of the buildings and by the outrageous un-Americanness of the ape who in our filmic dreams tried to climb to the Center's top. So very un-American was Kong, indeed, that we can see him as the ideal immigrant—the Other—to screen, bound, contain, disinfect, reeducate, and assimilate. (How gauche of him, and how presumptuous, to have his own ideas about the world we so graciously dangled before his eyes. Sander Gilman might have described this immodest upstart as yet one more immigrant Jew.) If the saga of the WTC is a racial story, so, surely, is *King Kong*. The frame story, for example, is that an American oil conglomerate exploits the natural resources of a fourth-world island. The locals are treated as ignorants who, like the original citizens of Manhattan, will barter for "shiny objects." The native fertility dance, led by a writhing pent-up monkey-man (Keny Long) strangely resembling the aggressive ape in the prologue to *2001*, suggests primitivity as an uncontrolled and ignorant sexuality. And Kong himself, of course, a primal roaming id, is visible to some extent as an icon of hairy and unsocialized darkness, the epitome of the white man's burden.

This theme has been explored by both Doherty and Rony in terms of the relationship between *Kong* (both scholars study the 1933 version) and the racial, ethnographic, and expeditionary films of the pre-Code era. White imperial civilization not only invades the space and culture of the Other but arrogates to itself the mandate and privilege of seeing it, that is, photographically recording and transporting the "primitive world" westward for cataloguing and profit. Rony in fact positions her discussion in terms of the late-nineteenth-century and early-twentieth-century exhibition of foreign persons as "freaks." In that light, Wilson's capture of Kong for display in New York is a plain analogue to Samuel Verner's capture and display at the Bronx Zoo of the Chirichiri man, Ota Benga.[2] When *Kong* is examined from this point of view, the fault of the ape is his presumptuousness in attempting to bond with a white woman and in trying to give himself the advantage of the position at the top of the tallest building, a position reserved for the cultural elite and one that is, simply, the best point of view around. That his affection for Ann Darrow (Fay Wray) in 1933 or Dwan in 1976 softens him in our eyes does not blur his transgressive character, his willingness to go where he cannot be thought to belong, to secure for himself a vantage no beast has had before.

But by invoking Horatio Alger, Carr allows us to imagine Kong's presumption in yet another way. He has taken a giant liberty, fashioning himself in the image of the common man who by struggle and constant endeavor can hope to succeed in Western culture. For Kong is the ultimate man of the street finally making it—there, and anywhere. If for Carr the WTC—and for others the Empire State Building before it—was "built atop" ethnic ruins, perhaps the great ape in some way represents the untimely rebirth of that trampled ethnic anlage, the outsider come to life again (or at least to social membership), and yet again vying for position at the top of the cultural scale. In that he, too, came distinctly from the outside; in that he, too, kept on coming though he was a product of a civilization the imperial technology of the West had thought to have superseded and trampled into the dirt with its vast military-industrial potency; in that he, too, took the liberty of imagining himself to properly belong at the "top of the world"—at least the top of the world in New York, a city which is the top of the Western world—and in that doing all this, intentionally or not, he had found a way to take some of our women with him, was Osama bin Laden, or his agent Mohammed Atta not, for a dazzling moment, the Kong for the twenty-first century?

It is de rigueur in accounting *King Kong* to describe the tale as a grand myth of heterosexual possibility. Carroll, for instance, notes that the film

> abounds with interpretations. These come in many shapes and sizes—Kong as Christ, Kong as Black, Kong as commodity, Kong as rapist, Kong enraptured by *L'amour fou,* Kong as Third World, Kong as dream, Kong as myth, Kong according to Freud, according to Jung, and even according to Lacan. The 1976 version of *King Kong* selects a few of these interpretations—notably Kong as Third World, Kong as commodity, and *L'amour fou*—and makes them explicit; the helicopters seem to sweep in from the Mekong Delta and the swooning heroine suggests that Kong is not always alone in his madness. (215–16)

Of the original *Kong,* Doherty reminds us that

> the high concept for the film grew out of a waking fantasy from Merian Cooper, the core of which was a single image: "a beast so large that he could hold the beauty in the palm of his hand, pulling bits of her clothing from her body until she was denuded." (289)

Cynthia Erb declares that it is "not my intention to contradict the many readings of *King Kong* that focus on the racial and sexual implications of the relationship between Kong and Darrow, for *King Kong* is undoubtedly a drama that operates on the 'dangerous' border of miscegenation" (93). De Laurentiis himself touted his film as "the world's most beautiful love story," and in a circumlocution of Kongish proportions, the *New York Times* issued the warning that the film includes "some intimations of unrealizable bestiality that small children everywhere will recognize as simple friendliness"

(Canby). The great ape, then, is ultimately nothing less than an apish Caliban, who would people his isle with Kongs if given the chance. Dwan is his Miranda; Grodin her Prospero-in-loco, Prescott her Ferdinand. Lowest of the low, yet not quite nonhuman, and at the same time magnificent in his magnitude, Kong dominates physically but apparently in an entirely presumptuous manner, since ugly beasts such as he should never set hands on beauties such as Dwan. If Dwan spends a great deal of time agape in the great paw, she may be a counterreaction with wide eyes to our own assumptions about his boldness and curiosity.

Reading about the film, indeed, makes it difficult to escape the assumption Kong has sex on his mind, especially, perhaps, when he reaches out and fingers Dwan's blouse. Rhona Berenstein describes the girl played by Fay Wray in 1933 as "a potential romantic partner to the monster" and goes on to report that Wray

> reconfirmed her intimate bond with Kong when she opened her 1989 autobiography with a candid letter to her 1933 costar: "Dear Kong . . . I feel that you never did mean to harm me. My children knew that when they saw 'our film' for the first time: 'He didn't want to hurt you,' they said, 'He just liked you.'" (192)

While the extreme close-ups of Lange reduce the texture of the gorilla's hand to a dark backdrop and shift the proportion of her figure to match our own, we can safely imagine her as a sexual object from a conventional sadistic or masochistic position. This is the traditional moment of intercut subjectivities that implicates us in the emotion of the story. As J. P. Telotte describes it with reference to the original *Kong*,

> As they look, *we* by turns stand in for each character, assume his or her supposed position just off-screen, and thus draw what has been termed "blind space" or outside realm into the specular world of the narrative. . . . Of course, this effect is crucial to any romantic scene, for it lets us participate in the vital interaction, the lovers gazing into each other's—and into our—eyes. ("Movies" 394)

But the editing jumps from close, suturing shots to medium and long placements. In these latter, as we see all or part of the gorilla in relation to Dwan and she immediately shrinks, our suture is broken, *since we identify with him.* Alternately, the closer we look and the more credible the sexual motive, the more feminine our experience is, too, because as viewers invested in it, we identify with Dwan. Rape is less thinkable—indeed, I would claim it is unthinkable—when we see Kong carrying Dwan around in a full shot, and it is especially unthinkable when he mounts the WTC with her in his grasp. It is surely for security, not romance or sex, that he affiliates with this woman, to gain whatever protection she can afford from the perils of the urban, capitalist scene. The hijacker's seizure of commercial aircraft carrying women and children was similarly, and strategically, self-protective.

This is hardly to claim that *King Kong* of 1976 offers a blueprint for the al Qaeda attack of September 2001. But there are disquieting similarities, strange echoes. This reflection of Erb's about *King Kong,* for instance, could as well have been written about the WTC catastrophe:

> it stages a monstrous reply to the colonialist adventure narrative: throwing off the evolutionist fantasies that had lured him into captivity, Kong makes a titan's effort to throw evolution into reverse. In this sense, the film's final scenes generally upset the evolutionist "order of things" so carefully established in the prologue. Pacing through the streets, using all his fighting movement to evoke memories of his actions on Skull Island, Kong exacts vengeance by reintroducing the primitive into the realm of the civilized, making an effort to return the spaces of New York to the topography of the wild.

If we concentrate on the territory that came, with the queerest kind of affection, to be known as "ground zero," for example, and where a rather primitive ritual of remembrance is scheduled to be enacted September 11, 2002, we see the text of the "spaces of New York" returned "to the topography of the wild" spelled out in plain sight. Whether true or not, it has been the conviction of the Western popular culture and press that the hijackers were in fact invoking in the airspace of Manhattan "memories" of American "actions" committed, if not on Skull Island, then in some less remote but equally obscure "home environment" utterly hostile to the ethos of the West. While the al Qaeda and the Taliban are no less human, no less advanced tactically, and no less credible in their own eyes than anyone else, nevertheless they have been painted religiously by government spokespersons and the media as evolutionarily low. According to a wall of press reports, they "hate" us, plain and simple—that is, they are capable of only an aggrandized emotional assessment. And they constitute an "axis of evil." Anyone who can grasp the proportions of the American government's colonialist imperative in Asia, and globally, can surely see the attack as a "monstrous reply." Monstrous it surely is: awful, yet also gigantic and compelling. If its central icon is the pillar of dark "satanic" smoke rising as the WTC burns, it may serve us to remember that each man's darkness is in part his own: both Kong and bin Laden are products of capitalism gone spectacularly wrong. Our mythic alienation of such forces betrays our own historical amnesia.

A more troubling fact about the collapse of the WTC surely must have galvanized millions as they watched, and yet paralyzed the public voice, namely, that the sight was not only a diabolical horror but also a wonder. Just so wondrous, indeed, are those exciting and also relieving implosive blowdowns of hotels, skyscrapers, and stadiums by TNT experts who make tall buildings vanish in a cloud of dust and leave not a rack behind. Again, and again, and again, and again, and again, we were shown—and continue to be shown: even as I write this sentence, the second plane is finding its target again on my television screen—the video replay of the two towers coming down in those quivering, suffocating pillars of smoke. Every time it is unbelievable again, as though, stunted from shock or oversatiation, we simply cannot learn from our own incredulity and must repeat it. Our intelligence tells us how brutal is the scene. But our hungry eyes are only shocked and astonished. Later—months later—we discover inexorably again and again that the culture has been attacked economically, politically, historically, psychologically, and neurologically, as well as militarily. But still we cannot get enough of the vision of the collapse, as though something in these towers of Babel was calling out for an end all along (the tower finally a story, its beginning begging for its end) and only a vision of an end could bring satisfaction. We do not find it difficult to imagine, at least, that the enemy may have thought, "This is a culture waiting to die." What I mean by this is not that I wish to regard our culture in this way but that on some level we already do, because the hostile statements of intention attributed to the hijackers *are sensible to us as such;* they constitute a kind of logic—not one we admire, to be sure, but one we understand. The WTC constituted what we can already comprehend as excess; reflected the excess of the culture that built it, the excess of capitalism, the excess of ethnocentric superiority. It is this guilt about excess that is relieved and re-relieved as we watch the edifices turn to dust and ruin in videotape replay. But immediately, as the tape loop circles, we have the buildings whole again, presto!, and we can taste triumph and power, the recipe for disaster. Later we are reminded the buildings were not *only* infrastructures but also habitations. Inside were people, whose presence and death must be reiterated so that we can grasp them in the face of the compelling vision, which would otherwise blot them out. Indeed, we *must* be reminded, because the vision *is* blotting them out.

It is a similar vision—a primitive vision, one might as well admit—that empowers us to marvel at the great ape Kong tumbling from the top of the world. As Patrice Blouin writes (of Jacques Tati's *Playtime*), "The madness of greatness, the romanticism of disaster, and the staggering collapse of yesterday's still-worshipped idols constitute the real stuff of American cinema, its day-to-day story and its eternal legend, its most perfect script" (44; author's translation). James Sanders, displeased with the WTC in general, one suspects, and certainly with De Laurentiis's film, complains that "[s]ome effort has to be made, in fact, to ensure that Kong actually falls over the side, rather than simply plops down on this football field of a roof" (101), and to be sure, we are desperate for this effort, we want to see the Fall. We gaze at the foreplay—the attack of the biplanes in the original film and the helicopters seeming to "sweep in from the Mekong Delta" in the re-make; Kong's putting the girl down (she "famously refuses to respond" [Erb 118]); the close shots of the ape being strafed, bullets passing quite through him; his dumbfounded gaze outward at the great vista of the incomprehensible, now utterly unreachable, metropolis; then his precarious loss of balance—finally, anticlimactically, as though it might never have come, the fall. The fall is ever greater for us because of the extenuation and development of the "foreplay"; and indeed, it may be apprehensible to us as he loses his perch that the building has been insinuated into the film not only to symbolize New York and civilization and hegemony and technical capacity but also to make pos-sible this devastating plunge. "Whom the gods wish to destroy they first raise up," Shaw wrote of Caesar. The fall, in fact, is what we came to see, and the stilled body in the WTC Plaza, coldly lit by klieg light, is proof that the fall has taken place. While in the original *Kong*, a shot of the ape falling had to be excised because of flaws in the matte process (Sanders 100), in the 1976 film, there is an emphatic shot taken from below as he drops toward the camera, moaning as he drops into us.

Only afterward need we reflect upon the fact, as Dwan slowly circles the great face, that Kong was "alive"; that the crash had vital implica-tion. As we appreciate it in its presence, the crash is first and fore-most—like the WTC destruction—a wonder of gravity, a new Titanic sinking. To some degree, we must feel that what can cause such an event must itself be a force of nature. We felt this inchoately on Sep-tember 11. Hence the propaganda value of the WTC attack, since not only the economy and the population were violated but also the Western *Weltanschauung*, the sense of what the world is, where we are in it, where nature is and we are not.

If Kong is a replacement for man, a fetish, he is hardly the only—or even the most fascinating—replacement in the film. The girl Dwan, named for Allan Dwan (1885–1981), the maker of *The Iron Mask* (1929) and *The Gorilla* (1939) and discoverer of Carole Lombard, Ida Lupino, and Natalie Wood (Bogdanovich 42), is not only a stand-in for film itself, because of that relationship, but a stand-in, too, for a woman—not metaphorically, in the sense that she has not yet come to terms with her social position or her self-concept, not yet accepted the responsibilities of facing up to her cultural position, but literally, in every one of a number of shots to which we are treated very frequently and which constitute a spectacular highlight of the film. I refer to the process shots in which she inhabits the hand of Kong, picked up, grasped, ferried, tickled, gazed at, moistened, blown dry, ogled, even "spoken to." Here, after all, if we adopt Kong's perspective—as we do both when he looks down upon her (and we grasp his lofty perspective) and when we see him with her from a distance—she is no person but only a figurine. Such is the fate, too, of those unfortunates trapped in the WTC, waving out of the windows, so long as we view them against the frame of the building as central figuration. They are fetishes for our most abject fear, perfectly suggesting—but safely, pictorially— vulnerability, mortality, innocence. At the same time, they are the diminishment of human importance and capacity in the perspective of a global capitalism that can erect such monuments to cupidity and mastery as the WTC around the world. Dwan is not Kong's presumptive lover; she is his toy, his fetish, his protecting spirit that he must carry with him everywhere. Not merely a token "female," then, Lange is playing a token human. In the same way, demonically, Atta, the American aircraft and passengers, and the Trade Center and its inhabitants, were the fetishes of bin Laden.

In this respect, Dwan is not only a child's delight but also a deeply chilling figuration, an idol. Discussing voyeurism in *Psycho* (1960) and the viewer's "divorce from the situation or abdication from any demands of involvement," J. P. Telotte adduces Owen Barfield's definition of idolatry, a "tendency to abstract the sense data from the whole representation and seek that for its own sake, transmuting the admired image into a desired object" ("Faith" 29). When a child, such as Kong (and why might he not be considered a child, regardless of his size?), abdicates from involvement through the use of a fetish, he is prone to emotional engagement exactly in his withdrawal and abdication. As Dwan is his plaything, then, he can be fascinated by her exactly to the degree that he cannot know her. We, I submit, are in the same predicament with respect to him, since he is our fetish. The difference between us is that we are more lethal than he is, in the end, unwilling to put him down before he gets hurt. If the WTC from which Kong tumbled in 1976—"a very boring piece of architecture," according to Vincent Canby—became our own fetish twenty-five years later, we understood its fall, came to terms with the terrorist attack exactly by withdrawing and abdicating ourselves. Television helped us in our withdrawal, no doubt, but did not create the preconditions for it. Ours is perhaps a more destructive potentiality for coldness even than the terrorists' who razed the buildings, since their dark potency fulfilled itself with a grandiose but yet a limited horror, a reflection of the great gorilla, if you will. But we watch videotape replays. Even now, in the summer of 2002 with ground zero cleared away, there is much talk of planning the tomb, the memorial, the reconstruction. Our capacity to see all this, and to repeat seeing it, is fetishism of a higher order.

Our capacity to stand back for a vision of the buildings coming down, like our stunned but pleasured sight of Kong dropping to his end, signals our own gross idolatry. We have fetishized the WTC itself, and all those who worked and lived therein, to the degree that documentaries and sermons need to be fashioned for us, that we might shudder with some tinge of genuineness at the vast multiplicity of death and sadness. As in the exploding architecture of *ID4,* the devastation of Tokyo in *Godzilla,* the wholesale flooding of the east coast in *Deep Impact* (1998), and the destruction of downtown Baltimore in *The Sum of All Fears* (2002), the image of disaster permits us to stand back from it and gasp, a reaction of such complete uninvolvement, even superiority, that we stun ourselves into guilt by experiencing it as beautiful. Then, quickly, we leap into sensitivity for the families of the dead; hero worship of the brave workers who must dig through the rubble; virulent and blind hatred of all aliens everywhere who must be thinking in their unknown abodes how to attack us once again. Manifest Destiny lives.

In ends are beginnings. Instead of seeing *King Kong* as a film about a mysterious island actually existent in some undeclared topography, where resides, in at least fictional truth, a beast of magical proportions; and therefore the story of a supernatural prize it is only natural for men to lust after, quest for, slyly capture, bring home, and show off; what if, instead, we begin with the Fall? Desperate to abdicate from our own experience and culture, to watch the giant world come down with an expressive crash, what heights must we first invent, what story tell that will inflate the object of our vision so it can thrill us when it lies in rubble at our feet? Kong is only in the jungle to be raised to a height. His love for Dwan is only the goad to make us love him and leave him, that we may be exultant upon his corpse. For surely, as Henry Louis Gates Jr. wrote of James Baldwin, "We like our heroes dead" (20).

In such a scenario, and only there, absence makes the heart grow fond. Here, the WTC of September 11 and the WTC from which Kong fell are no longer divided by the fictional membrane but are one and the same. Our thrill at devastation is hardly in itself the story of our civilization in fact, but it is the story of *Kong* and, as such, the story of the way we have chosen to tell the story of our civilization. Indeed, our fascination with *King Kong* continues unabated. Peter Jackson is now shooting a new version of *Kong* in New Zealand, which will be released in 2005.

Notes

1. See Farrell.
2. See Rony.

Works Cited

Arnold, Gary. "The New Kong Is Dead, Long Live the Old." *Washington Post* Dec. 18, 1976: B1.

Berenstein, Rhona J. *Attack of the Leading Ladies: Gender, Sexuality, and Spectatorship in Classic Horror Cinema.* New York: Columbia UP, 1996.

Billington, David P. *The Tower and the Bridge.* New York: Basic, 1983.

Blouin, Patrice. "*Playtime:* Bienvenue à Tativille." *Cahiers du Cinéma* 56 (May 2002): 44–47.

Bogdanovich, Peter. *Who the Devil Made It.* New York: Knopf, 1997.

Burns, Ric, and James Sanders. *New York: An Illustrated History.* New York: Knopf, 1999.

Canby, Vincent. "*'King Kong'* Bigger, Not Better, In a Return to Screen of Crime." *New York Times* Dec. 18, 1976: 16.

Carr, Steven Alan. "From Street Scene to Dead End: Naturalism, Hollywood, and the Urban Ethnic Immigrant, 1931–1937." Society for Cinema Studies Annual Conference. Denver. May 2002.

Carroll, Noël. "*King Kong:* Ape and Essence." *Planks of Reason: Essays on the Horror Film.* Ed. Barry Keith Grant. Metuchen, NJ: Scarecrow, 1984. 215–44.

Doherty, Thomas. *Pre-Code Hollywood: Sex, Immorality, and Insurrection in American Cinema 1930–1934.* New York: Columbia UP, 1999.

Erb, Cynthia. *Tracking King Kong: A Hollywood Icon in World Culture.* Detroit: Wayne State UP, 1998.

Farrell, Kirby. "Aliens Amok: *Men in Black* Policing Subjectivity in the '90s." *Bang Bang, Shoot Shoot! Essays on Guns and Popular Culture.* Ed. Murray Pomerance and John Sakeris. Needham Heights, MA: Simon, 1999. 35–46.

Gates, Henry Louis Jr. *Thirteen Ways of Looking at a Black Man.* New York: Random, 1997.

Gilman, Sander L. *Jewish Self-Hatred: Anti-Semitism and the Hidden Language of the Jews.* Baltimore: Johns Hopkins UP, 1986.

Johnson, David. "World Trade Center History." Aug. 15, 2002. <www.infoplease.com/spot/wtc1.html>.

Rony, Fatimah Tobing. *The Third Eye: Race, Cinema, and Ethnographic Spectacle.* Durham: Duke UP, 1996.

Sanders, James. *Celluloid Skyline: New York and the Movies.* New York: Knopf, 2001.

Sontag, Susan. 1964. "Notes on 'Camp.'" *Against Interpretation and Other Essays.* New York: Delta: 275–92.

Telotte, J. P. "Faith and Idolatry in the Horror Film." *Planks of Reason: Essays on the Horror Film.* Ed. Barry Keith Grant. Metuchen, NJ: Scarecrow, 1984. 21–37.

———. "The Movies as Monster: Seeing in *King Kong.*" *Georgia Review* 42.2 (1988): 388–98.

Wray, Fay. *On the Other Hand: A Life Story.* New York: St. Martin's, 1989.

The author thanks Nellie Perret, Steve Alan Carr, Jane Hoehner, Scott Preston, Mike Anderson, and Gwendolyn Audrey Foster for their perceptive comments on various drafts of this chapter.

4

Representing Atrocity
From the Holocaust to September 11

David Sterritt

The attacks of September 11 unleashed waves of media representation that both recall and contrast with representations of the Holocaust and its horrors. On one hand, the 9/11 attacks were widely seen as acts of flat-out destructiveness that differed from genocide only in their more limited scale. Media coverage emphasized their horrific nature in graphic and even lurid terms, with such periodicals as *Newsweek* and *Time* publishing special editions containing color-drenched images of blood-smeared survivors, bodies falling from windows, and the iconic World Trade Center crashing to the earth. One might easily think this was the Holocaust in miniature or the first act in a larger Holocaust-like tragedy fated to unfold in days to come. Video coverage shown on television took similar tacks.

Yet there are key differences between accounts of the Holocaust and those of the 9/11 events. Chronicles of the Holocaust necessarily contain little authentic moving-image documentation, while the occurrences of 9/11 became internationally visible when they were still taking place. Conversely, the physical tortures of the Holocaust have reached public awareness most vividly through images of atrocity captured after the Nazi camps were liberated, whereas the physical containment of the damage inflicted on September 11—facilitated by the nature of the attacks and the fact that the World Trade Center towers imploded instead of scattering their wreckage outward—rendered the destruction of human life almost invisible to the eye. The popular media rushed to compensate for this invisibility with a blitz of belligerent journalism on related matters, hammering incessantly on aspects of the case that are readily turned into narrative (e.g., the hunt for Osama bin Laden) and seizing on a fitfully fought, nebulously defined "war against terrorism" as a durable support for commercially marketable "public affairs" coverage.

In this context, note the progression of Holocaust representation through several stages, beginning with the poetic evocations of Alain Resnais's *Night and Fog* (*Nuit et brouillard,* 1955), then moving through more conventional documentaries and such widely disseminated narrative movies as Otto Preminger's *Exodus* (1960) and Stanley Kramer's *Judgment at Nuremberg* (1961), and turning in more recent years to the intellectually sophisticated accounts of such cinematic historians as Marcel Ophuls and Claude Lanzmann, who have chosen to omit "atrocity footage" from their works. Also interesting are the parallels among the avoidance of atrocity images in films by Ophuls and Lanzmann, the homemade tributes placed near the World Trade Center site by survivors and mourners, and the work of an artist like Christian Boltanski, who has skirted the twin pitfalls of sensationalism and sentimentality by exploring the Holocaust through ephemeral materials that achieve resonance through their very refusal of monumental form.

Conventional wisdom about the events of September 11 is clear: Everything has changed since the terrorist attacks on New York and Washington, and nothing will be quite the same again. We are still waiting to see what long-term forms this transformation will take. Responses by ordinary citizens during the first months after the attacks have run along traditional lines. As someone who lived one minute away from the World Trade Center at the time its towers fell and walked past it several times each day in the weeks afterward, I have had a good look at the gestures made on the outskirts of Ground Zero—photos of lost loved ones, children's toys and stuffed animals placed as tributes to slaughtered or orphaned youngsters, countless American flags, and other items that one might expect to find at what newscasters like to call a "makeshift memorial."

As a film critic, I have also looked closely at how filmmakers—from Hollywood moguls to independent auteurs—have debated the propriety of representing 9/11 in popular terms, trying to calculate when the public would be ready to relive it at the multiplex or on living-room video screens. It was not hard to foresee that films about September 11 would start flowing sooner rather than later, and that like the makeshift memorials at Ground Zero, they would take predictable forms—news hour specials reprising the tragedy with retroactive commentary and recycled video, and docudramas recreating individual and collective traumas of the apocalyptic day.

It was also obvious that full-fledged theatrical features would take a bit longer to arrive, given the lengthy turnaround time for feature-length narrative movies from initial conceptualization to the completion of final release prints, but that they would surely reach the screen as soon as producers grew confident they would not face charges of exploiting or capitalizing on the disaster. It seemed equally probable that their focus would be on the terrors faced by victims, heroic acts performed by rescue teams, and (more ambitiously) reasons why the cataclysm was not prevented (or, according to some theories, why it was actually allowed to happen) by law-enforcement and national-security agencies. Anticipating the inevitable onset of Hollywood responses to 9/11, representatives of George W. Bush's administration (including Karl Rove, the president's chief of staff) met with the chief of the Motion Picture Association of America, Jack Valenti, and other powerful figures of the film and television world to discuss options for handling the newborn "war on terrorism" and related matters. While the treatment of on-screen violence was a subject of ostensible concern, reports of the conclave indicate little serious thought about altering Hollywood's longtime status quo vis-à-vis this issue—nobody appears to have suggested that in-production films like *Black Hawk Down* and *We Were Soldiers* be aborted, for instance, or that depictions of wartime mayhem be stripped of the heroic and "patriotic" overtones traditionally draped upon them in mass-media entertainments.

Sure enough, movies dealing directly or indirectly with international terrorism and xenophobic paranoia are now positioned at various points along the production pipeline, preceded by a faltering parade of features that gained secondhand relevance to 9/11 by virtue of shots depicting the twin towers themselves (such as *Spider-Man* [2002], which was reworked to eliminate potentially distasteful World Trade Center action) or sequences with problematic images of urban disaster. The latter category included the Arnold Schwarzenegger vehicle *Collateral Damage* (2001), which the Warner Brothers studio moved from an opening date of October 5, 2001, to February 8, 2002, because of nervousness over the premise of the story, which has a firefighter embarking on a vigilante-style hunt for the Colombian drug merchants who killed his wife and child when they bombed a Los Angeles building to assassinate a political enemy. Although it was widely reported that Warner Brothers delayed the film's release because its depiction of fiery disaster in an urban building might be too disturbing for audiences in the immediate aftermath of 9/11, skeptics have suggested that its view of a fictional cataclysm, juiced up with standard-issue special effects, might have appeared not too troubling but too *tame* after ubiquitous television coverage of the real thing. Be this as it may, the studio did its best to protect its investment in the movie, prevailing on Schwarzenegger to preside over a Manhattan premiere accompanied by representatives of the Twin Towers Fund, a charitable organization. Ironically, the main controversy that greeted the release came from Colombian Americans who complained that the movie was ethnically biased, citing the hero's hunt for evil-looking Colombian bad guys in far-flung jungle villages. Few people seemed very exercised over the urban-disaster imagery.

Not long afterward, the release on May 31, 2002, of *The Sum of All Fears* (2002) sparked widespread media speculation as to whether Americans were "ready" for an action-adventure melodrama in which nuclear bombs decimate Baltimore; they proved to be very ready indeed, making the picture an immediate box-office hit. One short week later, on June 7, 2002, the question returned with a different twist, asking whether Americans were "ready" for a rollicking *comedy* about a streetwise Central Intelligence Agency recruit (Chris Rock) racing to head off a nuclear device smuggled into Manhattan by terrorists. *Bad Company* (2002) fared less well financially than *The Sum of All Fears* did, but blame for its lackluster performance falls more on its dubious entertainment value than on its relationship to 9/11. In any case, one wonders whether the "readiness" debates had any relevance to a moviegoing public that was clearly ready for anything that provided a sufficient number of entertainment bangs for its ticket-window bucks.

As film and video representations of September 11 multiply in time to come, I expect most critics will respond to them as they respond to other movies on "sensitive" issues: assessing the effectiveness with which they convey facts, elicit emotions, and accomplish the other audience-pleasing tasks traditionally associated with mainstream cinema. More thoughtful critics will also consider how earnest and responsible the representation appears to be—whether it seems motivated by a sincere desire to inform the living and memorialize the dead, or by the money-driven imperatives of Hollywood's never-ending quest for cutting-edge subjects and stories. Anticipating this, producers will try to balance what they perceive as the requirements of entertainment against the special need for sensitivity and seriousness called for by such a topic. Examples of this high-wire act arose immediately after 9/11, in network decisions about what to show and not to show in initial coverage of the catastrophe. One network played video of flaming victims leaping from the towers, for example, but withdrew the footage after a single late-night broadcast. Others chose not to display such material at all.

To show or not to show. This is one of the issues that led my mind from the horrors of the World Trade Center disaster to the radically different horrors of the Holocaust, and to the ways in which filmmakers have struggled to come to terms with them over the past half century. A retrospective look at Holocaust representation in cinema provides revealing insights into paths that responsible film and video makers might choose to follow or to avoid with regard to the 9/11 cataclysm. One reason why I find the comparison between historical representations of the Holocaust and present-day representations of September 11 so compelling is that, as already noted, the respective histories of these representations begin on such starkly opposite terms. In the case of the Holocaust, no imagery of any kind was publicly shown until the death camps had been liberated and the worst of the horrors were over; and even then most images necessarily depicted not the horrors themselves—aside from bits of footage shot by Nazis—but the appalling aftermath of these horrors as captured by Allied soldiers with sixteen-millimeter movie cameras. In the case of the World Trade Center, television video gave the entire world instant access to the traumatizing sight of hijacked planes crashing into the towers' walls and those walls crumbling under their own awesome weight as thousands struggled to escape and flee. Is it true, as Adorno resonantly wrote, that after Auschwitz, the act of writing poetry is barbaric? As horrendous as they were, the events of September 11 were far less sweeping and staggering than the Holocaust's unimaginable evils. Yet the question of artistic representation versus the pitfalls of vulgarizing barbarity remains an urgent one. Much light can be cast on it by observing how filmmakers have confronted it in the context of the Holocaust.

On the level of content and technique, can images capture, reproduce, or convey the essence of events and situations more vast and horrifying than anything encountered in everyday life or the so-called normal world? And on the level of philosophy and ethics, is it decent or permissible to make the attempt in the first place? This issue has long prompted debate among film theorists and historians, with regard not only to documentaries but also to fiction films that incorporate documentary material, such as the prizewinning *Judgment at Nuremberg,* which incorporates film footage from the liberated camps, and the TV miniseries *Holocaust* (1978), which employs still photos from sites of the atrocities.

The question of whether displaying death-camp footage is appropriate did not trouble the makers of *Night and Fog,* the first Holocaust documentary to become an enduring classic. Resnais was less concerned about the legitimacy of using authentic Holocaust images than about the even more basic question of whether he had a moral right to deal with the Holocaust at all, since he had not been personally involved with the camps in any way. He told film scholar Annette Insdorf that he decided to proceed with the project only on the condition that its voice-over commentary would be written by Jean Cayrol, a Holocaust survivor (213). This pairing of narrator and image maker is a key to the distinctiveness and power of *Night and Fog,* since as Insdorf notes, it juxtaposes the perspective of a witness with that of an artist working to make sense of the witness's survival and of the appalling circumstances that he overcame. So far at least, media representers of 9/11 have shown little of Resnais's scrupulous hesitation.

Later documentaries about the Holocaust have taken a wide variety of approaches—some relying heavily on archival film footage, others supplementing or partly displacing such images with didactic narrations, interviews with Holocaust survivors and participants, and the like. In positive or negative ways, all inevitably have some relationship with the issues I have mentioned above, which are also crucially relevant to present and future representations of the World Trade Center tragedy: whether filmed images can capture "truths" about sets of events so extraordinary, and what boundaries are established around representations of such events by moral and ethical considerations. The mightiest of all Holocaust documentaries are implicitly addressed to these questions, as well as to events of the Holocaust itself. I have in mind three films by American director Marcel Ophuls—*The Sorrow and the Pity* (1970), *The Memory of Justice* (1976), and *Hotel Terminus: The Life and Times of Klaus Barbie* (1988)—and two by Israeli director Claude Lanzmann, the epic *Shoah* (1985) and the more specifically focused *Sobibor, October 14, 1943, 4 p.m.* (2001).

The Sorrow and the Pity was recognized as an unprecedented work from its first appearance, and its reputation has scarcely dimmed. Film historian Marc Ferro has called it "a kind of October Revolution" in documentary filmmaking, since it introduces a novel use for the time-tested device of the filmed interview (142). I second this view. The interviews in *The Sorrow and the Pity* not only confront individuals with the past and challenge *versions* of the past that they would like to retain and promulgate but also are so richly structured and artfully interwoven that Ophuls is able to substitute them for the voice-over commentary that had been a commonplace in previous Holocaust documentaries.

A key element in this important film is therefore not a presence but an absence—the absence of anything corresponding to a "voice-of-God narration" in the traditional sense. In a 1988 interview with me, Ophuls explained his disdain for conventional narration in both practical and ethical terms. On one level, he said voice-overs are "too easy to do" and reduce films to "illustrated editorials." On a deeper level, he argued that narration "lends itself to propaganda [and] the legitimizing of all kinds of 'isms' [and] ideology." It seems to me that the implications of Ophuls's view are even larger than these statements indicate. For one thing, the omission of voice-of-God commentary puts the burden of expression on actual documentary materials rather than on the guiding and explaining presence of the filmmaker; such expression heightens the authenticity of the film while it enhances the ability of verbal and visual montage to throw past and present into mutually illuminating relief. For another, as critic James Roy MacBean has suggested, it facilitates the collapsing of past and present in a de-poeticized way—contrasting with the manner of a *Night and Fog*—by using a "window-on-the-world" approach to puncture time-honored myths about the film's primary topics, French resistance and collaboration during the Nazi era (478).

Ophuls continued his avoidance of conventional narration in two subsequent Holocaust documentaries, in which he also explored a new tendency in his work: a wish to project his own personality, opinions, and directorial problems visibly into the film. In *The Memory of Justice,* a massive work about the Nuremberg war-crimes inquiry, he includes conversation with his wife and daughter, and a remarkable sequence during which songs on the sound track comment mischievously on the more commercial activities that his friends and colleagues might rather see him pursue. He escalates this personalized filmmaking even further in *Hotel Terminus,* with more ironic music and his own personal, sometimes fierce confrontations with interview subjects. Ophuls may have eliminated traditional narration, but commentary continues to play a key role in his work, albeit in novel and increasingly personal ways. In *Hotel Terminus,* Ophuls also confronts the main issue that concerns us here: that of when *utilization* becomes *exploitation* in the handling of actual Holocaust images. Lanzmann has come to grips with this issue as well, arriving at even more radical—and radically effective—conclusions.

Fred Camper has suggested the possibility that "the photographing of any cinema image of a part of the actual world is an act of aggression," since the photographer "wrenches a specific part of reality from the context with which it makes a whole, places that fragment in a rectangular frame, and further delimits it in time" (par. 13). Turning to the issue of proprietorship of the image, Camper notes both the filmmaker's "need to exercise control over what is in front of [the] camera" and the tendency of passive spectators in darkened theaters "to feel that the images are in some sense [their] own." (This tendency might be even stronger in TV and video viewing, where the images are viewed at close proximity and can be stopped, started, fast-forwarded, and replayed at will.) Such considerations must weigh heavily in the minds of Holocaust documentary makers, who do not wrench, place, delimit, and control just any "part of reality" but parts that are directly connected to this century's most overwhelmingly horrific crime. If one grants film theorist André Bazin's contention that photographic images are literal "tracings" of reality, the moral ramifications are profound.

The situation is even more serious if, as Camper further suggests, film images viewed in big-screen splendor are "inevitably glorified by the projector's beam" in such a way that, in artistically successful films, they are "charged with a certain aesthetic beauty, or at least a kind of energy [which] it is hard to imagine . . . being utterly controlled by [feelings of] condemnation." Again, this must be carefully pondered by any filmmaker who aspires to depict an event as purely evil as the Holocaust—or the destruction of the World Trade Center—without giving it any hint of aesthetic beauty or artistic energy, however subtly, subliminally, or unwittingly.

Camper makes a sweeping statement when he suggests that a component of aggression may be inherent to the act of photography, regardless of the particular object being photographed. In her book *On Photography*, critic Susan Sontag makes a similar suggestion that refers specifically to the photographing of human beings. "To photograph people is to violate them," she writes, "by seeing them as they never see themselves, by having knowledge of them they can never have; it turns people into objects that can be symbolically possessed. . . . [T]o photograph someone is a sublimated murder" (14–15). Judith Doneson takes a somewhat more benign view, seeing the issue of who took the photographs, and under what circumstances, as deciding factors. Since some Jews documented life in the ghetto with photos, she says, "Using these testimonies today would . . . comply with the wishes of the Jews to have their history remembered" (178). What such differing views have in common is recognition of the fact that to depict the Holocaust in any way and for any purpose is to depict an event that must be measured entirely on the scale of human anxiety, human suffering, human death. Photographs of human beings must be used, whether these are authentic Holocaust images or statements by Holocaust survivors—and this raises a moral conundrum if we see the photographed individuals as being in any way victimized by being filmed as human beings and as objects in the material world.

One must add to this difficulty the even more profound problem of capturing the inhumanly vast magnitude of the Holocaust and its apparatuses of death. Holocaust film historian Ilan Avisar cites Lawrence Langer's study *The Holocaust and the Literary Imagination* on several points relevant to whether the enormities of the Holocaust can be conveyed through photography or any other means designed for realistic depiction: *(a)* that the Holocaust was "so fantastic and so extraordinary that it defies our basic notions of empirical reality, the raw material of every mimetic art"; *(b)* that "realistic accounts are limited by conventional patterns of thought and therefore cannot penetrate the darkest recess of human experience"; and *(c)* that literary "disfiguration" is preferable to realistic depiction because (in Avisar's phrase) it can "eliminate the possibility of aesthetic pleasure" (1–2). Avisar takes issue with Langer's last point, noting (among other things) that modernism often returns to "the raw material of reality" in order to "seize and grasp its ontological dimension." It is worth stressing, however, that both Camper and Langer see the dangerous possibility of aesthetic pleasure being proffered by realistic accounts of even the most hideous possible human event. Writing on Hans-Jürgen Syberberg's neoexpressionist epic *Our Hitler, a Film from Germany* (1977) in "Eye of the Storm," a 1980 essay in *The New York Review of Books,* Sontag strikes a similar note by suggesting that Syberberg could not "rely on documents to show how it 'really' was [since] the display of atrocity in the form of photographic evidence risks being tacitly pornographic" (qtd. in Insdorf 169). Many critical assessments of Leni Riefenstahl's documentaries on Nazi subjects describe an incipiently pornographic effect in them, as well.

This is precisely the point addressed by Ophuls in *Hotel Terminus* and by Lanzmann in *Shoah* and *Sobibor,* by means of yet another absence—this one even more profound and far-reaching than the absence of spoken commentary discussed above. These documentaries make extensive use of interviews shot in diverse locations, but neither contains any trace of so-called atrocity footage from the Holocaust itself. Both films undertake to document the Holocaust entirely through the recollections of individuals who went through it. As with his dislike of voice-of-God narration, Ophuls tends to explain his avoidance of atrocity footage in simple and perhaps oversimplified terms. Such footage "doesn't get the job done anymore," he told me, indicating his feeling that audiences have become desensitized to it by seeing it in so many previous films (Ophuls). But his decision to make a four-and-a-half-hour film without a single minute of such material points to a deeper motivation, and clues to this may be found in *Shoah,* a film that Ophuls deeply admires.

One of the most memorable elements in *Shoah* is the film's obsessive return to shots of the front gate of the Auschwitz camp, filmed with a camera moving along the railroad tracks that once carried trainloads of Jews to their deaths. Once it has reached the gate, the camera continues along its trajectory into the camp, but as Camper observes, it does so by switching to a zoom lens instead of moving physically ahead. "If camera movement tends to suggest movement through space, as of a human body," writes Camper, "the zoom tends to represent the movement of the mind, shifts in human perception." On this view, Lanzmann fulfills his film's obligation to take us into a concentration camp—yet by physically stopping his camera at the gate, he acknowledges the inability of present-day observers to truly enter such a place or truly comprehend what occurred there. He also tacitly acknowledges the "violation" that might take place if his camera *were* to penetrate the cursed space about which we hear so much from the witnesses he interviews. Lanzmann's refusal to use archival material of any kind, including film footage and still photos, may be understood in the same way: as a suggestion that to use *any* product of the death camps, for however well-meaning or enlightening a purpose, might be to participate, in however small a way, in the Nazis' enterprise.

All of this is worth bearing in mind as we come to grips with present and future 9/11 documentaries and docudramas. The nature of contemporary media technology adds additional cause for concern, moreover, especially when recycled video images of the World Trade Center disaster are put into play. In an essay exploring contrasts between traditional Hollywood moving-camera shots (made with cumbersome dollies and cranes) and the effortless perfection of modern Steadicam techniques, Jean-Pierre Geuens uses *Night and Fog* as an example, noting how differently today's new technology would have rendered the film's long traveling shot along a string of Auschwitz latrines. Arguing that "the entire gravitas of the scene would be lost," Geuens notes that in this sequence the filmmakers "enlist the slow, determinate, carefully executed dolly movement to interrogate the palpability of the cracks in the concrete, conveying, through the intentionality of the motion, their concern with the very muteness of the photographic image and its failure to evoke but the phantom of an event that was then and is now truly unspeakable." By contrast, a high-tech Steadicam shot would have seemed "respectful, but thoroughly incapable of interpreting the traces in the barrack or of questioning the failures of one's own memory. . . . The burden of the historical reflection would be replaced by mere externals, timeless surfaces without connotations" (15). One wonders whether the crushing reality of 9/11 was diminished in the instant of its first telling by the evanescent look and feel of the instant-video images that appeared on television screens around the world—however much the inherent characteristics of video are conventionally assumed to convey an automatic sense of on-the-spot actuality and infallibility.

The issues I have explored so far relate to the possibilities and pitfalls faced by documentary filmmakers who seek to convey unthinkable realities through cinematic images. The producers of forthcoming September 11 films will not all be practitioners of nonfiction, however. Some will be dramatic filmmakers, and their motives will vary widely, ranging from the responsible to the reprehensible. If we are fortunate, the responsible ones will emulate a creative and conscientious filmmaker like Israeli director Amos Gitaï, whose drama *Kippur* (2000) finds an extraordinary array of ways to depict the horrors of war as exactly what articulate veterans often tell us they are— an appallingly repetitive series of physical and psychological torments conspicuously lacking in the guts-and-glory heroics that war movies have fed us for decades.

Steven Spielberg tells us the same thing in the first twenty minutes of *Saving Private Ryan* (1998), then falls back on those very guts-and-glory clichés for another two hours or so. Given the enormous box-office success of that film and the same director's Holocaust drama *Schindler's List* (1993), it is likely that the makers of future 9/11 films with theatrical and major-network ambitions will draw more inspiration from these, and a thousand other Hollywood epics, than from the Ophuls and Lanzmann masterpieces I have been focusing on. The products of their labors may reinforce Adorno's contention about the impossibility of civilized art in a world where civilization itself stands on shaky foundations. Adorno himself later modified his views, however: "Perennial suffering has as much right to expression as a tortured man has to scream," he wrote in his *Negative Dialectics;* "hence it may have been wrong to say that after Auschwitz you could no longer write poems" (362). And the work of some principled artists has borne out the possibility that poetry after Auschwitz is possible, as it will surely remain after September 11. To suggest just one example, French artist Christian Boltanski has crafted his works from the most fugitive and transitory of materials—often visual materials like old photographs and newspaper pictures, sometimes more tactile kinds of ephemera like bits of clothing, clumsily strung lightbulbs, and candles casting shadows that are at once celebrations of life and dances of death. Through such materials he has evoked the most repugnant and the most poignant aspects of modern Jewish history without crossing the slippery line between exploration and exploitation, and without sliding into the pitfalls presented by the supposed certainty and transparency of overused 9/11 video images.

Looking at the less imaginative contributions to Ground Zero's makeshift memorial, it is hard to escape the conclusion that they are inspired less by heartfelt grief than by reflexive reactions to the shallow patriotism being pushed by TV pundits and radio talkers. The immediate aftermath of 9/11 brought scandalous displays like (to cite one of countless examples) WABC radio's coverage, "Our War Against Terrorism," complete with rock-style background music and crash-boom sound effects, shamelessly illustrating how our allegedly responsible media have turned what is supposed to be a holy war for democracy into entertainment of the crudest, crassest sort. Months later, a *New York Times* photo spread called "Get Your Souvenirs Here" documented such items as a key chain with a picture of Plane No. 2 about to strike, a "World Trade Center—We Won't Forget" snow globe with ashes swirling around two miniature WTC towers, and a twin towers piggy bank. (Is one supposed to smash it when full?) I have seen hawkers peddling toilet paper with "Wipe out terrorism" emblazoned above Osama bin Laden's portrait. And so on.

Such embarrassments contrast vividly with the appearance on Ground Zero's fences of point-and-shoot snapshots, Xeroxed drawings, informally scrawled poems, and other such items bearing the mark not of knee-jerk jingoism but of deeply personal responses to an ultimately incomprehensible event. It is probably asking too much, but one hopes professional chroniclers of September 11 will partake of their introspective spirit—which I take to be Boltanski's spirit as well—rather than the noisy extroversion that has hijacked most of the media so far. As artists like Ophuls and Lanzmann have discovered, the truest memorial may be built from the most unmonumental materials. And the image not shown may be the most telling image of all.

Works Cited

Adorno, Theodor W. "After Auschwitz." *Negative Dialectics*. Trans. E. B. Ashton. New York: Seabury, 1973: 361–65.

Avisar, Ilan. *Screening the Holocaust: Cinema's Images of the Unimaginable*. Bloomington: Indiana UP, 1988.

Bazin, André. *What Is Cinema?* Trans. Hugh Gray. Berkeley: U of California P, 1967.

Camper, Fred. "*Shoah*'s Absence." *Motion Picture* 4 (winter–spring 1987). Rpt. in <http://www.fredcamper.com/Film/Lanzmann.html>.

Doneson, Judith E. *The Holocaust in American Film*. Philadelphia: Jewish Pub. Soc., 1987.

Ferro, Marc. *Cinema and History*. Trans. Naomi Greene. Detroit: Wayne State UP, 1988.

Geuens, Jean-Pierre. "Visibility and Power: The Work of the Steadicam." *Film Quarterly* 47.2 (winter 1993–94). 8–17.

Insdorf, Annette. *Indelible Shadows: Film and the Holocaust*. Cambridge: Cambridge UP, 1989.

MacBean, James Roy. "*The Sorrow and the Pity:* France and Her Political Myths." Ed. Alan Rosenthal. New Challenges for Documentary. Berkeley: U of California P, 1988: 471–79.

Ophuls, Marcel. Personal interview. New York. Nov. 1988.

Sontag, Susan. "Eye of the Storm." *New York Review of Books* 27.2 (Feb. 21, 1980). Qtd. in Insdorf.

———. *On Photography.* New York: Anchor, 1990.

The author thanks Mikita Brottman and Fred Camper for their helpful insights during the writing and revision of this chapter.

5

"America under Attack"
Pearl Harbor, 9/11, and History in the Media

Marcia Landy

September 11 and Remembering Pearl Harbor

On September, 11, 2001, CBS News anchorman Dan Rather referred to the aircraft-missile attacks on the World Trade Center and the Pentagon, and the crashing of a plane near Pittsburgh, as "the Pearl Harbor of terrorism." The visuals that accompanied this pronouncement, emphasizing the crashing of the planes and the images of people leaping to their deaths from the windows of the World Trade Center, were described as "unimaginable. But part of today's reality." The constant news reports and television specials that emanated from CNN, NBC, ABC, CBS, and Fox on September 12 inundated the public with images of the disaster, and commentaries by anchors such as Dan Rather, Peter Jennings, and Tom Brokaw and interviews with government officials, historians, and even psychiatrists were quick to locate an historical analogy in December 7, 1941.

Repeatedly, images of the New York skyline minus the twin towers were interspersed with references to Pearl Harbor and "the day of infamy." Rather talked of how that earlier event "brought the United States of America together and propelled it to victory." On the same program, Rather interviewed the Israeli foreign minister, Shimon Perez, in Jerusalem, who commented, "The most important consequence today is to develop a strategy against terror." When asked whether there was a connection between the attacks and the U.S. support of Israel, Perez responded, "Terror is a new phenomenon, and

Israel is not the only target." This interview was interrupted by Karen Hughes, who reported on the whereabouts of the president and other high officials, also a matter of confusion and concern in the first media responses to the day. The program ended with Bob Schieffer interviewing Chuck Hagel, Republican senator from Nebraska, about the setting in place of security precautions at airports and other strategic sites. Hagel described the attack as a direct assault on the freedom of every American and, indeed, on the freedom of anyone who has it around the world.

On CNBC the following day, September 12, historian Doris Kearns Goodwin was interviewed by anchor Chris Matthews about the historical import of September 11. Matthews questioned her about the pertinence of the comparisons of September 11 to December 7. She replied that the assault at Pearl Harbor was on a military base where people felt vulnerable after the attack but that the September 11 bombings were on "people in their everyday lives and offices, walking on the streets." Unwilling to relinquish the analogy with Pearl Harbor and the retaliation by the United States, however, she stated, "It's high time now" for all the countries in the world to whom we have provided World War II support in the form of Lend-Lease, the Marshall Plan, NATO, and foreign aid to show their support for our nation. Recalling war efforts during World War II, she asserted that there is again a need for trained air marshals, the creation of war bonds, and more recruitment of competent individuals into intelligence agencies. She described the enemy as exemplifying how "the fire of anti-Americanism . . . has been bred into their system." The interview ended with her exhortation, "We have to allow our commensurate power as a superpower to be mobilized . . . now . . . and unto twenty years from now." Her interpretation of history is consonant with the other media events described above—selective in its choice of analogy and combative.

On September 13, Peter Jennings anchored "Special News Report: America under Attack," in which he joined with a number of reporters and specialists to evaluate the events to date. He, too, had on hand an historian to assess the events of September 11. Michael Beschloss described the attack as unique, not to be compared with earlier events such as Pearl Harbor, but he presented an ahistorical view that inevitably includes Pearl Harbor, since according to him, Americans are the same now as they were then: the American character has not changed. America is and has been "compassionate," with a great respect for civil liberties, thanks to a "national character" that is "woven into our genetic code." Thus he directly invoked biology as inherent to national character, responsible for compassion and benevolence, and presumably available as justification for war and violence. In terms that echo the numerous allusions to Pearl Harbor, Beschloss asserted that September 11 has "unified the nation." In talking about the effect of the casualties, Beschloss added another strand to the genetic character of the American—resilience.

Maintaining this optimistic and sociobiologic view of Americans, the program introduced reporter Dan Harris in an interview with a woman on the street who talked of the bravery exhibited by the New York firefighters and her appreciation of their work. Heroizing of the firefighters, as well as of Mayor Giuliani, began to emerge and would approach veneration in the following months. The next segment of the special was an interview with a spokesman for the National Football League, which had decided to cancel the weekend games to allow opportunity to "pause, grieve, and reflect." The baseball commissioner and several baseball team owners concurred with this decision. These instances, in Beschloss's terms, provided yet more proof of the "compassion" and "resilience" of the "American character."

After a report about the security precautions being instituted at airports, Jennings lauded "the unity and patriotism we have seen in the country today." However, the invocation of trauma was not neglected, as the story of Sheila Wood was presented. She told of her escape from death in the World Trade Center, her attempts to get air, her entrapment, her praying, and the appearance "of a man with a fire extinguisher" who was sent by an "angel to get me out of there." Immediately after this segment, psychiatrist Alvin Poussaint was asked by Jennings to comment on the woman's narrative. He described her as having suffered a great deal of "trauma, and it's likely that this may stay with her for the rest of her life." Comparing the attacks to a rape, Poussaint portrayed the victims in terms of similar feelings of violation. He described the "towers as phallic symbols" and the attack as "a kind of symbolic or attempted symbolic castration," thus reducing the public event to a subjective experience, completely unaware of the reductiveness of his analysis that fit in well with the popular psychologizing characteristic of this historical event.

Commenting on the anger that is endemic to analyses of trauma, Poussaint said that "it is part of the process" and recommended a supportive environment for the victims, asserting that community involvement and the church could aid them. Agreeing with Jennings about the great expression of national unity, the psychiatrist said that he hopes "it lasts a very long time, and crosses ethnic, racial, and religious lines." A report from Judy Muller in Salt Lake City followed; she interviewed various people about their anger over the attacks and the inconveniences caused them. Asked by Jennings to comment on how individuals could deal with this anger, the psychiatrist suggested that they "punch a pillow and say that they are angry." The close of the program emphasized the national resolve, the closing of ranks, and increasing approval for the president's management of the crisis.

An appeal to historical precedent is prominent in the newspaper reportage, where parallels are sought, located, and modified, quantitative similarities and differences highlighted—and the event of choice is December 7, 1941. For example, invoking President Roosevelt's response to the attack on Pearl Harbor in his "day of infamy" speech, a reporter from the *Daily Telegraph* expressed concern about President Bush's ability to "strike just the right note." The President's statement delivered on September 12, that "the attacks were more than terror, they were acts of war" were, according to this article, merely echoes of other government officials' statements (Harnden). Nevertheless, Bush's September 13 statement haltingly sought to provide the "right note" of "reassurance and determination" in saying, "These acts of mass murder were intended to frighten our nation into chaos and retreat, but have failed. . . . Our country is strong. A great people has been moved to defend a great nation" (qtd. in Stillwell).

Throughout the national and international news, other facets of Pearl Harbor analogies were multiplying, involving characterization of the enemy in the familiar language of difference from Americans in their hatred of democracy, in this case the "evil" character of Islamic militants. While acknowledging similarities between the attack on Pearl Harbor and the aircraft-missile attacks on the World Trade Center and the Pentagon, however, the language of outrage expressed by government officials and the news media also sought not to outdo the parallel to the element of surprise and anger of the Japanese attack but to intensify the responses to the September attack. In other words, September 11 is *another kind* of Pearl Harbor." While newspaper reports and editorials commented on a difference between the Japanese during a time of war and the perpetrators of the attack in September, the writing and television reporting maintained the analogy by emphasizing the surprise nature of the event and the demonstrations of patriotism and unity expressed in the aftermath of both. Both events were responsible for bringing "the country together" in the desire to "punish the aggressor," the ambiguity of "intelligence failures," and the display of heroism in the midst of disaster.

In particular, articles and editorials focused on the feelings of shock and alarm that came from the realization that "previously unthinkable actions had been inflicted on Americans in time of peace." A *New York Times* article declared, "There has been nothing like this since Pearl Harbor . . . though Pearl Harbor was a remote territory. . . . The country will never be the same" (Clymer). And again the analogy, expressed in the *St. Louis Post-Dispatch:* "Today's terrorist attacks evoke Pearl Harbor—in the planning, the carnage, the stunning impact, and the failure to sniff out what was coming" (Levins 48). The *Baltimore Sun* echoed these sentiments, stating that "I think we have another one," except that "this sort of concerted terrorism, attacking multiple targets is a first." The attack on the World Trade Center and the Pentagon "will likely dwarf Pearl Harbor" (Goodman 80). An article in the *Boston Herald* quoted House and Senate leaders' responses to the attack thus: "we are outraged at this cowardly attack on the people of the United States" (Battenfield and Miga).

The *Daily Telegraph* of September 12, 2001, referred to the attack as an "act of war—wicked in its meticulous planning, and brilliant in its appalling execution" (Robinson 62). On the same day, the *Denver Post* rehearsed the events that began at 8:45 A.M. (Eastern Daylight Time), describing the flowing blood, the chaos, the sights of people praying, and the commentary by asking (after a comparison but also contrast with Pearl Harbor), "Who do you fight?" (Olringer). *Business Week* reiterated this ambiguity, writing that the nation has been "rocked by a new day of infamy" in which the enemy is obscure and the threat of a loss of personal freedom, the fear of another wave of assaults, and threats to the economy loom (Walczak, Starr, and Dunham).

A couple of weeks later, the language of outrage subsided somewhat. *Business Week* opined that "America is slowly recovering its equilibrium . . . worried, sad and optimistic, resigned to the future and nostalgic for an era that ended 30 days ago" (Walczak, Starr, and Dunham). *USA Today* talked about a return to relative normalcy and how "out of this will come a bigger collective sense of national trauma than the attack on Pearl Harbor" (Hampson). The *Baltimore Sun* reported Condoleeza Rice as saying, "This isn't Pearl Harbor. It's worse" (Pitts). As calls for unity and patriotism continued, heroes began to emerge from the chaos, as did reflections on the analogy to December 7, 1941. For example, a discussion of the World Trade Center that appeared in the *New York Times* on October 7, 2001, focused on the importance of taking a long-range view of the events that transpired on September 11 and signaled a further need to create an historical context for the event. In a consolatory and elegiac mode, James Atlas wrote that it was necessary to find "a way to talk about what otherwise has no identity or no name." Invoking Caesar's march on Rome and the barbarism of the Middle Ages, among other historical events, and referring to Gibbons's *Decline and Fall of the Roman Empire,* Atlas asserts in Spenglerian fashion that "the highest civilizations have been brought down." Ruminating on the "proximity to death to September 11 as a common feature . . . of the landscape," Atlas concludes that to think historically enables one "to dispel the illusion that we stand alone in history, aloof from the wrack and turmoil."

On December 7, 2001, the sixtieth anniversary of Pearl Harbor, comparisons of September 11 to December 7, 1941, were again prominent in the television news as the president sought to legitimize the "war on terrorism." In a speech that day to veterans and survivors of Pearl Harbor, President Bush referred to the Taliban as fascists who cannot be "appeased" and echoed Roosevelt's position of unconditional surrender in flatly stating that "they must be defeated. This struggle will not end in a truce or treaty" (Bumiller). The President's language was again steeped in references to "our mission" and to a "great calling" as he told the grandchildren of the Pearl Harbor survivors, "[N]ow your calling has come." At the Citadel on December 11, the president again commemorated Pearl Harbor with a speech broadcast on *Talk of the Nation,* during which he again linked Pearl Harbor and September 11 and, in militant terms, stated, "No cave is deep enough to escape the political justice of the United States." Challenging the terrorists, he promised "new tactics, new weapons, informed intelligence experts" who "know the Taliban and who understand the local culture." After the speech and commentary by various news analysts, *Talk of the Nation* climaxed with the words of Theodore Olson, solicitor general of the United States, whose wife died in the plane that crashed near Pittsburgh. Olson charged angrily that "the atrocities of September 11th cannot prevail" and called the perpetrators of the attack "bigots, zealots, and persecutors" who hate "America's freedom, tolerance, and respect for all people." CNN's *Mornings with Paula Zahn* reproduced images of patriotism from December 7 newsreels, then from September 11.

Similarly patriotic, Tom Brokaw, in a December 8, 2001, interview on the Tim Russert CNBC show, reiterated comments from the *National Geographic* program about Pearl Harbor he had narrated (see below), stressing the "determination to defend all we believe in." An excerpt from his own TV show was shown, in which he commented on the lessons to be learned from September 11. He described Ground Zero as a "holy place to be enshrined" in the same fashion as the *Arizona* at Pearl Harbor. In another expression of patriotism linked to World War II, the *NBC Nightly News,* focusing on the dedication of the D-Day Museum, featured a reading by Tom Hanks of Roosevelt's speech after the attack on Pearl Harbor: "With confidence in our armed forces, with unbounded determination, we will gain the inevitable triumph. So help us God."

Thus the preponderant responses to September 11 in the newspapers have a consistency in which the Pearl Harbor analogy plays a central role, albeit with expressions of its far greater magnitude. As I indicate below, one finds in relation to the media coverage of September 11 and its link to Pearl Harbor the reiteration of innocence violated, the language of trauma, and the expression of the need for retaliation against a faceless enemy who has come to resemble earlier evildoers in the saga of Western civilization against barbarism. Particularly striking, since history and memory are so central to the language of national unity as reported on television and in the newspapers, is the absence of references to the Vietnam War, as if that event were expunged from American history. In other words, America failed to produce the decisive battle in Vietnam and the decisive victory in Iraq during the Gulf War of the early 1990s. With the elimination of references to Vietnam and the Gulf War, the numerous parallels to Pearl Harbor and victory in World War II have resurrected the sense of a divine mission. Equally striking in the evocation of memories of Pearl Harbor is the absence of questions about and critical commentary on the changed role of U.S. global politics that have transformed the nation into a policeman in a world order that many now see as an "empire."

Pearl Harbor, the Film, and Documentaries

In the entertainment section of the *Pittsburgh Post-Gazette* on December 7, 2001, Barbara Vancheri commented on the "timeliness and profits" of the Jerry Bruckheimer and Michael Bay film *Pearl Harbor* (2001). She quoted producer Bruckheimer on the patriotism of that earlier era: "We're seeing a lot of it again. The military is looking much differently since September." The film had been released months before the attacks on the World Trade Center and the Pentagon, and the plane crash near Pittsburgh. It was scheduled to commemorate the sixtieth anniversary of the Japanese attack of Pearl Harbor. The year 2001 also saw the appearance of two television programs about Pearl Harbor, one produced by the History Channel and the other by *National Geographic*. These three productions deserve examination for their resurrection of a traditional mode of narrating America history that, in the aftermath of the September 11, became all the more poignant.

The Pearl Harbor productions illuminating December 7, 1941, dramatize American exceptionalism and its sense of destiny in strikingly similar terms—a narrative of adversity and triumph exemplary for how much it reveals as well as for how much it elides. The main lines of this narrative involve a dramatization of the violation of innocence, a portrait of U.S. victimhood and of Japanese perfidy. The texts are constructed in elegiac fashion as a lament for the victims. While the survivors' accounts are replete with their detailed descriptions of horror accompanied by repeated images and reconstructions of the catastrophe, they are balanced by descriptions of extraordinary acts of heroism. The narrative of Pearl Harbor also focuses on the changes and the trauma wrought by the catastrophe on "the people" both at Pearl Harbor and at home, accentuating the patriotism that emerges from the event. The overriding insistence, in all of these productions, on national unity, the need for retaliation, the belief in a "mission," and the absolute necessity of "remembrance" are abundantly evident in the newspapers and television coverage of September 11.

Pearl Harbor is a genre film, a war movie in the spirit of such films as *So Proudly We Hail* (1943), *From Here to Eternity* (1953), and *Tora! Tora! Tora!* (1970), with added and updated elements derived from the technology of the later twentieth and early twenty-first centuries— the "realism" of loud Dolby sound, underwater cinematography, and digital effects to augment and intensify the battle scenes. In fact, this union of contemporary technology with 1940s genre conventions parallels the union of earlier World War II heroism with concessions to contemporary audiences in the toned-down treatment of the Japanese and the inclusion of an African American character. Also, in the conventions of contemporary mixed-genre production, the film seeks to anastomose three different narratives—romantic melodrama, action drama, and historical docudrama.

The melodrama features a romance between Rafe McCawley (Ben Affleck) and Evelyn Johnson (Kate Beckinsale) that begins with love at first sight, the promise of undying love, the belief in the virtue of chastity, and of course, an inevitable rupture that involves Rafe's best friend, Danny Walker (Josh Hartnett) in a not-so-chaste relationship with Evelyn after Rafe has been assumed dead. This triangle serves the discourse of the film well, invoking the familiar conventions of the action genre in which neither the conflict nor even the romance are between the man and the woman but between the men in their initial bonding, later antagonism, and finally reunion, if only through the death of Danny. One of the dominant themes of the romance is, in familiar generic terms, the transformation of the protagonist from a state of innocence into knowledge of "a world forever changed" but a reconstituted one of national unity, family, and restoration of a belief in the future.

The love narrative separates Rafe and Evelyn when Rafe volunteers to serve in the British Eagle Squadron. Thus the film provides a brief excursion into the war in Europe, as well as complicates the lovers' relationship. Visually these episodes at the air base and in combat evoke images from British war films of the 1940s and an opportunity to recapitulate the prowess of the Yank in Europe. Rafe's assumed death enables the coming together of Evelyn and Rafe's "best friend," Danny, in their shared grief. Rafe's return, however, produces antagonism between the two men that is resolved only in the shared dangers of combat against the enemy. This narrative is closely tied to the family romance. *Pearl Harbor* is framed by images of family in an

American rural, not urban, context, thus suggesting the organic, hence normal, imperative of continuity within nature through the sanctity of the land. This reconstitution of "normality" at the end of the film in the image of united family relies on sacrificial death in the martyrdom of Danny, alter ego for the protagonist Rafe. Predictably and conveniently, Danny dies, a martyr in the arms of Rafe. Danny's memory is safeguarded, since Evelyn has been carrying Danny's child, also to be named Danny, as a consequence of her affair with him.

The second line of narrative in the film, paralleling the romance, entails a portrait of the peaceful and idyllic world of Pearl Harbor before the attack, a world of camaraderie and innocence that is violated. To reinforce the element of surprise, the film contrasts scenes of military personnel and nurses enjoying the Hawaiian milieu—dancing, drinking, lovemaking, and images of an empty hospital ward as a contrast to the frenzied action that takes place there after the Japanese strike. The disintegration of Rafe and Danny's relationship over Evelyn, culminating in a barroom brawl between the two men, anticipates the "betrayal" by the Japanese (then suing for peace) of the United States. The action scenes dramatically reconstruct the disaster wrought on land and sea, the strafing of civilians, the explosion of Red Cross ambulances, the devastating attacks on the ships in the harbor, and the desperate struggles of sailors to escape from the burning and sinking ship. As the relationship between the two men is restored through the unity engendered by means of combat with a common enemy, so their reconciliation serves as a prolepsis for the collective overcoming of national defeat. In the spirit of the war film, this dimension of the narrative anticipates victory by including the two men's volunteering for a dangerous mission organized by Jimmy Doolittle (Alec Baldwin) to bomb Tokyo. In the dramatization of the successful attack, the vicissitudes of the romance narrative are paralleled in the action sequences that stress the romance of heroism, sacrifice, bonding, and remembrance in the harrowing but exhilarating experiences of danger in fighting the enemy and inflicting losses on him in the air strike over Tokyo. Danny's death also serves as a parallel to the martyrdom of the sailors entombed in the *Arizona,* sunk by the Japanese.

The third trajectory of the film involves historical reconstruction of the events leading up to the attack, conflicts in intelligence, and refusals to interpret signs properly. This narrative line especially involves President Franklin Delano Roosevelt, played by Jon Voight, portrayed as lamenting U.S. lack of involvement in the European war. Other historical episodes in the film involve the reconstructed roles of admirals Kimmel and Short; Doolittle; Admiral Yamamoto, played by Mako; and a black sailor, Doris "Dorie" Miller, played by Cuba Gooding Jr. These portraits are largely drawn from Pearl Harbor archives, interviews with survivors, and reconstructions of Roosevelt's response to the attack and pleas for preparedness: "We're building refrigerators, while our enemies build bombs." Roosevelt's concern for impending war is reinforced by the images of Admiral Yamamoto and other Japanese military and government officials as they draft, train, and execute their plan "to annihilate . . . [the] Pacific fleet in a single blow at Pearl Harbor," the motivation articulated as a response to the U.S. embargo, shortages of fuel, and control of the Pacific. Intercut with these scenes are those involving the role of intelligence agencies, the deciphering of codes, the relay of messages, and instances of belated or intercepted messages. Several portents of the impending disaster do not rouse admirals Kimmel and Short.

This historical segment of the narrative film makes the most use of newsreel footage, and where that was not available or feasible, animation or computer simulation fills the gaps. The film does not evade documentation, providing newsreel footage of Hitler and his conquest of the masses along with images of the Japanese incursion into Manchuria and the massacre of Nanking. Other than this footage, the treatment of the Japanese from Yamamoto to the pilots and submarines is, in the film, concentrated on the stages of the planning and the attack itself. The two-hour-long attack by the Japanese is presented in great detail, if only with the help of exquisite computer animation, producing a vivid sense of the devastation wrought on the people and naval fleet. The film laboriously reconstructs the destruction of the *Arizona* and the images of the many men who tried to escape but were entombed in the sinking ship or drowned in the sea.

But the film does not end on a note of defeat. Proleptically, Yamamoto is shown to say, "I only fear that we have awakened a sleeping giant." And Roosevelt, as if reinforcing Yamamoto's words, is presented in a meeting with his cabinet, saying, "We have been trained to think we are invincible. . . . We have to strike back now." The element of U.S. indomitability and invincibility is reinforced in a scene reminiscent of Peter Sellers's role in *Dr. Strangelove, or, How I Learned to Stop Worrying and Love the Bomb* (1964). Struggling from his wheelchair laboriously to stand without aid, Voight's Roosevelt challenges the "defeatists" who say a quick response is impossible, explaining to them that he now realizes that he has been "brought low," for a higher purpose—the salvation of the United States.

Images from newsreel footage of sped-up production to "avenge" Pearl Harbor are conjoined to the development of the Doolittle mission to bomb Tokyo, signs of the rousment of the "sleeping giant." "Let them repeat that we are a nation of weaklings and playboys," Roosevelt intones. The Doolittle episode will show otherwise, and the ending of the film centers on reflections concerning the "war that changed America." Thus the film has orchestrated the themes of blamelessness, the profundity of the trauma that transformed the United States, the element of "surprise" necessary to reinforce the sense of innocence unprotected, and the coming of age of the nation in the resurrection of national honor. In a sense, *Pearl Harbor* suggests the oft-repeated phrase associated with the Holocaust—"never again." At the end, the unity of the family is conjoined to revitalized images of manifest destiny and American uniqueness, themes that have resonated loudly since the Reagan years but have their source in a history and literature that far precedes the present.

The film was not reviewed kindly. In commentaries on *Pearl Harbor* before September 11, one reviewer for *Variety* described the film as exemplary of "the anti-historical approach that Hollywood seems to think the modern public prefers" (McCarthy). In line with this assessment, an anonymous article in *Time International* quoted the comments of a contributor to an Internet chat room as saying, "They'll probably make a movie called *Hiroshima* next in which the heroic American soldiers bomb those evil Japanese and save the world" ("Make"). A major share of the complaints against the film involved the view that, though "it gets a lot of things right," it does not "finally paint a clear picture of the attack or the political events leading to it" (Cagle), which seems naïve both in relation to commercial war cinema and as an assessment of what is problematic about the representation of the past: not its fidelity to fact but its failure to be critical of cultural politics.

The most strident criticism came from Rand Richards Cooper in a review in *Commonweal* that linked the film's point of view to Reagan conservatism and to its backlash against contemporary opposition to U.S. foreign policy. For Cooper, the film is an anachronism: "It's startling to see an essentially nineteenth-century romantic vision assembled so faithfully in a twenty-first-century movie. And discouraging, too." Also in a critical vein, Stanley Kauffmann in the *New Republic* of June 18, 2001, concluded that "the film compel[s] the viewer to look not for the truth of that hour but for the schemings of today" (26), though the nature of these "schemings" was not detailed. The initially negative critical reviews of *Pearl Harbor* disappeared with the post–September 11 media responses to the attacks on the United States. Whereas before September 11, *Variety* had claimed that the film exhibited a "*Classics Illustrated* fifth-grade approach to one of the most literally explosive moments" in United States history (McCarthy), such responses were no longer in evidence after the attack.

A brief excursion into the History Channel's production *Pearl Harbor* echoes the theatrical film's "romance of nation," drawing on similar newsreel footage, the same moments from the archive, and repetitive statement. As befits a television documentary, the program relies on conventions of the form: the use of narrator (in this case, *History Channel* host Roger Mudd) to set the stage and offer wisdom and counsel to the viewer, and the reliance on words of the survivors intercut with images of the disasters they describe. Once again is conveyed the idea that Pearl Harbor was a "turning point in history" when "the era of confidence" was "forever lost." In predictable fashion, the program rehearses, with the aid of "documentation" obtained through newsreel footage, the tension between the growing power of Hitler and the dominant "isolationist" sentiments as uttered by Charles Lindbergh. Also central to the unfolding of the narrative is the image of Hirohito, who is introduced with a voice-over explanation of the concept of Bushido, a Japanese belief in the sense of duty and patriotism owed to the nation on the part of its warriors. This concept is presented as something alien, marking "differences" between Japanese imperialism and the U.S. notion of patriotism. The documentaries, like the film, also present the event of Pearl Harbor as "a turning point of history" that "changed the world."

In the spirit of reinforcing an image of U.S. victimhood, the History Channel program begins its recounting of the events of December 7 with an invocation of the sunken *Arizona,* "a ship of destiny," a synecdoche for the nation, and the victim of Japanese aggression. This memorializing moment is a prelude to a breakdown of events, moment by moment, that interweaves the political elements that were slow to recognize the impending danger; the images of Pearl Harbor as "a paradise on earth"; accounts of survivors who validate the newsreel footage, albeit with personal accounts; and the images of the attacks themselves. In search of a reassuring closure, the program adopts two strategies: One entails an emotional treatment of the memorial built above the *Arizona,* as well as one in Japan, involving survivors and tourists. Keeping with the commemorative spirit of the documentary, Roger Mudd comments that survivors and their families are determined to "keep the memory of Pearl Harbor alive for all eternity." The other strategy that the program conveys to avoid defeatism and pessimism is "never again"—by invoking images of great men that saved the country from defeat—in particular, Admiral Chester Nimitz, who assumed control after Kimmel was disgraced and engineered victories in the Pacific Theater, and Roosevelt, whose leadership is credited with uniting the nation morally and militarily. The documentary parallels the Bruckheimer and Bay film in its emphasis on destiny, invincibility, betrayal, and ultimately, victory.

The *National Geographic* program, although cast very much in the mold of memorializing and the importance of "history" to that process, includes a narrative thread that highlights the concrete attempts to document December 7 by Bob Ballard (of *Titanic* fame through his underwater explorations). His mission, for which he is granted only two weeks, is to locate the remains of the Japanese minisub that was attacked by the U.S. Navy but never considered as a warning before the arrival of the planes. The narrator for this production is Brokaw, author of *The Greatest Generation.* The question animating the program as articulated by Brokaw is "what happened that fateful day?" Also drawing on accounts by U.S. and Japanese survivors, historians, newsreel footage from U.S. and Japanese archives, as well as maps and animation, the program presents Pearl Harbor as a place of pilgrimage and as a museum, emphasizing especially the memorial to the USS *Arizona* and the sailors interred in it. To reinforce survivors' accounts, the program provides the familiar blow-by-blow description of the day's events intercut with Ballard's ultimately futile attempt to locate the downed Japanese minisub. Ballard remains convinced, however, that "history tells us what you need to know," thus strengthening the film's claims to monumental history. Unlike the History Channel's explanation of Japanese militarism in the context of Bushido, however, this program describes the attack as a "suicide" mission.

In the spirit of memorializing, the documentary especially highlights one survivor, Carl Carson, who now has a fatal illness and is determined to finally tell his story after many years of silence, recounting his involvement in the gruesome nature of the events of that December 7 morning, his own wounding, and sense of helplessness before the wounded and dying. The program climaxes with a service on the memorial for the *Arizona* and camera shots of the names inscribed on a large tablet, as well as underwater shots of the various quarters and their remains on the ship.

In the documentaries, the question of conspiracy, incompetence, and disbelief are evident as they describe the several events that could have tipped off the United States to an impending attack. In line with the film, however, they seek to enact the event "as it really was" and end with an emphasis on U.S. victory. In a sense, the three productions are cast in an elegiac form, a memorial for the dead, especially in the case of the documentaries in that they rely on survivors to tell their stories of that day, on their memories, on their pain and inability to forget, and on the hope for a better future.

These three productions, while exhibiting some formal differences in their reconstructive modes, uses of documentation, treatment of the politics, and questions of failed intelligence processes, are emblematic of the process of what Friedrich Nietzsche terms "the uses and disadvantages of the past for the present moment." In their styles, they are faithful to the conventions of historical representation as exemplified by media—radio, film, and television. They all invoke a sense of national tradition and an implied sense of abiding national virtue. They are narratives of innocence and experience, coming-of-age rituals, and melodramas of betrayal based on the perfidy of the Japanese Other. They express a belief in American uniqueness, democracy, justice at home, righteous imperial power globally in the name of civilization and the injunction to "remember."

Epilogue

Television and newspaper reportage has seized on the event of Pearl Harbor to name and situate the events of September 11 and even when they claim that the 2001 event dwarfs Pearl Harbor, they recapitulate traditional forms of explanation and forms of response to confront the two events, reaching backward into American history rather than confronting critically the exigencies of profound global changes in which the United States plays a predominant role. In this sense, the film *Pearl Harbor* and the two commemorative documentaries produced before September 11 set the stage for this retrospective and regressive view of U.S. history and politics.

As a film critic who has sought to understand the character of popular culture without consigning it to oblivion, I have regarded the reliance on tradition and commonsense thinking as revealing important and complex insights about contemporary culture and politics. Thus the dismissive reviews of *Pearl Harbor,* in retrospect, ought to be reexamined. They offer insights beyond mere thumbs-down responses and aesthetic failure. In their cryptic fashion, they are revealing about the problematic legacy of the past sutured onto the exigencies of the present. For example, the romantic vision offered by the film and attacked in *Commonweal* deserves further examination. What is it that these narratives of Pearl Harbor expose about the persistence of history and its usefulness to contend with the present? On what historical resources does the film draw? Why is Pearl Harbor a yardstick for understanding the "American character" in crisis?

The film and the manifold reports in newspapers and on television do not rely directly on the film, but the film in its style and discursive strategies embodies strikingly similar assumptions about the American nation, its people, and its mission in the world. It is insufficient to describe its conventions as clichéd, because they address a way of organizing and aestheticizing knowledge and politics that requires tracing in terms of antecedents and conceptions of history. The very notion of historicizing demands examination. The film *Pearl Harbor* relies on a form of historicizing that could be described as monumental and antiquarian, relying on approximations and generalities, making "what is dissimilar look similar," and ignoring causes (Nietzsche 70). Monumental history thus "tends naturally toward the universal," considering effects in themselves, and "the only causes that it understands are simple duels opposing individuals" (Deleuze 148, 150).

Thus the narratives of Pearl Harbor that filter through most of the commentaries on September 11, emphasizing a sense of uniqueness, manifest destiny, paradise lost and regained, and the righteousness granted by divine mandate to set wrongs aright, are inherent to all these accounts but are not deeply indebted to Hollywood; rather Hollywood is indebted to these visions of American exceptionality.

Hence conceptions of America's role as policeman of the world not only are divinely sanctioned but thrive on creating a melodrama of good and evil that cannot tolerate ambiguity or contradiction. Therefore, despite contemporary concessions to political correctness through multiculturalism, as updating notions of the American melting pot and versions of populism, these narratives must be built on an edifice of Truth based on the essential goodness of the American character and its mission and calling. Moreover, in relation to internationalism and to the current moment described in terms of globality, this monumental and antiquarian vision of history must be adapted to current economic and political realities. This vision must be augmented and accounted for in relation to media representations of December 7, 1941, and September 11, 2002—namely, the uses of popular psychology under the rubric of "trauma" to reinforce the "infamy," "surprise," and "horror" of violations to American sovereignty.

The injunction to remember is allied to biological and psychological conceptions of the permanent damage to the individual and national psyche and the need to rehearse and mitigate the conditions of the shock attendant on the unexpected and inexplicable events. Thus, though the film *Pearl Harbor* and the two television programs preceded September 11, they exemplify a way of thinking that allows the continuity of religious notions of the sacred sense of place and of the sense that Americans have an ordained destiny in the world, which may involve the uses of war and violence to stop those forces that seek to impede this "progress."

While the documentaries and the film *Pearl Harbor,* like numerous reports and editorials about September 11, justify war and violence in the name of democracy, and while they rely on selective versions of history to underpin U.S. sovereignty, they reflect little on the terms of another aspect of history—namely, the transformations that have taken place in the United States from early founding conceptions of constitutional democracy to its present role as the world's policeman, a mantle inherited from the legacy of European sovereignty. Of this transformation, Hannah Arendt wrote,

> The American government, for better or worse, has entered into the
> heritage of Europe as though it were its patrimony—unaware, alas,
> of the fact that Europe's declining power was preceded and accom-
> panied by political bankruptcy of the nation-state (and its concept of
> sovereignty). . . . [W]ar is still the *ultima ratio,* the old continuation
> of politics by means of violence. It is a secret from nobody that the
> famous random event is more likely to arise from those parts of the
> world where the old adage "There is no alternative to victory" retains
> a high degree of plausibility. (6)

These statements describe what the Pearl Harbor productions expose
but do not regard it critically, mired as they are in the language of an
earlier mythology of America. Speaking specifically of a tradition of
organic thought that underpins the justification of politics by means
of violence, Arendt identifies it as the tendency to think in biological
terms, particularly of the sick body and its correlative, the "sick society," which she believes "enables the glorification of violence . . . [to]
appeal to the undeniable fact that in the household of nature destruction and creation are but two sides of the creative process . . . as a continuing prerequisite for continuing life in the animal kingdom"
(Arendt 75).

The trope of disease relies on a conception of crisis, catastrophe,
and rupture from a previous balanced state. One can see this in the
frequent recourse after September 11 to the language of injury and
trauma, and the quest for restitution or compensation endemic to
many of the pronouncements by the government and the media in
relation to World War II and the "war on terrorism." In relation to
traditional and dominant expressions of the American reliance on a
form of historicism based on biological, organic, and teleological
thinking, the monumental narratives that link December 7, 1941, to
September 11, 2001, raise important questions concerning the means
and ends, the strategic uses of traditional modes of historical representation as expressed through media.

Works Cited

Arendt, Hannah. *On Violence.* New York: Harcourt, 1969.

Atlas, James. "Among the Lost: Illusions of Immortality." *New York Times* Oct. 7, 2001, sec. 4: 5.

Battenfield, Joe, and Andrew Miga. "Attack on America: Bush—America Will Pass This Test." *Boston Herald* Sept. 12, 2001: 4.

Bumiller, Elisabeth. "Remembering Pearl Harbor, Bush Ties It to the Current Campaign." *New York Times* Dec. 9, 2001, sec. B: 1.

Cagle, Jess. "*Pearl Harbor*'s Top Gun: Fighting His Own Past, A Nervous Studio and (as Always) the Critics, Producer Jerry Bruckheimer Goes to War." *Time* June 4, 2001: 70.

Clymer, Adam. "In the Days of Attacks and Explosions: Official Washington Hears the Echoes of Earlier Ones." *New York Times* Sept. 12, 2001, sec. A: 20.

Cooper, Rand Richards. "Bombs Away: *Pearl Harbor.*" *Commonweal* June 15, 2001: 22.

Deleuze, Gilles. *Cinema 1: The Movement-Image.* Minneapolis: U of Minnesota P, 1986.

Goodman, Melvin A. "Clean House at the CIA." *Baltimore Sun* Oct. 11, 2001: 23A.

Hampson, Rick. "A Month Later, 'Normal Is Relative.'" *USA Today* Oct. 11, 2001: 5A.

Harnden, Toby. "Bush Fails to Capture Nations's Mood: America Looks in Vain for a Sense of Reassurance and Security." *Daily Telegraph* Sept. 13, 2001: 2.

Kauffmann, Stanley. "On Films—Looking Back." *New Republic* June 18, 2001: 26.

Levins, Harry. "Terrorist Attacks Evoke Pearl Harbor in Complexity, Impact: But Today's Enemy Is Essentially Unknown." *St. Louis Post-Dispatch* Sept. 11, 2001: 48.

"Make Love Not War: Disney Is Spending $10 Million to Convince the Japanese *Harbor* Is a Romance." *Time International* July 16, 2001: 41.

McCarthy, Todd. "*Pearl Harbor.*" *Variety* May 28, 2001 (383.2): 17.

Nietzsche, Friedrich. "On the Uses and Disadvantages of History for Life." *Untimely Meditations.* Cambridge: Cambridge UP, 1991.

Olringer, David. "US Watches Terror Unfold in Disbelief: Another Pearl Harbor Televised." *Denver Post* Sept. 12, 2001: A6.

Pitts, Jonathan. "Difference in Attacks Is Enormity, Experts Say." *Baltimore Sun* Sept. 12, 2001: 80.

Robinson, Stephen. "This Outrage Will Hit Americans Harder than Pearl Harbor." *Daily Telegraph* Sept. 12, 2001: 62.

Stillwell, Paul. "Another Kind of Pearl Harbor." *Naval History* Dec. 2001: 4.

Vancheri, Barbara. "Heroes of Dec. 7: Loaded *Pearl Harbor* Release Couldn't Be More Timely." *Pittsburgh Post-Gazette* Dec. 7, 2001: 42.

Walczak, Lee, Alexandra Starr, and Richard S. Dunham. "Terror in America." *Business Week* Sept. 24, 2001: 32.

6

City Films, Modern Spatiality, and the End of the World Trade Center

Juan A. Suárez

History unfolds forward as well as backward; the present forces us to rewrite and recreate the past, its focus, perspective, and framing undergoing constant change by the moving vantage point of the now. This retrospective awareness informs the present chapter, which seeks to reconsider the city film, an important subgenre in the experimental tradition, in light of the events of 9/11 and, conversely, to relate the rise, demise, and mourning of the World Trade Center (WTC) to the modernist regimes of spatiality and representation that inform city films. The attack on the WTC indelibly linked the spectacle of modernity, of which the twin towers were a prominent emblem, with urban ruin and devastation. Skyscraper architecture and gridlike design, signifiers of modernist utopia, universal rationality, and technological control, could not stand the return of modernity's others. Ruins, fanatical fundamentalism, and impoverished peripheries came back to haunt a center that had at once created them and turned them into its absolute others. Inaugurated by Paul Strand and Charles Sheeler's *Manhatta* (1921), city films, also called city symphonies, dwelled extensively on the dialectics of center and margin, spectacle and counterspectacle, novelty and ruin. Their style and iconography embodied many of the tensions that have recently exploded in the face of the metropolis. For this reason, it seems urgent to reconsider the genre as an incisive meditation on the embattled spaces of modernity and on the imbalances and contingencies of an aesthetic and social project that seems, today more than ever, dangerously out of reach.

I vaguely conceived some of these ideas as I screened *Manhatta* for my students in Spain in the fall of 2002. Shot in 1920 and early 1921 in downtown Manhattan and shown for the first time later that year in a commercial theater as lead to a feature, the film is usually considered the first significant title in the history of American avant-garde cinema (Horak 269–71). It is a seven-minute portrait of New York that juxtaposes shots of skyscrapers, traffic, crowds, construction sites, trains, the waterfront, and boats in the harbor with intertitles containing a number of quotations from Walt Whitman's poems "Crossing Brooklyn Ferry," "Mannahatta," and "Broadway Pageant." I included the film in a survey class on twentieth-century American culture that (predictably) moved from 1920s modernism to the post-1960s regimes of cultural production usually labeled postmodern. I had planned for *Manhatta* to be part of a unit on modernist depictions of urban space in combination with John Dos Passos's novel *Manhattan Transfer* (1925) and with a number of texts by contemporary sociologists, such as Georg Simmel and Robert Park, and visual artists, such as Joseph Stella, John Marin, Edward Hopper, Alfred Stieglitz, and Alvin Langdon Coburn. I was (and am) particularly invested in this unit, since I have spent years studying New York–based experimental cultures and have a long-standing fascination with the city, its history, and its spaces. I had, besides, spent the summer in New York doing some writing and research, and seeing friends. I was there when the planes hit the towers. I saw them wrapped in smoke from the platform of the Seventy-fourth Street elevated train station, in Jackson Heights. Unaware of what had just happened, I intended to board the train on my way to the Butler Library at Columbia University, where I had spent a good many days that summer. As I arrived at the station, the trains into the city were no longer running owing, as the voice on the public address system repeated, "to an ongoing police investigation in Manhattan," a message that, with the towers burning in plain sight in the distance, sounded to me unnecessarily cryptic and grotesquely euphemistic. By the time I left the platform and gained the street, I overheard that the north tower had collapsed.

As I watched *Manhatta* a few weeks later, I could not help but notice how elegiac it had become under the pressure of recent events. What had always seemed a rather "full" text, a self-assured homage to New York and its modern cityscape, had suddenly become mournful, inhabited by a loss—by the open wound of the bombed WTC. It was impossible, for me at any rate, to ignore that most of the sights in the film, such as the Woolworth Building, Saint Paul's Church and its graveyard, Trinity Church, the Morgan Bank on Wall Street, Broadway, City Hall, the Brooklyn Bridge, the old Custom House building, and the old Staten Island Ferry slip on South Street, were within walking distance of the site of the attack. In the course of a day, which is *Manhatta*'s time frame, the rotating shadow of the twin towers might have touched every one of these spots. These sights had suddenly become landmarks of loss, not only because they were metonymically contiguous with the WTC but also because its collapse somehow truncated the utopian aspiration that the new spaces of modernity signified, an aspiration that was the focus of Strand and Sheeler's film. This utopia is attached to skyscraper modernity, that is, to an organized, objective, legible, engineered society. In many ways, the WTC, and the twin towers in particular, could be seen as the culmination of this utopia and its contradictions; and their collapse, as a symptom that this ideal of endless rationality and scientific organization has limits marked by history, by the return of what this modern ideal represses.

Juxtaposing Strand and Sheeler's film with the destiny of the towers is less arbitrary than it may seem. *Manhatta* premiered the year that the Port Authority of New York, the public corporation that promoted the construction of the WTC, received its charter through a joint legislative initiative by the states of New York and New Jersey. The Port Authority was the first public corporation in the country; its mission was to act as a regional planning body in charge of promoting the efficiency of the New York port, whose functioning was indispensable to the region's economy at the time (Boyer 181–85). It was to do so not only by regulating maritime traffic and waterfront activity but also by facilitating the passage of commuters and goods between Manhattan and the mainland—by promoting, in short, mobility and communication. In fact, one of its first projects, which, in rather typical Port Authority fashion, took decades to be completed, was the construction of an underwater train that would replace the Manhattan Transfer ferry, which connected New Jersey and Manhattan's West Side.

Probably unwittingly, *Manhatta* points to the importance of the Port Authority's mandate by emphasizing, as Whitman's poetry and Alfred Stieglitz's photographs had already done, Manhattan's insularity and highlighting its identity as a hub of maritime and terrestrial routes. The film's opening already suggests this. A painted view of New York from the water is followed by shots taken from the bow of the Staten Island ferry approaching the slip and disgorging masses of passengers onto Wall Street. Later segments show barges, tugs, and passenger cruisers, such as the famous *Lusitania,* traversing the waters of the harbor and trains crossing the city's surface, advancing through the narrow canyons between skyscrapers. (The shots of steaming locomotives were probably taken at the old Hudson Terminal, one of the more than one hundred sixty buildings demolished in the early 1960s to make way for the WTC). These perspectives depict Manhattan as a porous, open territory of arrivals and departures, a symbol of the eminently modern qualities of transit and speed. Sixty years later, these very qualities were used to justify the construction of the WTC on the site of an old, established commercial area. The ostensible goal of the center was to centralize all the commercial and financial activity attached to the port in a modern office space, and to maximize the financial potential of New York as a world city. The undeclared goal was the promotion of real estate values in lower Manhattan, where both the Port Authority and the Rockefeller family had considerable holdings. David Rockefeller, president of the Chase Manhattan Bank, was one of the project's main promoters, and his brother Nelson, at the time the New York state governor, was its most energetic backer (Darton 58–59, 75–79).

Manhatta also foreshadows the rise of the twin towers through its fascination with the rectilinear shape, dimensions, and height of the downtown skyscrapers. These are the dominant visual motif in the film and provide its main ocular perspective. The film insistently frames ground-level activity (moving cars, horse-drawn carriages, and pedestrians) and the sights of lower Manhattan through high-angle shots and vertical pans taken from the rooftops of skyscrapers. These aerial perspectives imply that vertical thrust is the essence of modernity and is nowhere better embodied than in Manhattan, which becomes then a hieroglyphic not only for American modernity but for modernity at large. This syllogism, implicit in *Manhatta*'s visual terms, was an expression of cultural nationalism seeking both to underline America's contribution to modernity and to modernize America by proposing that the skyscraper fulfills some form of manifest destiny. This is what some of Whitman's verses quoted in the film suggest. For example, the quotation "High growths of iron, slender, strong, splendidly uprising toward clear skies!" introduces a number of takes of building sites and of finished structures. Written decades before skyscraper architecture was a reality, they become premonitory when crosscut with shots of early 1920s Manhattan. Whitman's lines lend cultural authority to the verticality of modern construction and push the skyscraper from the messy entanglements of contemporary history, technology, and real estate speculation into the serene realm of myth. Skyscraper architecture is then presented both as an emblem of the modern and as the fulfillment of a mythic vocation to rise above the ground.

These notions are considerably mystified and, as is the nature of myth, they serve to naturalize history and to appease its conflicts. They hide the fact that the origin of the skyscraper lies in not myth nor manifest destiny but the desire to maximize the return of investments on land purchase and construction. Hence the modernity of high-rise structures is attributable not only to their state-of-the-art technology and functionalist design but also to their offer of an apt image of the inflationary nature of modern capitalism. For Marx this nature was most evident in real estate and financial economy, where value is, more than ever, separated from actual use and where capital most clearly fulfills its intrinsic nature: its ability to multiply itself seemingly ad infinitum, to grow to astonishing mass on a proportionately meager base, just like a skyscraper.

Manhatta's mythic perspective also highlights, even as it occludes, the complex cultural work that architectural height performed in modernity as a mode of visibility and a form of social spectacle. Height made visible, and therefore seemingly objective, such ineffable notions as "progress" and "development" and elided, at the same time, their most disturbing implications. Making visible, translating into observable structures is itself an important modern imperative shared by modern medical science, the electronic media, experimental art, and popular culture. The ocular centrism of what Martin Heidegger called "the age of the world picture," which made seeing, knowing, and controlling tightly interdependent, had one of its most spectacular instances in the skyscrapers. They visualized "progress" by reifying it, translating it into size and height. Thus monumentalized, it appeared incontestable and universal. Who could argue with the sixty stories of Cass Gilbert's "cathedral of commerce," as the Woolworth Building was called, with the 102 stories of the Empire State, or the 110 stories of the twin towers? As these structures rose as universally available spectacles that presided over the city's public space, the progress they were meant to embody appeared within everyone's reach. One could touch with one's hand the buildings that signified it; one could linger in their lobbies, walk down their corridors feigning purpose, and ride the elevators as in a theme park of finance and wealth. (Stringent security has made this kind of *dérive* increasingly difficult nowadays). Such universal accessibility, whether visual or tactile, hid the fact that these signs of corporate power too often rest on the dispossession of the many. At the same time, their monolithic shape counterbalances the fragmentary, conflictive nature of the modern polity. Consider: one of the main spates of high-rise construction in Manhattan took place in the bleakest years of the Depression; the Empire State, the Chrysler Building, Rockefeller Center, and the Waldorf-Astoria all were built during the 1930s. In turn, the construction of the WTC took place in the mid to late 1960s, a particularly fractious period in American culture. It was part of an important wave of city renewal and architectural monumentalism that also generated the Cross-Bronx Expressway, the Lincoln Center, and several cyclopean office developments in lower Manhattan. Their ostensible goal was to help unify the city and to concentrate financial services, perhaps in an attempt to counteract, at least symbolically, the centrifugal pull of disintegrating social tensions.

Seen in this light, skyscraper architecture can be interpreted as a late descendant of the city beautiful movement, in vogue in the first decades of the century, and whose main ideologue was Daniel H. Burnham, designer of the White City of Chicago's 1893 Universal Exposition and also of some early high-rise buildings such as the Flat-iron in New York. The goal of the movement, which at the time ex-erted considerable influence among planners and policy makers, was to provide cities with monumental public spaces and open vistas. These should give urban centers a recognizable outline and an aes-thetic unity; civic landmarks should act in turn as a repertoire of com-munally shared symbols expressive of the city's self-image and aspira-tions (Boyer 43–55). At bottom, this was a form of environmental behaviorism: an attempt to unify the disparate urban masses through unitary design and to reach social through aesthetic harmony. One can find considerable parallels between administered urban space and the sort of filmic space promoted by classical cinema. Both are forms of spectacle that substitute "synthetic" for lived space and standard-ize visual perception, as they direct the free-floating gaze of the ur-ban dweller or film spectator to predetermined points of interest, to particular meanings and narratives.

Manhatta reedits Manhattan into a unified, monumental "city beautiful" and celebrates the extent to which its skyline may act as a cementing social symbol. In the process, the film reduces city life to geometric space, to a collection of surfaces and planes, and completely elides its dwellers. In the towering perspectives of the film, these ap-pear as moving dots scurrying along the sidewalks, milling on the ferries and crosswalks, or reclining on park benches in some rare moments of leisure. The modern city is reduced to its structures, its hardware, while the people who inhabit it are volatilized, turned into an undifferentiated accretion on its surface. Seen from the heights, they are interchangeable and ultimately equivalent in a grotesque reduction to absurdity of the idea of democracy. The extreme long shots of skyscraper perspective impose this sort of equivalence. Skyscraper architecture itself was the result of construction based on prefabricated, interchangeable components that could be welded and riveted together on site. In this respect, its main antecedent is the assemblage of railroad lines from standard lengths of steel. The application of this method to architecture was first tried in railway stations; in the first shopping arcades built from the late 1820s on; in the glass palaces at the world exhibitions, like the first one in London in 1851, or the one in Bryant Park in New York City a few years later; and in the first department stores (Schivelbusch 161–89). All these were designed for movement and consumption. Walter Benjamin has stressed that they were "dreamhouses of the collective," since these activities were connected with reverie and mystification but were also ruthlessly rational, governed by technological control, standardized measurements (of time and space), and systems of equivalence (405). These were places where one traded in fixed amounts and where money (exchanged for train fare, goods, services) was the universal code into which everything else was translated. And this carried over into the skyscrapers, which were frequently palaces of financial capital, headquarters of banks, insurance companies, and corporations. Is it any wonder that one can see from the tops of these buildings not actual people but only exchangeable parts, countable units, the geometry of dots and lines?

Manhatta shares such geometric reductionism with a number of contemporary ideologies and formations. Among these were the theories of scientific management formulated by F. W. Taylor (his *Principles of Scientific Management* appeared in 1911) on the basis of chronophotographic studies of workers' movement undertaken to reduce unnecessary energy expense. Taylor's proposals were first put into practice on a large scale in steel mills, providers of H-girders indispensable for skyscraper construction, and subsequently adopted by other branches of industry (in car manufacture, as in Henry Ford's assembly line) and by the military. When applied to urban space, scientific management gave rise to city planning, which sought to rationalize land use, to turn the city into a controllable mechanism where distinct areas were assigned particular uses and shapes, and to superimpose linear designs on the unpredictable effervescence of quotidian practice. But these tendencies also had aesthetic ramifications. These were theorized, among others, by Wilhelm Worringer, who connected modern abstraction to the atavistic attempt to gain some control over an unpredictable environment, and by Adolf Loos, who linked it to the functionalism of machine design and condemned the undulating excesses of ornamental art-nouveau architecture as symptoms of criminality, decadence, and primitivism. Attached to widely diverging ideological agendas, geometric reduction was also practiced by Cézanne, cubists, futurists, Kandinsky, Russian constructivists such as Malevitch and El Lissitzky, De Stjil, and a long line of modernists that reaches all the way to 1960s minimalism and beyond. In architecture, geometric formalism was most eminently practiced by the Bauhaus, Le Corbusier, futurist Antonio Sant'Elia, Eliel Saarinen, and an influential line of American designers, such as Frank Lloyd Wright, William K. Harrison, Raymond Hood, and William van Alen, among others. At the end of this long genealogy stands the stark shape of the twin towers.

The underlying principle in all these formations is a particular conception of modernism: one that has been theorized in terms of efficiency, streamlining, standardization, and mechanization. It is the kind of modernism that proclaimed "less is more" and conceived modernity as a process of simplification and paring down, of increased control and management, or in Walter Lippman's famous (and revealing) formulation, of "mastery" as opposed to "drift." This modernism, with its mythic overtones and its absolutist ideology, has tended to obscure the existence of another, equally important, form of modernism. This other modernism is vaguely discernible in the bird's-eye views of *Manhatta;* it stirs in the shadow of the skyscrapers or in those neighborhoods not yet fallen to frantic renewal. Its main symbol—perhaps *stage,* which connotes dynamism and performance, might be a better term—is metropolitan street life itself, with its ever changing human landscape, its ethnic, cultural, and linguistic mix, its impossible geometry and difficult formalization. It is a modernism that forgoes abstraction; rather than formalize, it seeks to chronicle (as modernist writer James Agee once put it) the "unimagined experience"—those parcels of social life not yet contained into discourse—and to do so without reducing them to pattern but respecting their opacities and irreducibilities. This form of modernism conceives modernity as a period of increasing relativism and complexity where universals must be powerfully inflected and nuanced. If this modernism has a geometry, it is not Euclidean but fractal, one that dissolves straight lines and stable planes into nearly unaccountable outlines.

What I am saying is not new, of course. It has been intermittently discussed under different headings not always explicitly connected with modernity or modernism. It can be traced to the conflict between what Marshall Berman called "the modernism of the expressway," embodied by Robert Moses' brutal public work projects of the 1960s, and "the modernism of the street," of some strands of 1960s experimental art (312–29). Berman takes as one of his sources of inspiration Jane Jacobs's indictment of modernist architecture and city planning, *The Death and Life of Great American Cities,* which rests on a similar distinction between regimented spaces and the complex, multileveled forms of social and spatial practice sedimented through spontaneous collective use (48–60). Jacobs's distinction is analogous to Michel de Certeau's opposition between the cartographable city of buildings and traffic routes, on the one hand, and the unmappable one of daily practice as lived and traversed by specific individuals, on the other (91–99). (This opposition was suggested to him by the view from the observation platform in the south tower of the WTC). In a more abstract manner, all these oppositions can be subsumed under Gilles Deleuze and Felix Guattari's distinctions between segmentarity and micropolitics; the molar and the molecular; the striated and the smooth (208–31, 474–500). These pairings express the opposition between abstraction, regulation, and reduction, on the one hand, and the free, unformalizable flow of practice and desire, on the other—an opposition that is not only social and aesthetic but discursive at large.

This distinction between two modernities should not be used to formalize the modern, to impose on it a rigid conceptual symmetry (or, in Deleuze and Guattari's terms, a striated, molar segmentarity) but, more loosely, to discern two of its dominant drives, which combine in all cultural expression, even though one of the two tends to predominate. *Manhatta* is a case in point. I have stressed so far its geometric reductionism but, as I have shown elsewhere, the film also owes much to a piecemeal inhabitation of the city environment and of urban popular culture practiced, for example, by the avant-garde magazine *The Soil* and the early city actualities to which its form harks back (Suárez). This is most obvious in the shots that purvey a backyard view of the city and show its unheroic, quotidian landmarks: ferries and tugs in the harbor, anonymous street corners, crowded sidewalks, parks, the quiet of the lunch break in a downtown square, the late afternoon shadows in a church graveyard. In the end, though, the film is more invested in molar accretions than in interstitial spatialities and ephemeral practice. By contrast, we could juxtapose *Manhatta* to a number of contemporary texts where the dominant drive is a micropolitical, molecular exploration of modern space and sociality. Some examples could be Paul Strand's candid portraits of urban types; Lewis Hines's photographic exposés of child labor and portraits of immigrants on Ellis Island; Dos Passos's *Manhattan Transfer,* much of which unfolds in *Manhatta*'s setting. And within the tradition of the city film, one could mention such titles as Jay Leyda's *A Bronx Morning* (1931) and Helen Levitt, Janice Loeb, and James Agee's *In the Street* (1952), or Joseph Cornell's and Rudy Burckhardt's films. In all of these texts, the city is not a spectacle to be consumed in detachment or to be regulated from above but a porous terrain that offers multiple points of entry, sites, modes of habitation, contacts, perspectives, and trajectories. From the perspective of yet another "molecular" modernist, the city emerges in them as a text of bliss: inhabited by multiple languages and voices in suspension and yet *"no sentence formed"* (Barthes 49).

Around the WTC, these two modernisms clashed dramatically. In fact the history of how this massive architectural complex came to be, wonderfully narrated in Eric Darton's indispensable piece of urban history, *Divided We Stand,* is the history of the victory of molar, lineal modernism over its molecular street counterpart. The WTC was the apotheosis of "city beautiful" monumentalism, gridlike linearity, and geometric reduction. Its designer, Minoru Yamasaki, was an epigone of International-Style architecture with ample experience in the design of boxlike constructions, which made exhaustive use of glass and steel and were usually commissioned by corporations. An early commission, the headquarters of Consolidated Gas, in Detroit, a building exclusively supported on a welded steel frame that used no masonry, was a trial run of what would later be the twin towers. At the relatively modest height of thirty-two stories, it was for a time the tallest structure thus conceived. For the twin towers, Yamasaki lengthened its basic steel frame and substituted solid beams for hollow tubes, an idea he derived from the layered tubular fibrillations of a bamboo stem. He borrowed the concept of a double structure from Mies van der Rohe's influential apartment houses at 860–880 North Lake Shore Drive, Chicago, dating from 1951. When finished, the twin towers at the WTC looked from the distance like solid metallic columns. As the steel tubes on the facade were set about twenty-two inches apart, no windows were discernible: it was truly the triumph of the geometric, mathematic, controllable space. In the innocent days before one became so aware of their tragic vulnerability, it was difficult to imagine them inhabited by people; they appeared completely self-sufficient, almost refractory to human use.

In a polemical move, Darton called Yamasaki "the architect of terror," which sounds a lot more incendiary today than when it was published in 1999. In part, he was interpreting the traces of violence, symbolic or real, that cropped up around his buildings. The most recent instance at the time was the February 1993 attack, when a van full of explosives was detonated in the WTC's underground garage, killing five people, injuring more than a hundred, and opening a crater five stories deep. There were others, though. An early Yamasaki commission predating the towers, one that contributed considerably, initially at least, to his reputation, was the Pruitt-Igoe public housing project in St. Louis. Declared by the mayor "a colossal failure," it was dynamited to the cheers of many former occupants on July 15, 1972, after more than a decade of conflictive habitation. For architectural historian Charles Jencks, this demolition confirms the bankruptcy of modernist architecture, which many, like himself, had been sensing all along, and closes its undisputed reign. What followed, at least in theory, was postmodern architecture, more human-scaled, playful, and indebted to vernacular styles (Jencks 34). In the meantime, though, terror continued to haunt Yamasaki's work. Of his 1975 Rainier Bank headquarters in Seattle, *New York Times* architecture critic Paul Goldberger observed, in a review titled "Seattle's Balance of Terror," that it seemed to have "blown out" from under the surface of the earth (Darton 121). Not long after the 9/11 bombing, early in 2002, the Spanish police intercepted documents belonging to the terrorist Basque group ETA that revealed detailed plans to blow up yet another product of the Yamasaki studios: Torre Picasso, in Madrid. Finished in 1989, it stands in one of the most inhospitable spaces in the Spanish capital: a barren concrete expanse bristling with office towers, desultorily adorned with scrubby gardens, and surrounded by multilane thoroughfares invariably jammed with traffic. This is a sinister roster that pits acts of terrorism against the terror these buildings often embodied; it describes a spiral of contagious violence that should make us ponder where terror starts. While it is never—and I want to be clear about this—defensible or justifiable, we are bound to learn nothing from it if we linearize it, abject it, and consider it an arbitrary unidirectional force that invariably comes from outside, from modernity's others, to attack us. It may be more productive, as well as more healing, to recognize the extent to which the terror also springs from our own spaces; the extent to which our modernity in general, and modern architecture in particular, are often in themselves regimes of horror. As Darton put it in his comparison of terrorism and Yamasaki's projects,

> To attempt creation or destruction on such an immense scale requires both bombers and master builders to view living processes in general, and social life in particular, with a high degree of abstraction. Both must undertake a radical distancing of themselves from the flesh-and-blood experience of mundane existence "on the ground." (Darton 119)

What was there on the ground where the towers were built?

The WTC was built on sixteen blocks of buildings dating mostly from the turn of the century and housing a large number of small specialty stores selling from pets to clothing to athletic supplies. City guides of the 1940s and 1950s frequently described it as a colorful street theater. The most salient feature in the area was Radio Row, also called "the radio district." One of the last specialized shopping districts in lower Manhattan, Radio Row was concentrated on Cortlandt Street. It was dominated by stores selling electronic appliances, but many also traded in discontinued components and spare parts extracted from old machines. Frequently these goods spilled onto the streets; they were held in crates and displayed on folding tables through which hundreds of ham radio operators and amateur electricians fingered their way. To judge from the record, the district must have offered a peculiar mixture of the old and the new: of old architecture with new appliances; of electronic technology with an atmosphere more typical of a souk or a bazaar. The landscape the center paved over was an example of "the other" modernity: fractal, street-based, hybrid, lived on intensely personal and quotidian terms. This gave way to the stern geometry of the towers at a considerable personal and economic cost. A report by New York's City Planning Commission estimated that there were about eight hundred firms and re-

tail businesses in the area in the early 1960s. Once plans for the construction of an office complex in the area became known, businesses
started abandoning the neighborhood in a steady trickle. Yet in early
1966, only a few months before demolition work was scheduled to
start, about 530 retail, office, and commercial firms were still holding out. The Planning Commission interviewed 221 of these. More
than half had no relocation plans; thirty-four were going out of business; and only eleven had definite plans for relocation. More than a
third had been in the neighborhood for over twenty-five years (Darton
109, 141). This kind of forced relocation was becoming a common
occurrence in lower Manhattan in the 1960s. The wholesale Washington Market, north of the future WTC, had been torn down and
the area "renovated" in the early 1960s; the Swamp, the old leather
district, was destroyed to make way for the Southbridge housing complex; and most of South Street was demolished to erect a number of
office towers.

As city renewal proceeded at a frantic pace and block after block
was slated for clearance, a number of New York experimental artists,
among them Allan Kaprow, George Brecht, Jim Dine, Red Grooms,
Claes Oldenburg, Robert Whitman, Renee Miller, and Martha
Edelheit, were generating a new artistic movement called, at the time,
"junk art," which reclaimed the outdated and the ruined. They produced installations and environments, which frequently took up an
entire gallery's space, combining street garbage, debris, and found
objects (Haskell 6–18). In an influential text often considered pro-
grammatic of this aesthetic, Kaprow, the movement's pioneer and
main theoretician, encouraged artists "to disclose entirely unheard of
happenings and events found in garbage cans, police files, hotel lobbies, seen in store windows and on the street" (55–56). Part of the
point in all this was to question the separation between art and life
by reproducing, in the spaces of aesthetic contemplation, the textured
decay of city refuse. (In this respect, Rauschenberg's pieces of the late
1950s, such as *Anagram* and *The Bed,* were the immediate antecedents for this ravenous recycling of found garbage; more distant ones

were early-twentieth-century dadaism, surrealism, and the work of a number of maverick American artists like Joseph Cornell, Louise Nevelson, and the "primitive" Clarence Schmidt, a sort of native *facteur Cheval* who had assembled around his house in Woodstock, New York, a massive environment of found objects.) Read against the backdrop of 1960s city renewal, junk art can be interpreted as an implicit protest against the megalomaniac designs of city planners and corporations. It drew attention to the intense affect attaching to the useless and old: to what had exhausted its run in the market but had once been object of desire.

Junk assemblages could also be seen as hurried attempts to compile traces of the city's memory before it disappeared under the advance of the bulldozers. The work of Jack Smith, an underground filmmaker and performance artist who was not part of the movement initially, is an outstanding example of this historical fascination with ruins and the outdated. These were the raw materials of his "moldy aesthetic," based, in addition, on rejected popular texts—old-fashioned films from his childhood, forgotten records—and on what he termed "human wreckage"—bohemians, glorious drag queens, and all kinds of urban misfits like himself. His first underground film, *Scotch Tape* (1962), was shot on the ruins of an old market torn down to build the Lincoln Center complex. A number of characters, the most visible one a black man wearing shades and a colorful turban that evokes Carmen Miranda's superlative headgear, dance to a mambo rhythm on a pile of rubble and twisted girders. These suggestions of the south and the exotic may be taken as reminders that the neighborhood now destroyed had been the Puerto Rican enclave of San Juan Hill. With their attention to heterogeneity, to piecemeal habitation, and to the layered memories attached to urban space, junk installations, like Smith's films, are examples of the fractal, molecular street modernism that the WTC rose to oppose.

And yet, it is this "other" modernity—this modernity of otherness—that has been extensively invoked in the wake of 9/11 to mourn the disappearance of the WTC in a number of art shows and web-based projects, as well as in some recent experimental film and video. What has prevailed in them is the intimate, close-up perspective of street modernism. The videos *First Person 911* (2001), by Luke Joerger and Ray Mendez; *911—Serra's Morning* (2001), by Saul Levine; *9/11 1st St. NYC* (2001), by M. A. Toman; *Periphery* (2001), by Illana Rein; and *Great Balls of Fire* (2001), by Leon Grodski and Pearl Gluck, all show how a historical event permeated the microhistory of particular individuals, who react to it from singular perspectives without any claims to representativeness. Brian Doyle's *Current* (2001) avoids the human-centered approach of these titles and focuses instead on the information-age debris: the clouds of paper and eddies of pulverized rubbish that drifted around the area days after the attack. A similar aesthetic of small gestures appears in more institutional contexts as well, such as the "September 11 Project" web site of the Museum of the City of New York and the web page of the WTC Association. Rather than the lost buildings, these two recreate the process of their construction. This information softens their scale and highlights their vulnerability and the laborious process of erecting what took so little time to collapse. The Museum of the City of New York also posted Richard Wellings's ink drawings of the towers under construction. Their intimacy emanates from their format and their focus: the human form in interaction with the building machinery and the rising structures. Lewis Hines's famous photographs of the construction of the Empire State, shown at the Museum of the American Indian, in lower Manhattan, nearly a year after the bombing evince a similar perspective. The pictures of workers, their bodies, and their physiognomies suspended above ground, framed against cables and steel beams are a lyrical homage to the people who actually raised the buildings, and draw attention away from the finished structures, "starchitects" (Rem Koolhaas's term), and designers who usually take center stage. These pictures have a joyful air, reminiscent of Ferdinand Leger's paintings of construction sites, with its cartoonish workers gleefully wielding their tools in defiance of gravity and exhaustion. While not conceived explicitly as a memorial, the exhibition of Hines's images does provide an indirect homage to the WTC by evoking the construction of another work of massive scale. In addition, they gesture nostalgically to a time when high-rise construction still had a considerable utopian charge that history has ended up denying.

In two photography exhibitions at the Jewish Museum ("New York: Capital of Photography") and MOMA ("The Life of a City"), the mourning is more indirect, since what is remembered is not primarily the WTC but the spontaneous street life of the city. Both are anthologies of New York street photography that culminate in pictures related to 9/11. At the Jewish Museum, the closing image is Jeff Mermelstein's picture of a man in a business suit checking the contents of his briefcase in the towers' vicinity, completely covered in white dust, surrounded by the fallout of the explosion. The last section in the MOMA show was a selection of images from "Here Is New York: A Democracy of Photographs," the project that collected pictures—most of them by nonprofessionals—related to the tragedy and its aftermath, scanned them into a computer data base, and sold digital prints to raise funds for the Children's Aid Society World Trade Center. Like the video work mentioned above, these photographs tend to focus on intimate reactions to the events. In all these examples, the WTC is mourned in the rhetoric of another modernity, the one it opposed and displaced. Why?

This may be in part because, while catastrophe is collective, mourning is usually private: a piecemeal process of reconstruction usually engaged at an individual level. This became most visible in the spontaneous memorials that sprung up in the immediate wake of the events: in the improvised shrines with mementos, photographs, and inscriptions; in the accumulation of tokens of affection and loss that still hang from the railing around St. Paul's Church, a block away from the site of the attack. These acts of mourning were performed in mass; yet each left behind the singular trace of an individual simply trying to cope.

From a different perspective, if mourning involves the internalization of loss, achieved by identifying and incorporating images of what we have been deprived of, what these exhibitions, web sites, and videos seem to mourn is, again, not the towers but the possibilities that street modernism embodied. The narrative implied in the shows at the Jewish Museum and MOMA in particular, the ones that most evidently bring the rhetoric of street photography to bear on the end of the WTC, is that 9/11 may mean the end of the innocent street life as we have (not) known it for decades: carefree, unpredictable, warm, full of unsung heroism and hard-boiled beauty. And while this narrative is to an extent true, it also conceals another one that does not lend itself so easily to clear-cut distinctions between now and before; us and them: this is the narrative that tells that street life has always been killed, in diverse places and times, by a predatory modernity, with its architectural gigantism, its geometric obsession, with the criminal cost it exacts in exchange simply for a place to live. Killed over and over again, however, the life of the street *always* recreates itself again—usually somewhere else.

Works Cited

Barthes, Roland. *The Pleasure of the Text.* Trans. Richard Howard. New York: Farrar, 1975.

Benjamin, Walter. *The Arcades Project.* Trans. Howard Eiland and Kevin McLaughlin. Cambridge: Harvard UP, 1999.

Berman, Marshall. *All That Is Solid Melts into Air: The Experience of Modernity.* London: Verso, 1982.

Boyer, Christine H. *Dreaming the Rational City: The Myth of American City Planning.* Cambridge: MIT P, 1983.

Darton, Eric. *Divided We Stand: A Biography of New York's World Trade Center.* New York: Basic, 1999.

de Certeau, Michel. "Walking in the City." *The Practice of Everyday Life.* Trans. Steven Rendall. Berkeley: U of California P, 1984. 91–111.

Deleuze, Gilles, and Felix Guattari. *A Thousand Plateaus: Capitalism and Schizophrenia.* Trans. Brian Massumi. Vol. 2. Minneapolis: U of Minnesota P, 1987.

Haskell, Barbara. *BLAM! The Explosion of Pop, Minimalism, and Performance, 1959–1964.* New York: Whitney Museum of American Art, 1984.

Heidegger, Martin. "The Age of the World Picture." *The Question Concerning Technology and Other Essays*. Ed. and trans. William Levitt. New York: Harper, 1977. 115–55.

Horak, Jan-Christopher. "Paul Strand and Charles Sheeler's *Manhatta*." *Lovers of Cinema: The First American Film Avant-Garde, 1919–1945*. Ed. Jan-Christopher Horak. Madison: U of Wisconsin P, 1995. 267–86.

Jacobs, Jane. *The Death and Life of Great American Cities*. New York: Random, 1961.

Jencks, Charles. *The Language of Post-Modern Architecture*. New York: Rizzoli, 1987.

Kaprow, Allan. "The Legacy of Jackson Pollock." *ARTnews* (Oct. 1958): 24–26, 55–56.

Loos, Adolf. *Ornament and Crime: Selected Essays*. Riverside, CA: Ariadne, 1998.

Lyotard, Jean-Francois. *The Postmodern Condition. A Report on Knowledge*. Trans. Geoff Bennington and Brian Massumi. Minneapolis: U of Minnesota P, 1984.

Schivelbusch, Wolfgang. *The Railway Journey*. Trans. Anselm Hollo. New York: Urizen, 1979.

Suárez, Juan A. "City Space, Technology, Popular Culture: The Modernism of Paul Strand and Charles Sheeler's *Manhatta*." *Journal of American Studies* 36.1 (2002): 81–106.

Worringer, Wilhelm. *Abstraction and Empathy. A Contribution to the Psychology of Style*. Chicago: Ivan R. Dee, 1997.

7

"Today Is the Longest Day of My Life"
24 as Mirror Narrative of 9/11

Ina Rae Hark

> When events seem unjust, when events seem chaotic, when things
> with the world aren't right, human beings try to attribute mean-
> ing and try to explain things away, in order to put it into some
> existing schema.
>
> —*psychologist Margaret Mitchell, on the confession of a*
> *police officer from Lockerbie, Scotland, that he had*
> *compiled a video from media reports on the terrorist*
> *bombing of Pan Am Flight 103 and replayed it obsessively*

In what appeared in retrospect an eerie sort of precognition, the television networks scheduled three new dramatic series about intelligence operatives *(24, The Agency,* and *Alias)* for the fall 2001 television season, to debut during the last week of September and into
October. Of these, the Fox series *24* had on the surface the most disquieting convergences with the events of September 11. Its pilot episode ended with the explosion of an airliner in flight, killing all aboard,
as part of a terrorist plot. The scenes of the plane's explosion, although
not the fact of its explosion, were edited out of the premiere episode
that aired on October 29.

Because the terrorist strikes on September 11 unfolded in several
locations, their collective occurrence is now evoked by the date, rather
than the place (cf. "Oklahoma City," "Waco," "Pearl Harbor"), in a
semiotic system more familiar to Americans as denotations of strikes
by their countrymen in the name of freedom (July 4, D-Day). Prob-

ably because of its ironic similarity to the country's universal emergency number, this day was soon rendered numerically in many media reports: 9/11. In a somewhat similar fashion, the multiple terrorist operations in the Fox show all occur during one single day, that of the California presidential primary. The numerical shorthand in the title of the series does not denote the actual day and month, which are never specified, but the day's duration, echoing the digital-age formula for uninterrupted temporal engagement, 24/7, and reinforced by the advancing digital clock that bridges segments of the "real-time" occurrences. The show's frequent use of split screen to render actions occurring simultaneously echoed the "multiple windows" technique increasingly utilized—and certainly during 9/11 and its aftermath—by another 24/7 operation, the cable all-news networks. Such windowing on 24 often portrayed the many cell phone calls that propel the plot. In another echo of the September tragedies, some of these calls are made to loved ones by people who fear that their deaths as a result of the terrorist activities are imminent. Like the doubling of the two plane strikes and two collapsed towers, 24 involves two different attempts on a candidate's life, two moles within the counterterrorism unit, and two separate kidnappings of and escapes by the daughter of protagonist Jack Bauer.

Nevertheless, as the plot arc of 24 is revealed, the politics involved, the targets of the villains, their methods and motivations are notable precisely for how much they vary from those that constituted the 9/11 attacks. Rather than being carried out by rogue terrorists who wish symbolically to attack the United States because of its superpower status, involvement in global capitalism, and pop culture colonization of other countries, the violence in 24 has narrow, personal motivations and results from the activities of competing state intelligence operatives. The disaster to be averted targets a specific individual, Senator David Palmer, and plays out more like a paranoid assassination thriller from the 1970s than an antiterrorist action narrative from the first decade of the twenty-first century. Although the last eleven episodes were plotted after 9/11, "real-life tragedy didn't alter the fundamental story they set out to tell. . . . 'We never intended the bad guys to be Middle Eastern because we felt that had been done a lot,' [executive producer Robert] Cochran said" (Owen).

Where *24* does significantly intersect with 9/11 is in the way it mirrors the television news coverage in the aftermath of the tragedy. U.S. television is rarely comfortable with abstractions or ideologies. From the outset, network news broadcasts and news magazines sought to personalize the tragedy, giving faces and voices to the victims and their survivors, and even to the perpetrators. (Barbara Walters, for example, interviewed the father of ringleader Mohammed Atta.) A political act metamorphosed into a family melodrama. This transformation is standard in the television coverage of disasters. The series *24* fictionally takes this approach back to the level of the attack itself, so that everything that initially seems political is actually personal.

The series also tells a story that coincidentally and unintentionally compensates for shortcomings that the events of 9/11 presented to media creators who wished to fashion a satisfactory disaster narrative from them. Because three of the horrendous events (impact of second plane, collapses of Tower 2 and of Tower 1) happened at the World Trade Center on live television, with the images subsequently available for endless recycling, it became the locus of media narrativization. The World Trade Center attacks posed difficulties as terrorist disaster narrative primarily because they made indistinguishable the fates of perpetrator, victim, and heroic rescuer. All three categories of people died and were literally compacted together. Thomas Lynch observes,

> So the further hurt of that late-summer Tuesday's dead is that it will not be kin that scatters them, or friends who carry them or family ground that covers them, or their beloved who last whispers soft goodbyes. They are the lost—too vastly buried, too furiously burned, too utterly commingled with the horror that killed them to get them back, to let them go again. We could not rescue very many. We will recover all too few.

"Ground Zero" provided only absences and disintegration. It provided no ground upon which to build compelling personal narratives. The media were left with loved ones and colleagues of the dead and the testimonies of those who would have been among the dead had not fate intervened.

Consider the differences presented by the 9/11 events and those surrounding the other major instance of terrorism in the United States, the bombing of the Murrah Federal Building in Oklahoma City. Less potent as spectacle than the World Trade Center (or *Challenger* explosion) because cameras were not present at the moment of disaster, Oklahoma City would lend itself well to the kinds of scenarios favored by network television. Although many died, many were rescued. Images of dazed children from the day care center in the arms of firefighters and Red Cross workers mixed with the iconic photograph of the firefighter cradling the lifeless body of one-year-old Baylee Almon. For several days after the bombing, survivors buried in rubble were found and brought to safety. Doctors, rescue teams, and their dogs all had their opportunities to wear the mantle of hero and give on-camera interviews. The national manhunt identified conspirators and the actual bomber, and over the ensuing years they were tried and punished.

Although the conspirators behind the 9/11 terror attacks are being hunted and may eventually be captured or killed, the actual perpetrators succeeded by choosing to die with their victims. Most of the rescue personnel who initially entered the towers died in their collapse. Only six people were ever pulled from the rubble, and most of them had not initially been in the towers when the planes hit. Newspapers and television news magazines reported that rescue dogs, who receive positive reinforcement when they locate a living victim, had become "depressed" by their lack of success, to the extent that their handlers would conceal themselves under coverings and allow the dogs to find them.

During the 1993 terrorist bombing of the World Trade Center, which Brigitte Nacos dubs "the first terrorist spectacular in the United States" (119), television crews were able to photograph people escaping from the building. On 9/11 the danger of being struck by falling debris, particularly the too-horrific-for-broadcast rain of human bodies and body parts, kept news crews at a distance. Photographers stationed at area hospitals could show only nurses and doctors waiting to receive injured survivors, who never arrived. While the terrible spectacle of the second World Trade Center disaster provided stunning and graphic images to fill television screens, there was a marked shortage of human survivors or rescuers to be shown or interviewed live on September 11. The abiding images were rather of still photographs of the dead or missing, posted or held in the hands of loved ones who sought them.

Journalism professors William Coté and Roger Simpson maintain that

> journalists and those in the audience understand that every story needs a "who," a person who will humanize the event, and stories about violence and victims of crime and disaster are no different. . . . The interview with a person caught in a violent event is a staple of news because it puts us in touch with the voice, face, and emotions of a person who is suffering. (85)

Such interviews, they say, allow the viewer to face his or her own fears of disaster by observing the behavior of someone who has gone through the experience. The obliteration of so many lives in the collapse of the towers robbed the media of countless potential "whos," and so it was obliged to recreate them. Even the staid *New York Times* ran a months-long series of brief profiles of the September 11 victims called "Portraits of Grief." Speaking in a forum "Time Stopped: 9/11 Coverage," sponsored by the Harvard University Institute of Politics and led by television documentary producer Callie Crossley, "Portraits of Grief" editor Jan Hoffman explained how the desired narrative to be gleaned from the vignettes was not always easily forthcoming. Sometimes survivors of the victim told conflicting stories or wanted to reveal information the victim had insisted on keeping private. Sometimes no one had anything good to say about the deceased.

Ms. Hoffman explained one case in which a man was a bad husband, the wife had very little to say, and the brother had a lot to say but all negative things. She explained that these are tributes and she does not want to write about negative characteristics of the victims but she won't publish lies. Instead she will work with the wording and try to paint the victim in a true, somewhat appealing light. (Crossley)

While the *Times* looked to make every victim a unique individual, there were some patterns to emerge from the casualty statistics, and some significant ones for considering media representations of the attacks. The two employers to lose the largest number of employees were the Cantor Fitzgerald brokerage firm and the Fire Department of the City of New York. Between the impacts of the planes and the collapse of the towers, a drama was unfolding in which working-class government employees committed to protection and rescue sought to deliver white-collar financial services employees from death. In the days and weeks that followed 9/11, it became clear that the self-sacrificing firefighter and not the savvy commodities trader would come to emblematize the victim of the attacks. Celebrities and politicians began appearing in FDNY caps and shirts, in a manner similar to the ways they sported red ribbons at the height of the AIDS crisis.

In the months that have followed 9/11, a certain gendering of the narrative has also occurred. Nearly three quarters of the victims were male, according to death certificates issued by the New York Office of Vital Statistics (Lipton). All the firefighters who died were men. These victims came to stand in for all rescue personnel in media representations. As the "Women in the Fire Service" web site reported

Many women in the fire and rescue service have commented to [us] about the lack of media visibility of women rescuers at the 9/11 incidents, and about the common and unapologetic use of the terms "fireman" and "firemen" by the news media. WFS has begun a project to collect and archive these stories, to provide a counterbalance to the growing perception that only men were involved in the response, rescue, and recovery efforts at the World Trade Center, the Pentagon, and the Pennsylvania crash site. ("Another")

Women did become a favored subject for attention from the network news shows and news magazines in features profiling the "September 11 widow," as Tom Brokaw of *NBC Nightly News* phrased it. The apotheosis of this type was Lisa Beamer, the pretty, blonde, and pregnant wife of Todd Beamer, a passenger on United Airlines Flight 93 that crashed in Pennsylvania. Beamer had communicated by cell phone his intention to band together with other passengers to foil the hijackers. His parting "Let's roll" has become a catchphrase to epitomize the dead male hero of the 9/11 tragedy. Indeed, the story of Flight 93 provides the one narrative to emerge from 9/11 that meets the requirements for entertainment television: a group of men, attractive and athletic, with a suitable range of diversity among them (the Jewish Jeremy Glick and gay Mark Bingham), refuse to accept their fates, declare their devotion to their loved ones, and then take heroic action against the villains. Whenever good taste gives way to the desire for profit, this will be the TV movie that comes out of 9/11.

In a July 8, 2002, commentary in *New York Magazine,* Michael Woolf noted that of late, the activities of al Qaeda have been transformed by the media into a narrative "of international shadows and intrigue" that "unfolds against a backdrop of summer spy movies.":

> People just can't stand being without a clear plot. They just don't want to hear (likewise, nobody really trusts them to hear) that the threat is scattered, inchoate, and random (the point about spy fiction is to reveal that the scattered, inchoate, and random are part of a greater devilish design), that there is no script, that men act and conspire inexactly and ineptly and mostly unsuccessfully. (15)

This narrative has also been generated after the first seasons of *24, Alias,* and *The Agency.* In the case of *24,* not only is the devilish design revealed but the arbitrariness of the deaths that occurred on 9/11, of people working in the wrong place or boarding the wrong plane at the wrong time, is countered by making the terrorists target specific individuals for specific personal reasons. Rather than construct a false ideological narrative, as Woolf accuses the U.S. media of doing in regard to al Qaeda, the series takes the step of reducing the plot to a tale of shattered, dysfunctional families linked through politics, replacing ideology with the "human interest" that network television coverage of 9/11 was simultaneously privileging over any foreign policy analysis of why the terror attacks occurred. The efforts of casually dressed federal agent Jack Bauer to prevent the death of impeccably tailored presidential candidate David Palmer loosely recapitulates the Fire Department of New York–Wall Street binary enacted on 9/11, except that the *24* narrative allows for successful rescue. In the most singular twist on the semiotics of television's 9/11 narrative, however, *24* disrupts the binary of male heroism and death versus female survival and anguished waiting by introducing into its diegesis the repeated figuration of female treachery. Jack and Palmer deal handily with the villainous men who threaten their lives, but women are an unending source of trouble and pain.

The situation that confronts Jack when he is called into his office shortly after midnight on the "longest day" appears to differ substantially both from the kind of terrorist acts committed on 9/11 and from what turn out to be the true motivations behind the plot his superiors charge him with thwarting. Terrorism carried out against the citizens of a nation by citizens of another nation or ethnic group that views the first nation as an oppressor or ideological foe rarely targets specific individuals. It is enough for the Palestinian suicide bomber that a targeted pizzeria is frequented by Israelis, enough for an IRA bomber that English shoppers will be harmed by his device, enough for the al Qaeda hijackers that the World Trade Center is a symbol of U.S. economic hegemony. None of these terrorists cares which particular Israelis, English people, or Americans they kill. The attackers are personally passionate in their ideological hatreds, but it is a diffuse hatred with no one individual as its target. Of course, such hate crimes do also occur within the borders of a single nation. Timothy McVeigh's anger was directed at the federal government, and he did not care which specific federal employees perished in the Murrah Federal Building.

Political assassinations, on the other hand, are usually carried out by disaffected citizens of a country against a specific political leader who advocates policies or represents constituencies that are anathema to that person and others of his or her beliefs. (Such leaders may also be targets of opportunity to deranged individuals who fixate on the person as an avatar for whatever bedevils them.) *24*'s premise that the first African American with a realistic chance to be elected president might be targeted for assassination by homegrown racist groups is supremely plausible, even though the spate of assassinations and assassination attempts that shadowed U.S. presidents and presidential candidates for two decades after John F. Kennedy was shot are now two more decades distant. Once the conspirators are traced to Germany and Serbia, however, this scenario rapidly loses credibility. Serbians, to be sure, would resent U.S. and NATO interventions (and bombings) meant to curb ethnic cleansing in Bosnia and Kosovo, but their involvement in either assassinations or acts of terrorism against Americans has never been documented to the American public. Despite the evocation of a "terrorist" threat in its opening voice-over, there is no terrorism in the sense of that in Oklahoma City or on 9/11 anywhere to be found in *24*.

There is much evidence that the media are simply not comfortable with abandoning the types of narratives that served so well in the past to describe external threats to America and Americans. Wolff notes that the developing media narrative concerning Islamic terrorist networks is "Cold War stuff. The ubiquitous and yet unknown and unknowable enemy. The international jihad, which, with only minor adjustments, replaces the international communist conspiracy" (15). The political narrative of *24*, both globally and within the agency, similarly looks backward to mid-twentieth-century models rather than forward to twenty-first-century ones. The villain behind all the machinations in *24* is revealed to be Victor Drazen, a fictional Serbian characterized as Milosevic's Eichmann, the director of all ethnic cleansing in the former Yugoslavia. Although Serbian ethnic cleansing and the intervention of the NATO allies to end it are phenomena of the past decade, the dastardly Drazens fit well into the mold of the Le Carré or James Bond villain. As Europeans committing genocide against other Europeans, they provide easy links to the media's still-favorite villain, the Nazi. (Asians or Africans who engage in torture or mass murders of their own citizens have never attracted similar media buzz.) Moreover, Serbia, as a close ally of Russia, easily calls up Cold War espionage, the glory days of the spy thriller.

Conflict within the counterterrorism unit, presumably of the CIA, the government agency that employs Jack, stems from corruption and infiltration by double agents. Doubtless the 2001 arrest of veteran FBI agent Robert Hanssen, who had spied for the Soviet Union for fifteen years during the Cold War and was motivated by profit more than ideology, influenced this portrayal. Many of the traitors depicted in the show are similarly driven by greed rather than politics. The apparent mastermind is named Ira *Gaines* (emphasis added), and as the Fox *24* web site proclaims in the synopsis of hour 10, "It becomes clear that Gaines has only a monetary interest in seeing Palmer killed." Computer analyst Jamey Farrell of the counterterrorism unit agrees to spy for him only because her government salary is not enough for her to support her son as a single mother.

Yet *24* is not about greed, racism, or Cold War ideology. The first twelve hours are essentially an exercise in misdirection. Beneath the international spy games and domestic power brokering that are its apparent subject matter, *24* is the story of three fathers whose government work has interfered with the well-being and happiness of their respective families. Senator Palmer's drive to become the first African American president left his family feeling that they had to handle the rape of his daughter Nicole and its aftermath on their own, concealing from him that his son Keith had angrily confronted her assailant, accidentally causing the man's death. Palmer's Lady Macbeth of a wife, Sherry, orchestrated a successful cover-up of Keith's involvement, but the news media got wind of the true story, threatening the senator's election chances. The stresses of Jack's job as head of the Los Angeles division of the counterterrorism unit had led him to separate from his wife Teri and have a brief affair with co-worker Nina Myers. His rebellious daughter Kim blames her mother for the separation and, once her parents have reconciled, tries to play them off each other. These two long-running soap operas were united when Palmer's senate committee authorized, and Jack was sent to carry out, "Operation Nightfall," an assassination of Victor Drazen. Suspecting the attempt on his life, Drazen sent a decoy into his home, which the counterterrorism team then bombed. Neither Drazen nor the assassins realized that his wife and daughter were in the house also, and they were killed. Complicating matters is the fact that the assassination squad was itself a decoy, enabling the agency to capture Drazen alive, presumably to learn the whereabouts of other Serbian war criminals, although their motives remain murky. The upshot is that what looks like a terrorist plot against a possible future president of the United States is in fact a grudge match. As Jack's supervisor George Mason remarks with bemusement during hour 18 of the longest day, "So correct me if I'm wrong, but what this day basically boils down to is a personal vendetta against you and Palmer by the family of Victor Drazen." The day of the California presidential primary is by coincidence the second anniversary of the deaths of Drazen's wife and daughter, and the masterminds of the highly convoluted conspiracy that *24* unravels are the grief-stricken sons of Victor Drazen, André and Alexis, who hope to have Palmer killed and Jack blamed, to take from Jack his own wife and daughter, and to help their father escape U.S. custody. (Ironically, the murderous Drazens are the most close-knit and nondysfunctional family in the show.)

The counterterrorism unit itself can be read as a dysfunctional family writ large. Jack's immediate superior, Walsh, informs him that a mole has probably infiltrated the Los Angeles office, but this father figure is killed after assuring Jack that he can trust Jamey Farrell, who is in fact one of two moles in the unit. Previous bribe taking in the Los Angeles office, on which Jack blew the whistle, has left him with additional colleagues who may not be traitors but resent his testimony against their friends. Early on, Jack shoots Mason with a tranquilizer dart and blackmails him because he refuses to reveal the source of the intelligence on the assassination attempt. Higher-ups are repeatedly willing to sacrifice agents in pursuit of murky national goals. There are even suggestions that whatever purpose the agency had in secretly detaining Drazen was so important that the Palmer hit would have been permitted rather than to reveal or compromise it.

Therefore the presumption that the assassination attempt on Palmer is a hate crime likely to tear the country apart with racial strife turns out to be a red herring. In the first episode, Tony Almeida says, "If it leaks out that we're screening Senator Palmer, people might think that it's because he's black." "Well, it *is* because he's black; it makes him the most likely target," Jack replies. Yet when Jack and Palmer meet for the first time and compare notes, Palmer exclaims, "What's incredible to me is that none of this has anything to do with me running for president, it has nothing to do with the primary, it has nothing to do with my being black. It's just revenge for taking out Victor Drazen." Indeed, there is no attempt to portray the Palmer bid for the presidency with any knowledge of racial realpolitik. As one critic notes, "that's my problem with *24*. As enlightening as the black-man-as-president story line appears, it is laughably underdeveloped. Sen. Palmer, played lamely by Dennis Haysbert, couldn't possibly be elected to the White House. He doesn't come across as intelligent or warm or funny or even politically savvy. He rarely smiles. He is the least complex character on the set. Are American voters supposed to believe this is the prototype for the first black president? Colin Powell he is not" (Merida). Moreover, the murderous and shadowy cabal of old white men who have underwritten his candidacy and think nothing of sending a hit man to silence Keith's psychiatrist or engaging in multiple additional acts of intimidation, seem highly unlikely to use a black liberal Democrat as their stalking-horse. One suspects that casting Palmer with an African American was merely a way for *24*'s creators to deflect censure of Palmer's previous unsavory dealings.

The metanarrative of *24* uses the Drazens and their many hirelings as catalysts to call Palmer and Jack to account for their failures to be good fathers, as well as to free them from their own bad institutional fathers. The crisis calls forth two different responses, however. What is required from Palmer is that he prove himself worthy to exercise the Law of the Father before he can go on to govern the country. His chief sin is that while he engages in authorizing clandestine intelligence operations, he is completely deceived about what has been going on in his own family for years and is apparently equally ignorant of the true nature and goals of his most powerful political backers. His narrative trajectory requires him to win back his son's love and trust, exercise his political clout to trump Jack's obstructionist counterterrorism unit bosses, and repudiate the dark side of his campaign, symbolized by his decision to divorce the scheming and duplicitous Sherry.

Jack discovers that his role is to act as Palmer's agent in all senses of the word. He has been handpicked to lead the off-the-books takeout of Drazen that the senator initiated, and the narrative requires him repeatedly to sacrifice those close to him to maintain that role. Drazen, when he finally appears on the scene in the unlikely incarnation of Dennis Hopper, is an eerie doppelgänger to Palmer. Just as Jack's attempt to assassinate him failed, Drazen's attempt to make Jack the agent of Palmer's death also fails. Unlike the increasingly decisive and powerful Palmer, however, Jack, the show's nominal protagonist, fails more than he succeeds. While able to refuse to be the instrument of Palmer's death, Jack has an alarming tendency to be fatal to those who ally themselves with him. He was the only member of the Operation Nightfall team to return alive, and he is implicitly still trying to expiate the guilt for their deaths. Yet his debts just keep piling up. Mason notes sarcastically, "Nice, Jack. Have you noticed there's a body count wherever you go?" Police Officer Jessie Hampton and CIA security agent De Salvo both are taken hostage while trying to help Jack, and both are killed despite Jack's agreement to surrender in return for their release. Five counterterrorism agents guarding Jack's family are gunned down. Able to rescue his wife and daughter once, he fails to have any effect on their various escapes and renewed perils in the last eleven hours, and the day ends with his wife Teri killed by the co-worker in whom Jack has put his greatest and most misplaced trust.

In essence, the David Palmer and Jack Bauer narratives adhere in broad contours to the characteristics Gilles Deleuze ascribes to the respective formal structures of sadism and of masochism. Most apparent, of course, is the masochism: "Sitting through an entire episode of the unnervingly suspenseful '24' is a gleeful exercise in masochism, both thrilling and torturous" (Rothkerch). Deleuze notes that "masochistic pain depends entirely on the phenomenon of waiting and on the functions of repetition and reiteration which characterize waiting" (119). For Jack, this is "the longest day of my life," during which repeated threats to him, to his colleagues, to the man he is charged to protect, and to his family delay and deny respite for twenty-four hours straight. During that time, Jack suffers verbal abuse; is shot, drugged, handcuffed, betrayed, and beaten; and is interrogated by his superiors after being compelled again and again to disobey or lie to them. Nearly every hour includes a scene in which Jack must implore someone to help him save his wife and daughter, and pleading for forgiveness is another frequent occurrence. As Jamey Farrell reminds him when refusing to trust his promise that he can obtain an immunity deal for her, "You have no power." The day ends with the exquisitely painful scene of Jack cradling the body of his slain wife, saying, "I'm so sorry, so sorry." Due to the program's unique real-time format and broadcast schedule that caused audiences to experience the twenty-four hours over a period of seven months, viewers likewise were subject to the phenomenon of waiting and the "thrilling" torture and suspense.

For the subject of masochism, Deleuze asks, "Is it not precisely the father-image in him that is thus miniaturized, beaten, ridiculed and humiliated? What the subject atones for is his resemblance to the father and the father's likeness in him: the formula for masochism is the humiliated father" (60). The series thus stresses the mirroring of Jack with all the bad fathers the narrative calls upon him to eradicate. When Jack faces a Victor Drazen who has run out of ammunition and so surrenders to him, Jack shoots him repeatedly in cold blood, emptying his own gun. Jack also kills Ira Gaines face to face, just after Gaines has spoken of the risks of "our business" and wished him "good luck" in a scene that suggests some sort of unholy connection between the two men.

Although the *24* narrative follows three fathers and seems on the surface to be about male-male battles for dominance, the show repeatedly highlights the power of women to control men's actions. The Drazens embark on their vendetta because Palmer and Jack are responsible for the deaths of their wife-mother and daughter-sister. Gaines depends on women for the success of his bizarrely convoluted scheme. The assassination attempt would be over before one A.M. if saboteur Mandy had not been able to seduce photographer Martin and obtain his ID card during a tryst in a 747 restroom. Gaines's ability to use Jack as both accessory and fall guy for the hit on Palmer depends on the certainty that his daughter Kimberly will sneak out of the house with her friend Janet to meet two college boys at a furniture store in a bad part of town, so that her subsequent kidnapping will put Kim and later Teri Bauer under his power for the purpose of bending Jack to his will. Likewise, his ability to monitor Jack's compliance with his instructions depends on Jamey Farrell's treachery. Jack defeats Gaines only after he is without female resources, either as accomplices or hostages.

When the Drazens resort to plan B, that is, decide to take care of the release of Victor and the murder of Palmer and the Bauers with an all-male, all-Serbian team, their lack of power over women is telling in comparison with Gaines's. Unlike Mandy's seduction of Martin, Alexis Drazen's seduction of Palmer advance woman Elizabeth Nash backfires. Sent in by the counterterrorism unit to plant a tracking device on the lover she has recognized as one of the potential assassins, she instead stabs him. Drazen hit men repeatedly fail to kill Teri and Kim, and when the Drazens briefly recapture Kim, she manages to escape on her own. The shooting of ally Mila, to prevent Jack from using her as a shield in an escape attempt, leaves them womanless, and Jack single-handedly charges in and kills them all. While it would seem that this happens while their most powerful female agent Yelena–Nina Myers is still at large, Nina insists that she is not really working for the Drazens, only using them. A phone call to her female superior in Germany seems to confirm this.

The foiling of the Drazen plot and thus the salvation of David

Palmer to assume his proper role as enunciator of the Law therefore requires an all-male playing field. While loyal and heroic women will either be killed or raped-terrorized and used as tools with which to blackmail virtuous men in the Jack-Drazen plot, at the heart of Palmer's sadistic narrative, which subsumes Jack's, is his eventual repudiation of powerful and grasping women in the harshest ways possible. Discovering that his speechwriter Patti has tried to seduce him to obtain information for Sherry, Palmer feigns interest only to sit beside her on the bed and deliver the following pronouncement: "There's something I want to tell you, Patti. You're fired. Pack up. Get out. . . . I want you out of this hotel in thirty minutes." When Patti makes the excuse that Mrs. Palmer "can be pretty scary," Palmer intones, "So can I." His banishment of his wife is even more scathing, "I'm not angry with you, Sherry. I feel sorry for you. You've lost touch with what it is to be a parent, a friend, a wife. After tonight I don't want to see you again. I just don't think you're fit to be the first lady."

Women like Sherry often play the cold and cruel tormentor in masochistic fantasies, and the narrative paints Palmer as the solution to Jack's suffering by portraying the ambitious Alberta Green, who "is trying to make a career move" at Jack's expense, as a dead ringer for Sherry. Palmer's abrupt putting of Green in her place when she objects to his ordering Jack's reinstatement foreshadows his tone with Patti and Sherry. All these women can be seen to represent the maternal figure who assumes power in the masochistic fantasy of paternal annihilation, while sadism "stands for the active negation of the mother and the inflation of the father (who is placed above the law)" (Deleuze 68).

And then there are the daughters: Kim Bauer and Nicole Palmer. The creators of *24*, Robert Cochran and Joel Surnow, have repeatedly said in interviews that the kidnapping of Kim is more central to the narrative of the show than any specifics about the terrorist plot. Cochran notes, "Jack's got this suspenseful thing he's got to deal with every week, but the center of it is his emotional stake. How's he handling it? How's it affecting him as a human being, as a husband, as a father? The terrorist part could have been anything without affecting that" (Owen). More specifically, the family crisis spoke directly to the anxieties of the two producers: "Then we had to do something that [made] it a personal story. Bob and I both have teenage daughters, so we thought, 'Wow. What if our teenage daughter disappeared?'" (Rothkerch). While this is certainly an event to galvanize sympathy for their tormented protagonist, the sadism directed at daughters by the narrative is so extreme, so beyond what is necessary to suggest a father's worst imaginings about a kidnapped child, as to give a viewer pause about the nature of Cochran and Surnow's paternal feelings. Especially gratuitous is the treatment of Kim's friend Janet York, whose father is killed and then impersonated by Gaines lieutenant Kevin Carroll. Relieved of the necessity to hold back on the sufferings of daughters who are to be returned to producer-surrogates, the writers cause Janet to be abducted, to have her arm broken when it is slammed in a van door, to be hit by a car during an escape attempt and left seriously injured in the street, and then, after a rescue and successful surgery, to be smothered in her hospital bed by her false father.

As I noted previously, it was the violation of daughter Nicole seven years before that precipitated the familial crisis in the Palmer household and that surfaces to threaten Palmer's election hopes. Thus all three young daughters portrayed in *24* have been forcibly assaulted in one form or another by men. The differing narrative functions of Nicole and Kim do, however, go along with the parallel sadistic and masochistic story lines carried by Palmer and Jack. Deleuze states that the daughter in a sadistic scenario is "elevated to the position of incestuous accomplice" while in a masochistic scenario "the young girl is the victim." Because the Palmer narrative on the day of the primary is a sadistic one, Nicole's victimization is in the past. Her only role, as accomplice, is to express her unqualified love for her father—she even goes so far as to blame herself for being raped and causing the current crisis—and to serve as a contrast to the rebellious, initially mother-allied Keith.

Kim's role as victim undergoes an interesting slippage within Jack's masochistic trajectory. After being rescued from Gaines's compound,

Kim in fact becomes more and more a double for the masochistic subject Jack. Subjected to one perilous situation after another—the typical pattern of suspense, repetition, and delay—she shows his pluck and ingenuity in extricating herself from all of them. Because the overall sadistic narrative of *24* authored by its creative team subsumes Jack's masochistic narrative, this shift of the daughter from victim to accomplice-double is appropriate, as is the death of the once and future mother Teri rather than the daughter, for as Deleuze repeats, "sadism is in every sense an active negation of the mother" (60).

An Internet commentator makes the following observation:

> Take the two main black female characters—Palmer's wife, Sherry (Penny Johnson [Jerald]), and Alberta Green (Tamara Tunie), the agent sent to take over the counterterrorism unit in Bauer's absence. Both are grasping, ambitious women, ready to sacrifice others' families or positions for their own gains. . . . At worst, the treatment of these characters smells of bias; at best it's just some crappy TV writing. (Thrupkaew)

That's putting it mildly. Despite its appropriateness to a sadomasochistic project, *24*'s habit of representing nearly every significant female character as either bitch-betrayer or terrorized victim is disturbing evidence of a profound misogyny that has received amazingly little commentary from the professional media. Cochran and Surnow's previous series, *La Femme Nikita,* featured a female assassin who worked for a corrupt intelligence agency, and there's clearly some spillover into *24,* especially in the character of Yelena-Nina. Yet this is an inadequate justification for the wholesale animus directed at female characters week after week, and someone should remind the two executive producers that sadism and masochism *are* perversions, no matter how thrilling.

How then do the narratives the networks derived from the 9/11 attacks compare with the narrative *24* unfolded during its longest day? Both efface ideology to concentrate on the personal and familial dimensions of those involved. The gendering of the narratives, however, are reversed. 9/11 coverage counters male terrorist "martyrs" who accomplished their objectives with a celebration of dead male heroes and their widows, struggling to recover from the emotional trauma and get on with their lives. The series leaves us with a devastated widower and a number of empowered males who have eradicated the male terrorists who opposed them, in a world where wives, mothers, and female colleagues have been killed or banished. Were Surnow and Cochran to have scripted the tale of United Flight 93, one imagines Beamer, Bingham, and Glick would have had to overcome controlling female flight attendants and haughty women passengers to make their move on the hijackers. They would have succeeded in crash-landing the plane, resulting in some deaths but many survivors, themselves included. Meanwhile, in New York City, debris falling from one of the World Trade Center towers would have crushed to death the pregnant Lisa Beamer.

The demographics of *24*'s audience make a fascinating footnote to the ways its narrative reflects the media narrative of 9/11. Final Nielsen numbers ranked the show, a darling of the media press from the moment the pilot became available for advanced review, a disappointing seventy-fourth among prime-time shows. It ranked thirty-ninth, however, among viewers between 18 and 49, "an audience craved by advertisers" (Battaglia). What's more, Sandy Grushow, chairman of Fox Entertainment, when announcing the show's renewal for the 2002–03 season, informed television reporters, "It was the No. 1 new drama series among high income homes. . . . Our sales department loves this show. This series is making money. The international revenues are immense" (Duffy).

The general television audience remained cool to *24* and its "catering to the multitasking tastes of savvy computer users and picture-in-picture geeks everywhere" (Howard), preferring more traditional twentieth-century aesthetic styles to cutting-edge twenty-first-century ones. Its devoted followers were the upscale market, the people more likely to have worked in the World Trade Center office suites than to have come to rescue its inhabitants, those who would have been equally well described by current New York City mayor—and wealthy businessman—Mike Bloomberg when he reviewed the 9/11 death certificates: "These were people taken from us in the prime of their lives. They worked to go to school, get an education and get a job, and right when they are starting to move up, they are just taken from us" (Lipton). These are not working-class heroes, this mayor is not the former cop and prosecutor who held the city together on 9/11, and this audience for *24* is thrilled by an account of a man who endures terrible physical and emotional distress, and loses more than two dozen of his fellow government agents and his pregnant wife, to preserve the life of the man deemed fittest by some television executives to serve as CEO of the United States, despite his tendency, as with many CEOs in the news in the months after 9/11, to keep some of his indebtedness off the books.

Works Cited

"Another View of 9/11: Women Tell Their Stories." *Women in the Fire Service*. Mar. 30, 2002. July 7, 2002. <http://www.wfsi.org/AnotherView. html>.

Battaglia, Stephen. "Clock Will Keep Running for '24'." *New York Daily News* May 17, 2002: 131.

Coté, William, and Roger Simpson. *Covering Violence*. New York: Columbia UP, 2000.

Crossley, Callie, ed. "Time Stopped: 9/11 Coverage." *Harvard University Institute of Politics Forums*. Mar. 6, 2002. June 4, 2002. <www.iop. harvard.edu/studygroups/s02-media-journal.html>.

Deleuze, Gilles. "Coldness and Cruelty." *Masochism*. Trans. Jean McNeil. New York: Zone, 1991: 9–141.

Duffy, Mike. "'24' finishes a tough day with a bang." *Detroit Free Press* May 21, 2002. July 23, 2002. <http://www.freep.com/entertainment/ tvandradio/duf21_20020521.htm>.

Howard, Douglas. "Time's Up: Fox's *24* and the Question of 'Real Time.'" *Pop Politics* Jan. 30 2002. June 4, 2002. <http://www.poppolitics.com/ 2002-01-30-24.htm>.

Lipton, Eric. "The Toll: In Cold Numbers, a Census of the Sept. 11 Victims." *Index of 9-11-01 Data.* Apr. 19, 2002. June 3, 2002. <http://members.dandy.net/~lulu/911-before-after.html>.

Lynch, Thomas. "The Dead and Gone." *Christian Century* Nov. 14, 2001: 6.

Merida, Kevin. "The First Black (Fictional) President?" *Washington Post Writers' Group* Mar. 20 2002. July 23, 2002. <http://www.postwritersgroup.com/archives/meri0320.htm>.

Nacos, Brigitte. *Terrorism and the Media.* New York: Columbia UP, 1994.

Owen, Rob. "Tuned In: There's Still Time to Get Caught Up in '24.'" *Pittsburgh Post-Gazette* Feb. 5, 2002. June 3, 2002. <http://www.post-gazette.com/tv/20020205owen0205fnp4.asp>.

Rothkerch, Ian. "A Day in the Life." *Salon.com Arts and Entertainment: Television* Feb. 5, 2002. July 23, 2002. <http://www.salon.com/ent/tv/int/2002/02/05/surnow/html.32>.

Thrupkaew, Noy. "Fox's *24* Could Be More." *American Prospect* Mar. 22, 2002. July 23, 2002. <http://www.prospect.org/webfeatures/2002/03/thrupkaew-n-03-22.html>.

Woolf, Michael. "Homeland Insecurity." *New York Magazine* July 8, 2002: 14–15.

8

The How-To Manual, the Prequel, and the Sequel in Post-9/11 Cinema

Rebecca Bell-Metereau

In the period leading up to and following September 11, 2001, a number of cultural critics have recognized what Umberto Eco calls "Ur-Fascism," a culture of paranoia that values sacrifice, obedience, the cult of the hero, and the doctrine of constant warfare. Eco observes,

> Since both permanent war and heroism are difficult games to play, the Ur-Fascist transfers his will to power to sexual matters. This is the origin of machismo (which implies both disdain for women and intolerance and condemnation of nonstandard sexual habits, from chastity to homosexuality). (59)

Women figure importantly as iconic devices in films that demonstrate the kinds of roles they play in the ur-fascist drama. Examples include the scapegoat and cause of downfall in *Independence Day* (1996), the sexual prize for which young men lay down their lives in *Pearl Harbor* (2001), and finally, the doyenne of the domestic world in *Panic Room* (2002). One may look at the growing number of militaristic movies, temporarily upstaged by real-life events but waiting in the wings like prima ballerinas, to see that the media not only reported but helped create a siege mentality, followed by a reaction of panic and consequent thirst for revenge. Clear patterns appear in the roles women have played in some of the most popular box-office films from before and after 9/11. They are viewed variously as scapegoats for blunders, as excuses for mayhem, and finally as participants in "justified" revenge, both in the public and private spheres of film narratives. With an array of Hollywood products prefiguring, instructing, and reinforcing a militaristic model, one can point to works that constitute the how-to, the prequel, and the sequel films for 9/11. An equally influential and yet more invisible instruction manual comes encoded in these films; gender role models are embedded in the characters and plots of narratives supposedly limited to pure action and adventure. If the events of September 11 made producers shaky about timing the release of war films, 9/11 firmed up their resolve on how males and females should be depicted. Many films made at the turn of this millennium restrict women to a set of types that harken back to Nazi Germany's vision of the proper roles for women, with the added variations of the avenging mother and the combat-ready sex kitten popularized during the James Bond era.

Gender roles are scarcely mentioned when people point to media complicity and agency in the events of 9/11. Rather, they tend to point toward film violence as a causative influence. Robert Altman brought a firestorm of protest when he delivered the following pronouncements after the terrorist attack:

> The movies set the pattern, and these people have copied the movies. . . . Nobody would have thought to commit an atrocity like that (the attack on the World Trade Centers) unless they'd seen it in a movie. . . . How dare we continue to show this kind of mass destruction in movies? I just believe we created this atmosphere and taught them how to do it. (qtd. in Roten)

Roten attempts to refute Altman's claim about Hollywood's culpability, noting that Tom Clancy's book *Debt of Honor* and Fox TV's *X-Files* spin-off, *The Lone Gunman,* actually come closer to predicting the exact methods of the suicide pilots. What both Altman and Roten neglect is another, more important influence that movies had on the events of September 2001. American blockbuster movies laid the groundwork for the public's response to the event as the beginning of war rather than as a terrorist attack, and that, as Robert Frost would say, "has made all the difference."

Altman was not alone in claiming media responsibility for 9/11. Even editorials in mainstream magazines like *Entertainment Weekly* and *Hollywood Reporter* "demanded a newer, kinder, softer industry" immediately after the event. With films like *Armageddon* and *Independence Day,* "Hollywood blockbusters, it seemed, had prefigured, even created September 11" (Roten 1). A web site on death in film speculates that post-9/11 films would depict more psychics, lost spirits, heroic and sacrificial deaths, along with more terrorists and natural, tame deaths ("Death"). Since the list includes most forms of death imaginable, this doesn't tell us a lot. It would, however, be safe to predict more depictions of death as uplifting, simply because this slant has been successful thus far. A film executive came out of the October 2001 preview of *The Sum of All Fears* gushing, "God, this is so positive and life-affirming, we could release it today!" Director Phil Robinson maintains that his depiction of nuclear war is in good taste, because it shows "no shots of charred bodies and no people disappearing in white flashes" (Maher 3). Apparently, for this filmmaker, what is more important than depicting war or terrorist acts in a realistic way that might upset people is portraying war in an uplifting and encouraging way that will inspire people to go to more movies. Robinson's notion of the ethical responsibilities of filmmakers is truly disturbing, especially if he accomplishes his apparent goal of making people feel good about armed conflict.

Given the attention span of the American public, the industry's initial hesitation over releasing the huge batch of war films already in the hopper may have proven somewhat overcautious. MGM's delay of John Woo's *WindTalkers* (2002, starring Nicholas Cage) did not save the hundred-million-dollar film from limping in with only a measly $40 million in domestic grosses. Another delayed film, Warner Brothers' Schwarzenegger vehicle *Collateral Damage* (2002), also grossed only $40 million. On the other hand, studio decisions to go ahead with the relatively low-budget *Training Day* (2001) and *Spy Game*

(2001) brought in $76 million and an Oscar for Denzel Washington, and $62 million, respectively. *Black Hawk Down*'s production date was actually moved up "to take advantage of the patriotic climate," a move that brought in $108 million in domestic sales. Of course, release dates are not the only factors in a film's success. Jude Law's "hunk" rating may have made teenaged girls more willing to go along with boyfriends to see *Enemy at the Gates* (2001), while the declining popular appeal of Cage and Schwarzenegger may have contributed to the failure of their films. Jack Mathews of the *New York Daily News* made the sarcastic comment, "Pity the film industry. It has to deplete an inventory that is eighteen months to three years behind the news before it can exploit the new, which means September 11, 2001, won't produce any significant post-9/11 movies at least until 2003" (25).

Kevin Maher argues persuasively that

> the aesthetic memory of 9/11 is perversely and irreversibly rooted in blockbuster movies. It's a fact that even Saddam Hussein, hardly the world's sharpest cultural critic, has famously acknowledged, declaring: "When we watched what was happening in America for the first time, we thought it might be another American movie. Later we found that it was a real movie." (5)

After the initial shock of September 11, all kinds of films underwent modifications, such as the digital removal of the towers from *Zoolander* (2001) and *Serendipity* (2001) and the reshooting of the *Men in Black II* (2002) climax with the Chrysler building in the original version's background. Yet even after all the hand-wringing and precautions delivered in the immediate wake of 9/11, within a matter of months, movies were "Back with a Bang," as Kevin Maher observes, with *The Sum of All Fears*' poster tag line: "Could Terrorists Actually Detonate a Weapon of Mass Destruction on U.S. Soil?" Joel Schumacher's *Bad Company,* Barry Sonnenfeld's *Big Trouble,* and Tom Tykwer's *Heaven* feature a terrorist in a subway, a bomb in a Miami airport, and a "queasily evocative skyscraper explosion" (3). All of these films were shot before 9/11, but they were edited afterward, marketed with an eye to the effects of 9/11. They also contain worldviews that support government policies and actions, particularly in the archetypes and stereotypes presented as models for behavior for patriotic American men and women.

While filmmakers have been struggling to find a surefire formula for action films, they have kept an eye on patterns of female viewership, a small but steadily growing market share of the war genre's box office. Various forms of combat and action movies of the last few years may offer isolated instances of female empowerment, but they generally present a clearly codified set of gender expectations following traditional behavior patterns. If the Great Depression gave birth to Steinbeck and John Ford's Ma Joad and Rosasharn in *The Grapes of Wrath,* the dawning of a new millennium spawned *Charlie's Angels* and *Lara Croft, Tomb Raider.* With the repositioning of women in traditionally masculine genres, images of domesticity and consumption are also retooled and refigured, and instead of featuring Rosie the Riveter on the home front, filmmakers give viewers something more like Rosie the Robocop. The archetype of the billowy, nourishing earth mother is replaced with the hypersexualized female, complete with firm, perky breasts, stiletto thin legs, a designer wardrobe, and black-belt karate skills. The woman as combat-ready sex machine reached its artistic zenith with *Crouching Tiger Hidden Dragon,* a film hailed by horny teenaged boys and art-house feminists alike for its novel presentation of a lethal woman warrior, climbing walls and floating through the air as in a dream of flying. A third popular alternative for women is the nurse-doctor or caretaker, as presented in *Pearl Harbor* (2001) and *The Sum of All Fears* (2002). This female figure hovers in the background, taking care of wounded until she can rejoin the hero at the end of the film, after he has performed all the exciting footage-worthy work.

If action film roles appear limited for females, the range of popular types is at least as narrow for men as well. The most popular figure in war films is the strong, silent man of action, who works from his gut instincts and acts without thinking—the true macho man. A couple of other, more androgynous figures are possible as well. The sensitive man, who is often younger and characterized as more emotional and ethical, usually learns from the macho man how to behave. Mr. Sensitive serves as the foil to the Action Man, and he will either sacrifice himself as a result of being inspired by the manly hero, or he will be the one to survive and admire the bravery and self-sacrifice of the macho hero, as in *Hart's War*.

Long before the terrorist attacks of 2001, the nation was already marching in step with a steady drumbeat of militaristic movies, cautionary tales that warned against being "soft" on enemies. Viewers watching the news of September 11 may have experienced an eerie chill of déjà vu as they watched footage of planes plowing into buildings. Only five years earlier, some anti-Clinton viewers cheered at *Independence Day* previews that depicted a similar scene in which flying ships blow up the White House. Such fictional depictions of national disaster were popular, with *Independence Day* coming in number one in 1996. That movie, which a number of astute viewers have recognized in retrospect as a kind of terrorist how-to, had two important messages: aliens are evil and women are trouble. Women in *Independence Day* give all the wrong advice, and when the president lets a woman lead, she and others pay with their lives:

> When Margaret Colin's Constance Spano, the president's press secretary, refuses to listen to her estranged husband about the countdown and the inevitability of attack, she causes the death of millions of people. Only after she and her husband reconcile is she able to become a savior. When Mary McDonnell's Marilyn Whitmore, the First Lady, first refuses to obey her husband and later pushes her daughter away, she is punished by death with little show of grief on the part of her husband or her daughter. (Hobby 52–53)

The film presents the lesson that naive assumptions about how enemies may be appeased represent a feminine or feminized mind-set.

A similar antipacifist note is sounded by *Saving Private Ryan* (1998), in which women are conspicuously absent throughout the bulk of the film. Even though there are no women in the war scenes, certain men take their place in being the spokesmen for a pacifist sensibility. Along with Private Richard Reiben (Edward Burns), the audience develops sympathy for the German soldier, who later betrays Reiben's trust by killing Private Stanley Mellish (Adam Goldberg). Captain John Miller (Tom Hanks) plays the more manly, tough, and realistic hero to Reiben's naive softy. The film invites viewers to wallow in the guilt Spielberg feels for never having entered combat himself, and it places a premium on sacrifice and blind obedience to duty. Ryan, like the viewer, is alive because others have died, and the framing tale—the only part of the film to feature females—hits viewers over the head with this sentiment, just in case the narrative doesn't make the point clearly enough.

The notion of sacrifice was already popular among male and female audiences, as it was presented in the number-one box-office film of 1997, *Titanic*. While *Titanic* was not a war film, it had several of the favorite features of combat pictures: frightening situations, action, mayhem, and sacrifice, all set in the context of a class-busting romance. Katha Pollitt observes that *Titanic* has it all from a feminist and a traditional perspective:

> The twentieth century, which for so many men is a saga of loss, decline, and displacement, has told a different story to women. So call Titanic a women's fantasy—of costless liberation brought to you by a devoted, selfless, charming, funny, incredibly handsome lover. He teaches you to spit, awakens you body and soul, points you toward a long, richly eventful future, and dies, beautifully, poetically, tragically—but not before he tells you that freezing to death in a sea full of corpses was worth it because it brought him you. (48)

When *Pearl Harbor* attempted to follow the same blockbuster formula—romance set against the backdrop of historical disaster—it failed to live up to its economic promise. Some might argue that the chemistry just wasn't there, but perhaps the real problem was that the film simply didn't calculate its audience well enough. *Pearl Harbor* has one foot planted firmly in the new millennium and the other in yesteryear, with a growing split pulling it apart right up its generously endowed middle. The formalist bipartite construction has worked before in war films, most effectively in Stanley Kubrick's *Full Metal Jacket* (1987), whose first half depicts the orderly indoctrination of boot camp while the second half shatters into the chaos and meaninglessness of Vietnam combat. In terms of its depth and complexity, *Pearl Harbor* should probably not be mentioned in the same breath with Kubrick's piece, however, in what is tantamount to comparing a McDonald's beefalo burger with a Ritz filet mignon. *Pearl Harbor* tries to repeat the success of *Titanic* by wedding romance and disaster, fiction and history, chick flick and action pic. During a three-hour labor, through half of which the audience may have dozed, nothing emerges but a stillborn giant. In a market-driven blockbuster industry, the filmmakers attempt to capitalize on the successes of predecessors, to read potential audiences, and to create a product that appeals to as many demographics as possible. What resulted in *Pearl Harbor* was a product hopelessly divided between efforts to please two irreconcilable audiences.

Another split reveals itself in the film's formal aspects. The opening idyllic scenes reminiscent of *South Pacific* contrast jarringly with the jerky handheld camera and slow motion of the battle field and the hospital, the filmmaker's failed attempt to capture the gut-wrenching charge of *Saving Private Ryan*. Nowhere is the film's split personality more apparent than in the feeble attempts to give birth to a "new woman" and a "new minority," a concept that is touted in female voice-over at the end of the film. Aside from these elements receiving only token minutes in a three-hour film, the way these actions are depicted also gives women and African Americans short shrift. Women and minorities are linked in the conversation between Evelyn Johnson (Kate Beckinsale) and Doris Miller (Cuba Gooding Jr.), in which Miller has a chance to complain about his role as dishwasher instead of fighter. Evelyn admonishes him to make the best of things, thus placing her, as white and female, in a position of superior wisdom and power. Evelyn later demonstrates her status as a superior woman, at the cost of another often vilified group—doctors. When hundreds of mutilated bodies are flooding the hospital, one of the doctors stands paralyzed with shock until level-headed Evelyn commands him to do something. While it could be argued that this scene demonstrates the plucky superiority of a woman, it is important to note who is diminished by this scenario—the trained professional or "intellectual." Just as *Forrest Gump* (1994) and a score of other films have touted the populist notion that simple guys really know better than "eggheads," *Pearl Harbor* presents a kind of faux populism that shows a common, ordinary dyslexic guy being the one who can handle the stress of warfare. The glorification of the rebel is another common motif, but this figure is not rebelling against the power of the state. Rather, he is breaking cumbersome rules in zealous support of the will of the state. This popular message paves the way for a mind-set that disdains overly conscientious civil libertarians or politicians who insist that the nation follow rules of constitutional or international law.

What is astonishing is that relatively few reviewers noted the prowar jingoistic message of *Saving Private Ryan* and *Pearl Harbor.* Instead, arguments popped up about how fair the film's depiction of the Japanese was. Two moments present themselves as instances of supposedly evenhanded treatment of the "enemy." In the opening battle scenes, one of the Japanese pilots waves his hand to indicate to a few women and children that they should seek cover. Later, we see pretty American women dressed in forties-style dresses and heels running from Japanese strafers. In the scene of Americans bombing Tokyo, we see a few seconds of women strolling along in kimonos under parasols in a peaceful garden, looking up as the planes fly overhead. The film takes great pains, however, to demonstrate that Americans don't harm civilians or women. The audience doesn't see the Japanese women running or actually being struck by bombs. The only American strikes we see are those of munitions plants and military targets, followed by cheers of "Take that, you bastards!" Women are used in both cases to "humanize" the soldiers, but clearly some humans are depicted as more humane than others. In a similar lopsided fashion, the film's attempt to depict the leading female character as heroic is also slanted in favor of the men's version of heroism. Men shoot down planes and accomplish dazzling flying and shooting maneuvers, while the woman saves someone's life by sticking her finger on a gushing artery. In terms of sheer coverage as well, men receive about ten times as much screen footage as women do in this film.

Even the romance of *Pearl Harbor* is weakened by its imbalanced and shallow depiction of male-female relationships. A few brief scenes show the hero as a bumbling, sincere hunk who is told what to do by the pretty nurse. No doubt this depiction is intended to appeal to female audience members, who can view themselves as powerful and in control of emotional relationships. When Rafe McCawley (Ben Affleck) does the honorable thing and doesn't sleep with Evelyn before his departure, the lesson for both genders seems to be that this restraint was an error. Later on, after Evelyn thinks he has died, she willingly has sex with his best friend, Danny Walker (Josh Hartnett), and the result of this union becomes the centerpiece of the film's climax. One might think that the final love scene would be between a man and a woman, but in *Pearl Harbor,* the romance occurs between the two men. Rafe, the more daring and masculine of the male duo, returns to discover his girl has been taken, and after a conventional barroom brawl, the two friends reach an uneasy reconciliation. Then, when Danny sacrifices his life for his friend, the farewell scene between Rafe and Danny provides the emotional and sentimental high point of the film. The climactic love scene between Rafe and Danny manages to efface the female entirely. When Rafe tells Danny that Evelyn is pregnant with Danny's child, Danny tells Rafe, "It's your child, too." The mother is erased from the formula, and the child, who turns out, significantly, to be a boy, becomes the child of two men in the schema of the film. Evelyn is pictured briefly with Rafe and the child, and then the film closes with a touching twosome, the young boy sitting on his father's lap, flying the plane that the dead man's father and the two young men had flown. Patriarchal heritage remains intact, with an all-male line of succession handed down through the symbolism of the airplane, the phallic symbol of dominance. The masculinization of cultural narratives does not mean that the feminine disappears completely. Rather, the emotions and characteristics associated with the feminine are displaced onto masculine characters. They express their love and tenderness, but only within the context of death. It is only when comrades fall and lie in each other's arms, ready to die or already dead, that the hero can express his love for his comrade.

Other functions of women are seen clearly in *Black Hawk Down,* including their use as icons of innocence—the justification for all the fighting. A few seconds of a shot of a woman or, better yet, a woman and children, may be used to humanize and soften the image of the macho soldier. For example, in *Black Hawk Down,* a movie from which women and girls have been effaced almost totally, there are only a few seconds of screen time for women. At one point, a red-veiled woman passes in front of the camera to provide local color. Another time, we see two small girls standing and looking at the soldiers as they pass by during the shooting. At one point, a soldier warns a passing woman to get down during the fighting. Then, later on, a soldier comes into a house for shelter, where he sees a woman huddling with several children. He indicates to them that they should be quiet, and then as he sneaks out, he waves good-bye to the children. One of them waves back, with a shy smile. The only negative incident with a woman occurs when a red-veiled woman (perhaps the same one from an earlier scene?) starts to raise a gun, while an American soldier shouts, "Don't you do it. Don't you do it!" Finally, the soldier has to shoot her, and later, as the soldiers run down the road, one of them vomits as they run, supposedly out of shock and revulsion over having participated in the shooting of a woman.

In describing Somalia, Mark Bowden's paperback edition of *Black Hawk Down* says, "The lesson our retreat taught the world's terrorists and despots is that killing a few Americans, even at the cost of more than five hundred of your own fighters, is enough to spook Uncle

Sam" (Doherty 5). According to Thomas Doherty, in *Black Hawk Down*, "the extraction film," "the profusely slaughtered Somalis might as well be crocodile meat" and "the African hordes circling around the Americans and lurking around every corner evoke nothing so much as the swarming aliens in the series originated by Ridley Scott and reinvented as sci-fi combat by James Cameron" (5, 6). Doherty notes, "Always entranced by uniforms, vehicles, and sleek weaponry, Scott fixes a caressing, fetishistic gaze on the fashion accessories of the modern military." The sensuous description of Scott's attitude underscores the homoerotic appeal of war films. Women are unnecessary in war films because all the real romance, intimacy, and physical thrills occur between men. Fondling a woman's breast seems tame in comparison to clutching a comrade's sucking chest wound. The intimacy accomplished by a single silent gaze from one suffering man to another speaks much louder to many male audience members than the romantic prattle of a woman ever could. In describing the sacrifice and bravery required during warfare, the male voice-over at the end of *Black Hawk Down* says, "It's about the man next to you and that's all it is." How true.

A similar sentiment appears in Randall Wallace's *We Were Soldiers* (2002), in which reporter Galloway (Barry Pepper) says the men fought "not for their country or their flag—they fought for each other" (Doherty 8). *We Were Soldiers* has more women and families in the background, once again to reveal the human, soft side of the military. One scene shows family man Lt. Col. Hal Moore (Mel Gibson) explaining to his daughter that people must have wars in order to get rid of bad men. While the film makes a nod to showing "both sides" of the conflict by crosscutting between the Viet Cong leader and the American leader, the essential humanizing element of women and children is missing from the depiction of the enemy.

Hart's War, an all-male film, presents dual gender identities in a single-sex setting. Adapted from John Katzenbach's novel (inspired by his father's World War II experiences), this film places soldiers in a German concentration camp. The son of a senator, former law student Lt. Thomas Hart is identified as weak for having yielded to torture. Played by the pretty and wholesome-looking Irish actor Colin Farrell, Hart's character, clothing, and demeanor are somewhat prissy, and for a prison camp resident, he maintains a strikingly natty appearance. The camera presents him in the soft focus usually reserved for women, and his body is exposed, in feminized poses. At one point, he crouches freezing and naked, and after this episode he points to a map, betraying his country and his gender. Clean shaven and vulnerable, he stands in stark contrast to the manly Colonel William McNamara, played by a stern Bruce Willis, whose long, stubble-covered upper lip, small, squinting eyes, and simian appearance fit perfectly his role as top gorilla of the pack. Hart is humiliated and placed with the enlisted men, and later joined by two black officers, one of whom is mysteriously killed and the other is later framed for murder of a white racist. Hart battles bravely for justice until he learns that the entire trial is set up to distract the Nazis from the Americans' planned escape. Hart attempts to sacrifice himself and claim that he was the murderer, but he is one-upped by McNamara, who returns to camp after getting his men out and takes complete responsibility for the escape of the other men. He is promptly shot in the head by the German Col. Werner Visser (Marcel Iotes). Hart's voice-over tells the audience that now the black man can return to his children and tell them the importance and meaning of words like *sacrifice, honor,* and *duty.*

The story demonstrates for audiences how maintaining group welfare and making sacrifices justify violating whatever shabby and tattered legal rights have managed to survive in a prisoner-of-war camp. Any civil libertarians concerned with the abrogation of legal procedures in the wake of 9/11 are encouraged to hang their heads in shame at the suggestion that individual human rights should ever take precedence over the demands of a society at war. This notion of the pettiness of demands for individual rights is echoed in an episode of the television show *The Practice* written specifically in response to 9/11. An Anglo-American woman married to an Arab American comes to the firm to find out what has happened to her husband, who has been picked up for questioning. She is not allowed to speak to him, and when he "testifies," he claims that he is willing to give up any rights whatsoever to help his country and demonstrate that he is a true patriot. None of the women, including his wife and the female lawyers, seems to understand his notion of self-sacrificing honor, and they all try to obtain traditional justice for him. While this episode initially appears to be giving an evenhanded take on the issue, perhaps slanting in favor of the outraged wife, by the end of the story, the implicit assumption is that, as tough as it seems, stoic silence and acceptance of enforced sacrifice is the best response. In both *Hart's War* and this episode of *The Practice,* the concern for injustice and sympathy for the plight of the individual victim are depicted as womanish, childish, and unrealistic.

Just as the society of post-9/11 finds itself in the peculiar position of being "at war" without the possibility of performing any of the usual wartime activities, the soldiers in *Hart's War* must invent ways to demonstrate their bravery and willingness to sacrifice. The message of self-sacrifice may be just what the Bush administration would like to see from a film, but it didn't seem to appeal to audiences as much as sheer escape did in 2001. Of the top ten highest-grossing films released in 2001, only *Pearl Harbor* had a war theme, and it limped in behind five fantasy and children's films and a sequel, *Rush Hour 2* (2001), for a disappointing seventh overall in box-office grosses. In 2002, half of the top ten highest-grossing films were fantasy or children's films, and although this may look like a pattern similar to that of 2001, the element of female-delivered revenge adds a new wrinkle to the formula.

Even revenge films like *Panic Room* (2002), which would not be categorized in historical, war, or action genres, can make powerful statements about historical events. Whether or not a film presents itself as history, it may provide some people with "information" and attitudes about history, culture, and society. Films that do not contain specific references to history may nevertheless alter people's views of historical events. For example, it has been argued that a number of science fiction films of the fifties fed into people's fears of communism by portraying the threat of mindless automatons or totalitarian worlds. Movies that glorify violence or military action probably affect people's attitudes toward war more than they realize. Many of our attitudes about other cultures come from subtextual and structural cues that are not even part of the main plot. Indeed, the absence of the "Other" is probably the single most important way in which our views of history and society are affected by popular films. Other cultural experiences are trivialized or simply missing in popular film, and the tendency of mainstream films to stick to certain narrative patterns reinforces our ethnocentric and patriarchal worldview. Most Americans have never seen a war story presented from the point of view of the "enemies" or women affected by wars, whether they are about World War II, Vietnam, or terrorism. Of course this erasure or distortion is not limited to war films. Despite (or perhaps because of) the scarcity or absence of women and girls in film, significant lessons about masculinity and femininity are conveyed through same-sex relationships in which one of the men "becomes" the woman. Stereotypical behaviors, dialogue, body positions, camera angles, and lighting signal the "feminine" man. When such imitators function as women, not as many real female characters are needed in a film, from the point of view of filmmakers. This situation works to the detriment of women characters within the film narratives and real women within the film industry. More important, the masculinization of the zeitgeist, as expressed through the popular storytelling medium of film, damages society as a whole, as a psychic entity, as revealed in its artistic and entertainment productions.

One of the most harmful effects is in creating a culture that fears the Other. In discussing the popularity of the film and the real-life phenomenon of the "panic room," Joan Ryan writes, "So-called panic rooms are just an exaggeration of what is becoming a preoccupation with keeping safe. We are becoming a bunkered nation, and it has little to do with Sept. 11. We don't fear terrorists; we fear each other." She observes that in fact from 1993 to 2000 violent crimes declined 44 percent, and household burglary declined 45 percent, according to the Department of Justice. . . . So why do we feel so much less secure? Because we see the outside world not through our windows, but through our televisions.

The plot of the film *Panic Room* substantiates this view. In it, Jodie Foster plays Meg Altman, a recently divorced mother, whose guilt-ridden husband has provided her with an enormous financial settlement. She and her diabetic daughter are in the process of moving into a gigantic house, complete with a "panic room," which turns out to be the repository for a bundle of cash hidden by the previous owner. A grandson, aware of this stash, plans to break in with his criminal friends, not anticipating that the house will be occupied by a couple of females. At first, the would-be robbers assume the heist will be simple, but the criminals end up becoming victims rather than victimizers. Jodie Foster's character is a cross between a badger and an enraged suburban mom, grim and tight-lipped in her determination to save her young. When she calls her ex-husband to enlist his aid, he is repaid for his efforts by becoming another victim of head-bashing violence. The criminals are portrayed as the usual low-life scum of mixed color and pedigree, and viewers cheer for the not-so-frail victims of crime. While the filmmaker and actors put in a workman-like performance on a script almost as claustrophobic as the tale's setting, the film fails to create much excitement. Nevertheless, this mediocre concept seems to have struck a chord with the viewing public. The film ranked eighth in overall grosses by July 2002. Unlike many of the so-called action heroines, Foster doesn't play the role for sex appeal, and one cannot help but wonder whether this one is aimed primarily at the soccer moms who feel so ill-used and put-upon that they need to drive gigantic SUVs and take kick-boxing classes to experience empowerment. This film's central fantasy seems to be one of isolation and an enforced return to a claustrophobic womb—the panic room. From a materialist perspective, the plot could be said to offer a mild critique of overconsumption in its negative portrayal of the luxury home. The closing scene shows the mother and daughter happily discussing the selection of a modest two-bedroom apartment, ringing a new-millennium variation on Dorothy's famous phrase in *The Wizard of Oz:* "There's no place like home; there's no place like home." For a society sensing itself on the outskirts of some mysterious "War on Terrorism," this sentiment was probably as comforting as the 1939 isolationist message of *The Wizard of Oz* (1939) was for a nation on the brink of World War II. The heroine of *Panic Room* takes revenge by setting on fire a bad guy, who apparently never learned the lesson of drop and roll. His shrieks as he runs through the house are quite a contrast to the cries of Dorothy's witch, who melts after Dorothy throws water on her. Despite differences in the level of violence, women in both films are encouraged to fight for their right to be domestic, and happiness is found in returning to a humble abode after a foolish foray into the threatening masculine realm of action and ambition.

The escalation in American women's penchant for violence is another sobering aspect of the millennial zeitgeist. Nicholas Kristof notes that "one of the most far-reaching consequences of September 11 is a surge in gun sales around the country," with women accounting for 60 percent of that rise. Women and girls figure importantly in another connection between media and education, the rise of ROTC programs throughout the nation: "$234 million of defense department money in 2002 was spent on JROTC," quadruple the amount of a decade ago (Goodman 58). Colin Powell comments on how positive this development is, noting that this gives youths a "good gang" to join (Goodman, 59) In an interview, "[a] cheerful 13-year-old named Lydia Banda thrusts her hand into the air. 'I wanna go into the military because I see it in the movies and it seems fun,' she declares. 'And when the war is over, you get famous and you make a lotta money'" (Goodman 81).

The idea of showing the "fun" side of the military is nothing new in filmmaking. After the grimness of the Cold War, Americans gobbled up images of the spy, whose gadgets, flair, and debonair urbanity set a new standard for masculinity. Women in these films were still sex objects, but they were tools with some possible bite. The 007 paradigm spoke to both sexes, and the emphasis on gadgets, clothing, and consumerism appealed to the commercial side of the industry. With more opportunities for sales of spy gear and clothing, everyone was happy. A resurgence of the cool spy appeared with the comic spoofs of the *Men in Black* and *Austin Powers* films, but even in more serious versions of the motif, the message is the same. Ordinary people should be glad that someone else is handling the dirty business of espionage. Whether it is the men in black knocking out aliens or Ben Affleck's character saving the world from a nuclear holocaust, audiences should be grateful that someone behind the scenes is making the right decisions and sacrifices for the greater welfare of society. This kind of ideology disguised as entertainment is couched in comedy or action pictures, two of the most popular genres.

The "uplifting" *Sum of All Fears* offers a perfect example of just such a propaganda vehicle. Under the guise of presenting a critique of the mutually assured destruction military model, *The Sum of All Fears* actually urges audiences to accept the practice of spying, deception, assassination, and invasion of privacy as a beneficial state of affairs. By showing a scenario in which a neo-Nazi terrorist organization fools the United States into thinking it has been attacked by Russia, the film reveals how well the system actually works. People behind the scenes on both sides are keeping track of what is really going on, and these people will take the appropriate action when it is necessary. Even if someone succeeds in detonating a nuclear device, it doesn't seem to have any long-lasting consequences. Only one person—an Arab peasant—is shown suffering any consequences as a result of radiation poisoning. The hero Jack Ryan (Ben Affleck) doesn't even have to lose any hair, let alone suffer cancer or radiation sickness, even though he drove through firestorms and was thoroughly dusted with radioactive ashes. His girlfriend Cathy Muller (Bridget Moynahan) is blown against the wall by the impact of the bomb, along with the shattering glass from the window in front of her. A short time later, the film features vignettes of her dealing with burn victims, with hardly a hair out of place. She manages to finish up her little activities just in time to greet Jack, once he is through saving the world as we know it.

In the final scene, the spy (Liev Schreiber) behind the scenes comes up to the couple, happily picnicking on the grass and listening to the president's words, with the White House featured prominently in the background. He presents them with an engagement present, and Jack asks him how he knew they were engaged, since he asked her to marry him only that morning. The friendly spy shrugs and the couple laughs, shaking their heads in amazement, with a grateful "Isn't that cute? Those wacky spies!" look on their faces. Instead of being outraged or threatened by being spied on in their most intimate exchanges, the couple gladly accepts the gift from the nice spy who manipulates not only their personal destinies but also the future of the entire planet. This scenario has the effect of making people comfortable with the notion of constant surveillance, since it is clear that this is for their own good. A look at the credits for this film makes it evident who would like to promulgate this worldview, with a list of cooperating and sponsoring entities that reads like a who's who in the military. Meanwhile, media makers and critics have been remarkably complicit in this effort to make us feel good about all things covert and military. Reviewers don't bother to subject the current rash of war and spy films to the kind of scrutiny they often apply to films of other genres. For example, none of the mainstream reviewers observed that characters in the aftermath of the nuclear explosion of *The Sum of All Fears* suffered none of the effects of radiation. In a similar vein, no mention was made in mainstream reviews of the dismal failure of the setting of *We Were Soldiers* to capture even a semblance of the jungles of Vietnam, whereas decades earlier, critics scoffed at Kubrick for importing potted palm trees to England in an attempt at verisimilitude.

Numerous conspiracy web sites posit the notion that the U.S. government had prior knowledge of the impending terrorist attack of September 11, 2001. While these theories may attribute more malice or organizational skills to the government than it actually has, they nevertheless point to an important aspect of the events before and after

9/11. There is a kind of seamless quality, a sense of inevitability and ritual repetition that pervade media coverage of the event. People fall into their roles as if programmed to respond, and films and news stories from the time preceding and immediately following the attack seem to prefigure, create, and promulgate a climate of terror. Even choices in games and clothing styles fall in line with a state of war. Combat gear and camouflage clothing hang in racks alongside soft, retro flowery gypsy blouses, a contrasting pattern reminiscent of styles from the Vietnam era. The world as depicted in film and media divides into a set of binary oppositions: patriotic versus unpatriotic, hawk versus dove, masculine versus feminine, hard versus soft, action versus indecision. Gender roles also split into a few narrow choices for both men and women, and with this paucity of choices, not just the cinema but also the art, thought, and spirit of a nation are impoverished.

Works Cited

"Death and Dying in Film." Aug. 15, 2002. <http://www.trinity.edu/mkearl/death02/deathflicks>.

Doherty, Thomas. "The New War Movies as Moral Rearmament: *Black Hawk Down* and *We Were Soldiers.*" *Cineaste* 27.3 (2002): 4–8.

Eco, Umberto. "Eternal Fascism: Fourteen Ways of Looking at a Blackshirt." *Utne Reader* Nov.–Dec. 1995: 57–59.

Goodman, David. "Recruiting the Class of 2005." *Mother Jones* Jan.–Feb. 2002: 57–62, 80–81.

Hobby, Teresa Santerre. "Independence Day: Reinforcing Patriarchal Myths about Gender and Power." *Journal of Popular Culture* 34.2 (2000): 39–55.

Kristof, Nicholas. "Post–Sept. 11 Fallout: Handgun Sales Rise." Rpt. in *Austin American Statesman* Apr. 13, 2002: A9.

Maher, Kevin. "Back with a Bang." *Observer* June 30, 2002. Aug. 15, 2002. <http://www.guardian.co.uk/Archive/Article/0,4273,4451271,00.html>.

Mathews, Jack. "Films 9/11 Catch-Up." *New York Daily News* Jan. 13, 2002: 25. Rpt. in *Santa Rosa Press Democrat.* Aug. 15, 2002. <http://www.pressdemocrat.com/goingout/movies/reviews/13films_914.html>.

Pollitt, Katha. "Women and Children First." *Nation* Mar. 30, 1998: 48.

Roten, Robert. "The Laramie Movie Scope: Hollywood and 9/11." Apr. 15, 2002. <http://www.lariat.org/AtTheMovies/essays/moviesand911.html>.

Ryan, Joan. "Too Panicked to Live." *New York Times* Apr. 17, 2002. Aug. 15, 2002. <http://www.yorknewstimes.com/stories/041702/edi_0417020010.shtml>.

9

The Fascination of the Abomination
The Censored Images of 9/11

Mikita Brottman

> Another waterproof sheet was spread over the table in the manner
> of a tablecloth, with the corners turned up over a sort of mound—
> a heap of rags, scorched and bloodstained, half-concealing what
> might have been an accumulation of raw material for a cannibal feast.
> —*Joseph Conrad,* The Secret Agent

When the half-wit Stevie trips and falls while carrying a bomb
intended to blow up London's Greenwich Observatory in *The
Secret Agent,* Conrad spares us nothing. Like Chief Inspector Heat who
is assigned to the case, we are forced to confront the "shattering violence of destruction" that transforms Stevie into a "heap of mixed things,
which seemed to have been collected in shambles and rag shops," "a
heap of nameless fragments" (81). "Look at that foot there," demands
the constable who was given the task of shoveling up Stevie's remains.
"I picked up the legs first, one after another. He was that scattered
you didn't know where to begin" (82). The news of the explosion
reaches Stevie's sister when she overhears Chief Inspector Heat informing her husband that Stevie was "blown to small bits: limbs, gravel,
clothing, bones, splinters—all mixed together. . . . [T]hey had to fetch
a shovel to gather him up with" (166), a description that leads her to
imagine vivid fantasies of "a rainlike fall of mangled limbs" (210).

The Secret Agent was based partly on the case of Martial Bourdin,
who attempted to blow up the Greenwich Observatory on February
15, 1894, and, in doing so, accidentally blew himself to pieces. The

163

case was reported in great detail in the following day's newspapers. More than a hundred years later, the bombing of the World Trade Center in New York—a far greater tragedy—resulted in the deaths of almost three thousand people, yet despite the thousands of witnesses and hours of footage, media renditions of the World Trade Center bombing are much less detailed than Conrad's fictional account of the death of poor Stevie.

Nevertheless, any discussion of the events of September 11 on American television is still characterized by highly overcharged rhetoric, including the widespread use of the word *horror*. Conrad's account of Stevie's death, however graphic and explicit it may be, is completely uncontroversial because it takes a literary rather than a visual form. In Western culture, particularly in America, we've come to associate "the horrifying" with visually explicit representations of violence, usually violence done to the human body (dismemberment, evisceration, decapitation, and so on). For anything to be considered truly horrifying, it has to be *seen*—and, preferably, rendered as graphic and lifelike in detail as possible.

However, despite all the rhetoric, television coverage of the events of 9/11 brought us no visual images to endorse these recurrent assertions of "horror." We saw planes crashing into the World Trade Center, which was spectacular. We saw the towers collapse, which was incredible. We saw huge clouds of smoke and piles of rubble, buildings covered in dust and ashes, people running in alarm through the streets of lower Manhattan. Later, we saw sobbing widows grieving over their missing husbands; we saw firemen and police officers mourning their valiant colleagues—but horror? If horror is defined as visual representations of violence done to the human body, most NC-17–rated films contain more horror than any station's broadcast of the events of 9/11. If the American television coverage of the events of September 11 had been an Arnold Schwarzenegger movie, people would be asking for their money back.

Six months later, with the events of September 11 a little more clearly in perspective, CBS brought us the two-hour-long documentary *9/11*. It was described by Melanie Lefkowitz in *Newsday* as "brutal," "dramatic," and "sickening," an experience that "brought the stark reality of the terror attacks home in a new, somehow even more powerful way" (15). Again, however, despite the hype, *9/11* contained no graphic footage of injuries, no falling bodies, no images of death—nothing anywhere nearly as "brutal," in fact, as the images we were shown on September 11 itself. To round off an already anodyne package, Robert de Niro was drafted to introduce the documentary with a warning that the program contained a certain amount of "earthy language" and, "numerous expletives"—perhaps an unprecedented amount for network television, speculated David Bauder in the *Nando Times*. Even the sound was edited to cut out the noises made by bodies landing on an awning outside the World Trade Center, in case some viewers might find them too disturbing. Incredibly, the CBS documentary *9/11* contains blood in only one single scene, when a firefighter, seen catching his breath after the towers' collapse, is shown to have a small cut on his upper cheek.

If you decided to change channels during the screening of *9/11*, you would have had little trouble finding the kind of graphic footage of human death so conspicuously absent from the CBS documentary. If you tuned into the Discovery Channel, for example, you might have been able to catch an episode of *Pile-Up!* or *Runaway Trains*, cable television shows devoted to footage of violent and often fatal accidents. Or perhaps you might have preferred to watch an episode of *Trauma: Life in the ER*, the Learning Channel's longest-running series, a fly-on-the-wall hospital show that allows us to experience a night in the emergency ward, including close-up open-wound sequences from the operating theater. It seems to be a requirement of the show that each episode involves at least one fatality. Other, similar shows on the Learning Channel include *High Speed Pursuit!*, *Paramedics,* and *Code Blue.* If none of this grabbed you, you might have been able to catch Court TV's *Cops,* a show notorious for its showcasing of scenes of real-life violence filmed by cameramen who follow an inner-city police force on their nightly rounds. On the other hand, *When Good Pets Go*

Bad on Fox is always good for footage of lions mauling overambitious photographers in safari parks, or foolhardy matadors being torn apart by bulls.

To find the most extensive coverage of real-life violent fatalities, however, you would have needed to tune in to one of the most popular channels on cable television, the History Channel. Specializing in footage of wars, military campaigns, assassinations, and the bombing of large cities, the History Channel offers a round-the-clock diet of shows like *Great Blunders of History, The Wrath of God, History's Crimes,* and *Caught on Film.* The last series has been especially popular, featuring rare footage of historical disasters, from student films of the Kent State University shootings and unedited images of the *Andria Doria* shipwreck to footage of the Nazi concentration camps of World War II. In fact, Holocaust footage is shown on television so frequently that scenes of skeletal prisoners pushing wheelbarrows full of dead bodies are familiar to us all. It is generally accepted that the viewing of such footage is a vital part of understanding the terrible horrors of the concentration camps, even if, inevitably, such footage soon loses its original capacity to shock. When faced with the grotesquely overblown media rhetoric surrounding the horror of 9/11, it is important to remember that graphic footage of "real-life" human death is shown all the time on television, and the broadcast footage of the collapse of the World Trade Center is remarkable not for its horror but for its *absence* of horror.

There are three main reasons for this. The first is that in the case of this particular disaster, there was relatively little explicit horror to see. Most of the people caught in the World Trade Center either escaped unhurt or vanished completely. Morgue workers reported that the body bags that were brought in contained nothing but unidentifiable pieces of charred, ashen meat. Paradoxically, then, we were given all the rhetoric of horror but none of its stock-in-trade images: no walking wounded, no suffering bodies, no wartime landscape of broken bodies and severed limbs. Hospital units waited in silence for the sudden influx of casualties that never came. There were no miraculous rescues for us to applaud, no half-dead bodies to be pulled proudly out of the rubble. No plucky survivors were rushed away for lifesaving emergency surgery; there were no pavements slick with blood. Although nearly three thousand people lost their lives in the destruction of the World Trade Center, even now, fewer than six hundred of the bodies have been officially identified. The rest of the bodies will never be recovered, because they no longer exist. They were instantly incinerated, transformed into cinders—destroyed and cremated in the same moment. Which really isn't such a bad way to die, if you have to die before your time. When confronting the remains of Stevie's body in *The Secret Agent,* the chief inspector finds it "impossible to believe that a human body could have reached that state of disintegration without passing through the pangs of inconceivable agony," and yet "his reason told him that the effect must have been as swift as a flash of lightening" (81).

The second reason for this paucity of graphic footage is that 9/11 was the first time America suffered a major foreign attack on its own soil. To show vivid images of suffering American civilians was considered too psychologically disturbing to the general public. Footage of people being blown apart at their place of work on an ordinary weekday morning is rather different from images of wars being fought in foreign lands. Any broadcast of such graphic footage would have been considered dangerously demoralizing, upsetting the ideological assumption that Americans are immune from the kinds of violent attacks on civilians that characterize war zones like Beirut and Northern Ireland.

The third reason for the absence of graphic footage is that the disaster is fresh in the collective memory, and there is still a great fear of upsetting those whose friends and relatives were killed in the attacks. Even if the bodies in the footage are rendered unrecognizable, there are still a significant number of people for whom such images may rekindle traumatic and terrifying memories. With the passage of time, however, these taboos will eventually relax. Once the events of 9/11 have become "historical" in the same way that the Holocaust has become historical, we will finally be shown whatever graphic footage exists. The argument that the bodies on screen might be the friends or relatives of television viewers will come to have less and less weight over time. After all, there are plenty of Holocaust survivors alive today, as well as people whose friends and relatives were killed in the concentration camps. Yet, as the History Channel's programming demonstrates, there are no longer any substantial taboos surrounding the television broadcast of Holocaust footage or images from the Japanese American internment camps, which are deemed adequately historical to be shown without causing shock or controversy.

It will probably be at least another ten years before any television network, even the History Channel, feels comfortable enough to broadcast the censored images of 9/11. How much of this repressed footage there is remains a matter of debate, but nobody is in any doubt that it exists, especially considering the number of news networks filming at the scene, as well as security cameras and individuals with video equipment. Few of us can forget the images of falling bodies shown briefly on some news channels on the day of the disaster itself, before the television networks came to a universal decision that such footage was unsuitable to be shown. After 9/11, we never saw those falling bodies again.

Many commentators have expressed fears that this graphic footage could make its way into the hands of evil individuals who might then exploit it for the sick pleasure of those voyeurs who collect such underground footage, or charge people to watch it on the Internet. There seems to be a widespread sense of anxiety about the fact that this repressed material will make its way to that frightening place known as "out there"—the dark boiler room of Western culture—presumably alongside footage of animal torture and prepubescent children involved in sexually explicit acts. This belief is itself supported by the assumption that it is the evil people "out there"—pedophiles, psychopaths, snuff movie makers, suicide bombers, Islamic terrorists, and other assorted sickos—who are responsible for the horrors that occur on a daily basis in American society.

The otherworld of "out there" used to be underground, as in "underground footage," but now can be accessed equally readily through cyberspace, where all kinds of distasteful things are alleged to go on. The Internet is becoming increasingly mythologized, leading to a new sense of domestic isolation that has been dramatically heightened by the 9/11 attacks on American soil. The original antihero of the Internet used to be the anonymous and unknowable hacker, but this evil individual has recently been usurped by the computer-savvy fiend who caters to the sick tastes of perverted voyeurs. In media discourse, such characters are usually conceptualized as lurking around on the Internet, which can in turn be accessed through the computer terminals in our own homes. The computer screen is therefore regarded as a kind of magic portal—the gate of hell—through which computer viruses can escape to infect your home, turning your husband into a porn fiend and your children into the potential victims of drooling pedophiles, maybe even pedophile priests.

"The social changes which have followed the Internet explosion," writes computer expert John Ives, "themselves quite abrupt, have led to stories which suggest near-apocalyptic scenarios in which innocent users find themselves at the mercy of forces beyond their control" (4). Ives explains how people's fear of the Internet's power to disrupt community stability and organization is typified by anxieties about computer viruses that are capable of physically eating their way through the materials of your hard drive or making your computer screen literally explode. To many people, especially those who don't understand how their computers work, the Internet is an unrestricted, unpoliced otherworld, where perverts swap tips, teenagers make suicide pacts, pedophiles lurk in the guise of pen pals, and the censored footage of 9/11 plays over and over again in an endless, blood-drenched loop.

The truth is a lot less dramatic. Television cameramen at the scene of any large-scale disaster, accident, or violent act regularly capture plenty of graphic material on tape. If, on return to the station, it is determined that this footage is too explicit to be broadcast, "DO NOT AIR!" will be written on the side of the tape in big red letters. If any of the material is deemed usable, it will be edited out of the tape and spliced into the broadcast. People who work at television stations sometimes become curious about these "DO NOT AIR!" tapes. They usually have access to duplicating facilities and will sometimes make their own copies of these tapes to take home. Temps or interns may make copies as a souvenir of their job at the television station; photographers may make copies in case the tape is needed as legal evidence, or in case the footage can be screened at some future date. Copies of these tapes may be kept in the television news archives and sometimes in private collections, especially if the events they document are of potential legal or historical significance. Occasionally, an individual with access to such footage will obtain copies for a producer, who will then put together a compilation of murders, suicides, accidents, assassinations, and other real-life disasters to be offered for sale to the public.

Far from being "underground," however, these tapes can be bought or rented at virtually any high-street video outlet. The most popular include the *Death Scenes* series, produced by Nick Bougas, and the *Faces of Death* series, produced by Conan Le Cilaire. The original *Death Scenes* (1989) is basically a catalogue of police stills from 1930s and 1940s Los Angeles, arranged according to manner of death. *Death Scenes 2* (1992) includes video footage of an execution by firing squad, footage of people leaping from a burning building, Holocaust footage, outtakes from drivers' education films, footage from Vietnam, tape of accidental deaths, lynchings, hangings, and the televised suicide of disgraced Pennsylvania state treasurer R. Budd Dwyer. The *Faces of Death* series combines genuine outtakes from news reports, nature documentaries, sports coverage, war scenes, and amateur footage of accidents and disasters alongside faked, pseudoauthentic footage purported to be taken from local news stations, closed-circuit television networks, and amateur camcorder enthusiasts.

It seems inevitable that repressed material from 9/11 will appear as part of one of these low-budget "shockumentaries" long before it becomes acceptable viewing on network television. The fact that it remains repressed, in fact, virtually guarantees a market for such footage. Some of these shockumentaries are produced in other countries, contrived to play on anti-American sentiments. A Japanese video called *The Shocks,* for example, released in 1989, consists of unedited news footage of American disasters and opens with the image of a tear of blood running down the face of the Statue of Liberty.

Future foreign shockumentaries will clearly make much of the "secret" footage of 9/11. There have already been reports of such footage being shown on video in the Middle East and China. Apparently, in the immediate aftermath of the attacks, workers at Beijing television worked round the clock to produce a documentary they called *Attack America,* which splices scenes from Hollywood films with shots of the events of September 11. As rescue workers pick through the rubble of the twin towers, according to journalist Damien McElroy, "the commentator proclaims that the city has reaped the consequence of decades of American bullying of weaker nations."

In his late essay "The Question Concerning Technology," Martin Heidegger writes that "the essence of technology is by no means anything technological" (14). What Heidegger suggests in this essay is that what we call "technology" is fundamentally no more than an extension of the relationship between human beings, and to think of it in any other way is to engender the kind of passivity and mystification that characterize public anxieties about underground videos and, in particular, the Internet. It is certainly true that still photographs of accidents and disasters, mainly grabs from "DO NOT AIR!" tapes, can be viewed on-line. Again, however, there is nothing secret or underground about these sites, like rotten.com, gruesome.com, scarystuff.com, and trauma.softcoma.com; most of them are even free to use. Some have recently begun to feature repressed material from 9/11, both still footage and video streams, mostly of people leaping to their deaths from the windows of the World Trade Center.

This footage of falling bodies, some of them on fire, contains what are perhaps the most memorable images of 9/11, many of which were shown live on the morning of the disaster. A man and woman jumped in tandem, holding hands. One woman jumped clutching her purse primly to her chest. On September 12, a few newspapers ran a haunting picture on their front page—a shot of a man dressed in suit and tie falling headfirst, captured in freeze frame on film, upside down, arms loosely at his side, one leg bent in a graceful pass. After September 12, however, there seems to have been a general agreement on the part of the media that the use of any images containing human beings falling from the towers was inappropriate and distasteful. Footage of the falling bodies has not been shown again in the mainstream media but can easily be found on-line.

For example, Ogrish.com, a free Internet site, features eight still photographs of falling bodies and a series of video clips of people leaping from the buildings, set to the song "Free Falling," by Tom Petty. Ogrish.com specializes in graphic pictures of dead and mutilated bodies, but the "Free Falling" clips were considered excessive even by fans of the site. "Please take that music freefalling from that clip," writes one correspondent. "Please understand that these people were falling to pretty soon hit the concrete and meet death. . . . i love watching shocking shitt too, but the music just doesn't show any respect." Another correspondent writes, "I used 2 have respect for the dry humor of the site, but u went and screwed it big time now. These people were victims of the worst massacre ever known in the free world and u see fit to make a cheap laugh at their expense?" Also included is an unofficial first request from an FBI agent to "please remove all related pictures regarding the world trade center attacks (mostly graphic with the people falling down) it is a discouragement to the american public." The agent appears to have no problem with the site's numerous graphic pictures of terrorism and executions perpetrated on non-American soil.

Most Internet sites that include images of human bodies falling from the towers show them from a distance, as large specks alongside a mass of falling debris. Yet however indistinct they might be, these images of falling bodies are the most haunting and memorable part of the tragedy. Children reportedly looked up at the sky and told their parents that "the birds are on fire." People escaping from the burning towers were apparently told by the police to "just run—and don't look back"—as though, like Lot's wife, they risked being turned into a pillar of salt. It is also significant that, although we may have seen these bodies falling, we never saw them land.

These images are reminiscent of reports about the Wall Street crash of 1929, when according to rumor, businessmen who had lost everything were throwing themselves out of their office windows into the street below. Most historians, however, will tell you that this never really happened. People throw themselves en masse from a building only when that building is collapsing or on fire. In the 1911 Triangle Shirtwaist factory fire in New Jersey, for example, more than fifty people jumped to their deaths from the ninth floor. The year before, nearly twenty people leaped from a burning tenement in Newark, New Jersey. In both cases, some people survived—or survived long enough—to explain why they had chosen to jump. Several said it was to make sure their bodies would be identified and not incinerated beyond recognition. Perhaps this was the motive of many of those who leaped from the burning World Trade Center, since they couldn't have known that the towers were about to collapse, destroying their bodies anyway.

It makes more sense, however, to assume that these people were escaping a more horrible death. If on the one side of you is unbearable heat, roaring flames, and acrid smoke, it makes sense to head for the fresh air outside the window. The response of leaping out must be almost instinctual, an automatic reflex rather than a conscious decision—perhaps the impulsive urge to take control over the way you're going to die. Officially, those who leaped to their deaths—were their bodies identifiable—would actually be classified as suicides, which seems rather ironic, since it's usually assumed that the suicide victim actually wants to die. Those who leaped from the burning World Trade Center may have chosen the least painful form of death possible at that moment, but given the choice, they clearly would rather not have died at all.

The images of people leaping from the buildings are disturbing, but the experience itself may not actually have been so bad. People who've attempted suicide by jumping from the Golden Gate Bridge—and survived—report that the fall was experienced as almost transcendental, that it went in slow motion, that the experience was virtually mystical. Those who leaped from the World Trade Center may have been jumping to certain death, but it would have been a death that annihilated consciousness in a way that was nearly instantaneous—far less painful, in fact, than the deaths most of us can look forward to.

One particular correspondent on Ogrish.com, Carl, defends the site's use of graphic images on the grounds that people have an understandable curiosity about the events of 9/11 that they have been given little opportunity to satisfy with the coverage of the tragedy in the mainstream media. "We are all curious to see what happened," writes Carl, "not only outside by seeing those men jumping, but inside . . . what went on? What were they thinking? Who ran where? Who collapsed in a second? Who had a heart attack? We are all curious about the facts."

This point is more important than it may seem. In *Moses and Monotheism,* Freud explains that repressed material will return in the form of obsessional thoughts or impulses capable of governing future actions (24). Since television coverage of the events of 9/11 brought us very few graphic scenes at all, many of us have been compelled to imagine these scenes for ourselves—what Joseph Conrad in *Heart of Darkness* describes as "the fascination of the abomination" (10). Whether or not the events of 9/11 affected us personally, it's difficult not to speculate about what went on that morning on the upper floors of the World Trade Center after the planes had hit. Most of us have imagined the scenes of terror and catastrophe, if only at an unconscious level. Most of us have wondered what it was like for those who were killed instantaneously, and what it was like for those who clung to life for another hour or so. How did it feel to jump from the buildings, and how did it feel to stay inside? How would we have reacted in the face of such a terrifying event? Would we have stayed calm, or would we have panicked? What is it like to choke to death? What is it like to burn alive?

According to psychologists, low-probability events, especially those that inspire extreme horror, can jolt us into this process of primitive thinking. The most frightening images of 9/11 are not "out there" in the dark places of our culture—in underground videos or on the Internet—but "in us," psychologically, in our shared cultural unconscious. This will remain true as long as the media continue to censor their coverage of the catastrophe and as long as the taboos surrounding the broadcast of 9/11 footage continue to be upheld.

It is often reported that people from cultures unfamiliar with photography sometimes display a morbid fear of the camera, believing that to take somebody's photograph is a way of stealing their soul. This fear is seen as primitive fetishism, but what could be more fetishistic than our own culture's superstition toward the photographic image? In Western culture, the photograph is surrounded by enormous structures of mystery, anxiety, and taboo; it is an ideological commonplace that video images have the power to harm, traumatize, and seduce, to overcome all ordinary rational logic and human reason. The media regularly convey moral tales about pornographic films turning home-loving husbands into sex-obsessed perverts, about video violence turning teenaged schoolboys into gun-toting killers. Evangelists have claimed not only that certain horror films are works of the devil but that evil resides in the actual celluloid of these films. All over the United States, people are currently serving custodial sentences for possessing photographic images considered so shocking and disturbing that those who own them are considered dangerous criminals and cannot be allowed to go free.

This extreme fear of photographs seems absurd when we stop to consider exactly what the photograph is—nothing more than a moment of light trapped on a small piece of celluloid. On the Internet, the photograph is transformed to something even less substantial than this—a series of pixels on a screen. Along with the images of falling bodies, Ogrish.com also displays four-color photographs taken during the collapse of the World Trade Center. One depicts six firefighters carrying a large tray containing the remnants of a charred, blackened human form. Two others depict what seem to be dead bodies partially covered by white sheets and surrounded by splashes of blood on the pavement. None of these pictures is especially disturbing.

The final image, a little more explicit, depicts a severed hand on the pavement surrounded by what appears to be office debris. The hand is closed into a fist, with the index finger outstretched, and shards of bone protruding from the wrist. The photograph, attributed to "Todd Meisel, Daily News," is a little shocking at first but quickly ceases to disturb and soon becomes poignant, resonant, and—in terms of its color, composition, and balance in the frame—even rather beautiful. And this is probably the worst there is to see. How much less explicit and disturbing is this picture than those repressed images of 9/11 that terrorize the public's imagination? Like footage of the Nazi concentration camps shown so frequently in documentaries about the Holocaust, this is the kind of image that cuts through all the media rhetoric and allows us to come to a straightforward, unadulterated understanding of exactly what happened in the World Trade Center on the morning of 9/11.

In the psychoanalytic process, patients are considered cured only when they are finally able to confront repressed material and come to understand once-terrifying events in their proper temporal context. In the same way, only when the events of 9/11 are understood in the light of a contextualizing distance will we be able to face the real images of the tragedy. Perhaps, in ten or fifteen years, such images as those described above will be as commonplace as television footage of the Holocaust is today. This transformation can happen, however, only when the media are prepared to abandon their bombast about "sickening horror," their rhetoric about "the day that changed the world."

Without this contextualizing distance, we fall into the trap of what Gary Saul Morson calls "chronocentrism," the arrogant "temporal egotism" that judges everything by the standards and "knowledge" of the present, as though our accidental lateness confers on us greater wisdom instead of knowledge of a greater number of facts (278–79). In his book *Plagues of the Mind,* classicist Bruce Thornton explains how "the lure of a distorting and self-flattering chronocentrism is sweetened by the technology of the image, with all its vivid immediacy and imperious novelty and rapid-fire turn-over" (86–87).

The final death toll of 9/11 is currently reckoned to be 2,843, a number vastly lower than initial reports of the disaster suggested. In March 2000, almost three thousand members of an apocalyptic cult in Uganda were immolated in their churches, a tragedy that—where mentioned at all in the American media—was relegated to the "foreign" section of a few of the larger newspapers. To make a comparison a little closer to home, almost four thousand people are killed every month in car accidents on the American roads. This death toll—far greater than that of 9/11—is all but dismissed as a by-product of progress, civilization, and the American way of life.

Works Cited

Bauder, David. "Entertainment: CBS to Air Documentary on Sept. 11 Attacks." *Nando Times.* Mar. 6, 2002. AP Online. <http://www.nandotimes.com/entertainment/story/283628p-2547173c.html>.

Conrad, Joseph. *Heart of Darkness.* New York: Norton, 1988.

———. *The Secret Agent.* London: Signet, 1983.

Freud, Sigmund. *Moses and Monotheism.* Ed. Katherine Jones. New York: Random, 1987.

Heidegger, Martin. *The Question Concerning Technology and Other Essays.* Trans. William Lovitt. New York: Harper, 1977.

Ives, John. "Computer Virus Hoaxes: Urban Legends for the Digital Age." *Bad Subjects* 37 (Mar. 1998): 4–8.

Lefkowitz, Melanie. "Watching the Horror Through Tears." *Newsday* Mar. 11, 2002: 1, 15.

McElroy, Damien. "Beijing Markets Film of American Attacks." *News Telegraph* (U.K.) Nov. 3, 2001: 10.

Morson, Gary Saul. *Narrative and Freedom: The Shadows of Time.* New Haven: ISI, 1994.

Thornton, Bruce. *Plagues of the Mind: The New Epidemic of False Knowledge.* Wilmington, DE: ISI, 1999.

10

Mohsen Makhmalbaf's *Kandahar*
Lifting a Veil on Afghanistan

Philip Mosley

The majority of Americans neither knew nor cared much about Afghanistan before the horrifying events of September 11, 2001. Thereafter they knew and for the most part cared considerably more, while the mass media quickly moved to saturation coverage in the aftermath of the disaster. Once American reprisals began against the accused terrorist group in Afghanistan and the regime that had harbored it, viewers soon grew familiar in word and image with such names as al Qaeda, Osama bin Laden, Taliban, Northern Alliance, Kabul, Tora Bora, and Kandahar. For those curious to discover more about the Afghan situation and its broader context, however, there was little material available beyond the often predictable media discourse and a small number of specialized documentaries. One of the few films about Afghanistan already in circulation was an Iranian feature, *Kandahar* (Iranian title: *Safar e Ghandehar*, 2000), directed by Mohsen Makhmalbaf, an important Iranian auteur but, like many of his fellow Iranian filmmakers, relatively unknown to American audiences.

Kandahar is a welcome addition to the rare film images of Afghanistan and its various native peoples. Apart from routine images of war and destruction purveyed by the news media, Western viewers have seen few films concerning Afghanistan beyond occasional television documentaries or Hollywood features often shot elsewhere (*The Horsemen*, 1970; *The Living Daylights*, 1987; *The Beast of War*, 1988; *Rambo III*, 1988). *Rambo III*, for instance, is worthy of little attention other than for the irony in hindsight of an American military hero teaming up with Islamist freedom fighters against Communists on behalf of the free world. Superpower politics, now as then, spawns unlikely bedfellows. As for a growing number of documentaries, most date from the Soviet period and during or after Taliban rule. These potentially hazardous undertakings, several of which were made by and about women, include *Beneath the Veil* (Cassian Harrison, 2001), *Behind the Veil: Afghan Women under Fundamentalism* (Ricardo Lobo, 2001), and *Afghan Alphabet,* Makhmalbaf's own documentary on the poor education of refugee children in the Iranian border villages, shot during the U.S. military campaign of late 2001. Much like Nelofer Pazira, on whose story *Kandahar* is based, Saira Shah in *Beneath the Veil* is an Afghan expatriate journalist traveling surreptitiously in Afghanistan and recording a voice-over narration of her experiences.

Kandahar at first attracted no more than a degree of polite critical attention and almost no commercial interest. Though it won the Ecumenical Jury Prize at the 2001 Cannes Film Festival, it was predictably overlooked by American distributors and in the end was picked up by a small company for limited theatrical release. The events of September 11 changed its fortunes. *Kandahar* was sold to more than forty countries, while critics in the United States and elsewhere in the Western world suddenly began to take notice. J. Hoberman crystallized this new interest by suggesting that "*Kandahar* may be the most fortuitously titled release to open here since Warner Bros. unveiled *Casablanca* only weeks after the Allies landed in North Africa."

Kandahar was made well before the September attacks, and it clearly engages with a chronic situation instead of reacting to specific political or military events. The film is therefore neither about al Qaeda nor about the Taliban as such, though it certainly helps to explain the particular set of circumstances that led to the influential presence of both organizations in Afghanistan. As a result, the film seems strangely prescient of, yet removed from, the events of September 11, which makes the film more difficult to situate as an exposé of the terrorist crisis. One may argue that many viewers confronted by sounds and images of an Other invariably and perhaps inevitably try to interpret them in terms they can understand. A Western viewer thus may seek in *Kandahar* what Hamid Dabashi calls "instrumental correspondence," an "aggressive reduction of a work of art" to what the viewer hopes or believes the film is "about," even if "this is not the way a work of art alerts, objects, condemns, or celebrates" (278). This search for "acceptable" meanings enters a discourse of interrogation, explanation, and reassurance that we construct in times of public crisis. Much of this discourse locates itself in official channels of information and in the media of mass communication. We also look to art forms in helping to make sense of how we are affected by a crisis, in proposing alternative modes of debate, and in suggesting answers to our (not always conscious) questions. In the wake of the September attacks, *Kandahar* may strike many Western viewers as a somewhat puzzling text, one that satisfies yet frustrates our desires and expectations. The film reaches (out to) us in a timely manner from within that Islamic world we now strive more than ever before to comprehend, offering us an imaginative vision grounded in formal elements (narrative, image, character, etc.) by which we may "frame" an emotional and intellectual response to Afghanistan. At the same time, precisely because it is "an/other" text, the deployment of these formal elements may perturb us because they answer to different aesthetic values or to different sets of cultural traditions and imperatives.

Kandahar is undeniably a polemical film, yet in keeping with the evolution of Makhmalbaf's work, his moral outrage finds expression in a humanistic vision (Makhmalbaf). This vision is one of sadness and compassion but also of hope and courage. Above all, the film is a call to attention and accountability inside and outside the Islamic world. As Kent Jones says,

> Makhmalbaf's film may not be completely "successful," but what would constitute success given the task he's set for himself, which is basically to ignite the conscience of his viewers—his Western viewers in particular—through a lesson barely disguised as a folkloric fictional journey? (26)

This journey is made by Nafas, an Afghan-born journalist in her late twenties, who is trying to reach Kandahar in three days from the Iranian border to save her land mine–disabled, Taliban-oppressed sister from committing suicide at the moment of a solar eclipse. The plot of the film closely follows the personal experience of Nelofer Pazira, who fled Afghanistan for Canada with her family in the late 1980s. Pazira, who plays Nafas, had been moved by letters from a friend who remained in Kandahar and was threatening suicide. More than a melodramatic convenience to the director of the film, this threat is real to many Afghan women in extreme duress (as attested by several interviewees in *Behind the Veil*). Pazira traveled to Afghanistan but failed to reach her friend. However, she had seen *The Cyclist* (1987), Makhmalbaf's film on Afghan refugees in Iran, so she contacted him in 1998 and suggested a film based on her dilemma. Makhmalbaf had already explored the long-term psychological effects of prolonged warfare in *The Marriage of the Blessed* (1988), a controversial critique of the eight-year conflict between Iran and Iraq. Though nothing came of Pazira's idea at first, Makhmalbaf did undercover research in Afghanistan in 1999 and, on deciding to make a film, contacted Pazira again, inviting her to play the leading role.

Makhmalbaf shot *Kandahar* with a small crew two kilometers from the Afghan border in Iran. As expected, the film proved extremely difficult to make. Rigid tribalism among Afghan refugees in the area allowed only cursory interaction between different groups. The environment was harsh, and living conditions in the refugee community were terrible. They endured official and unofficial harassment; at times Makhmalbaf disguised himself to evade apprehension by potentially hostile parties. They also discovered an almost total unawareness of cinema among the Afghans who formed the majority of the cast. The remaining parts were played by two Polish medics and Hassan Tantai. An expatriate African American convert to Islam, Tantai (also known as Dawud Salahuddin) has since admitted shooting an Iranian dissident near Washington, D.C., in 1980. His casting added controversy to the film in Europe and the United States.

The refugees' almost total lack of visual acculturation may be explained partly by the isolated nature of their agrarian and nomadic life. In any case, for all Afghans, possible exposure to visual media disappeared under the Taliban, who sought to eliminate all cultural activities as contrary to their severe interpretation of Islam. Afghans in urban areas once had been avid consumers of mainly Hindi films, and before the Soviet invasion of Afghanistan in 1979, a number of Bollywood imitations were made there. Domestic production then dwindled to a handful of Soviet or Mujahedin (Islamic holy warriors) propaganda films. Under the Taliban, there was nothing. Cinema, television, photographs, portraits, singing, dancing, playing of musical instruments were all banned, leaving only two hours daily of radio propaganda. Even allowing that the Taliban regime lasted only seven years, and thus for only a portion of most Afghans' lives—though a larger portion than one might imagine, given their extremely short life expectancy—it is hard to underestimate the devastating effects of these policies on a people deprived of those cultural enrichments that most other societies take for granted.

After production was completed, Makhmalbaf declared himself drained and demoralized by the rigors of shooting the film and by a feeling that it could do little to improve the lot of the Afghan people. He subsequently authored a long article (published in March 2001 and later accessible on-line) in the wake of an international outcry surrounding the Taliban's destruction of two centuries-old statues at Bamyan in central Afghanistan. The title of his article, "The Buddha Was Not Demolished in Afghanistan; He Collapsed out of Shame," refers to the shaming of the rest of the world for its ignorance of and unconcern with the Afghan situation beyond an understandable reaction to the desecration of priceless artifacts. Within half a year, that indifference had changed in a way few could have possibly foreseen.

Makhmalbaf says that since the mid-1990s, he has been preoccupied by the idea of human sorrow. Sorrow is the principal theme of *Kandahar*, caused in the Afghan case by the cumulative effects of war, disease, poverty, starvation, backwardness, and oppression. Makhmalbaf seeks, says Hamid Dabashi, an "emotional perspective . . . in the frame of human sorrow" (189), while for the director, his film "attempts to portray in personal terms the desperate situation that exists" (Interview). That situation is one the Afghan people have found themselves in for almost a quarter century. It began with a bloody struggle against the Soviet Union's occupation of the country from 1979 to 1989, an imposition known to proud and independent Afghans as "The Catastrophe." The Soviets were forced to withdraw by the dogged resistance of the Mujahedin. Drawn from disparate indigenous and foreign sources, these freedom fighters were armed and financed by Arab oil states and the Central Intelligence Agency. By 1992 the Communist administration had been replaced by a seven-party Mujahedin coalition, based on Loya Jirga (a federation of tribal leaders), a traditional system of governance offering then as now the only hope of fragile national unity. Furthermore, the production of opium had replaced agriculture as the mainstay of the Afghan economy. Against a backdrop of fierce ethnic rivalries and struggles for power and influence among competing warlords and drug barons, the country slid into four years of civil war. The authoritarian rule of the Taliban (Islamic religious students), who captured Kabul in 1996, proved to be a two-edged sword. Their severe interpretation of sacred law *(Sharia)* produced civil disarmament, an efficient if ruthlessly punitive judicial system, and a degree of order that proved—as in European fascist regimes of the 1930s—reassuring to many Afghans exhausted by years of lawlessness, division, and subjugation to a foreign yoke. Yet the Taliban also eliminated what little freedom or modernity had previously existed, especially for women, in Afghan society. After ruling most of the country with an iron fist for seven years, the Taliban was swiftly deposed after the September attacks because of their protection of al Qaeda terrorists. The stark consequences of these successive national traumas continue to hamper attempts at recovery. As Nafas confirms in her narration, out of a population of twenty-six million, one Afghan has died every five minutes for the last twenty years from land mines, war, famine, and drought. Six million more have been refugees, mainly in Iran and Pakistan.

Nafas's journey consists of four stages with major intervening scenes in which Makhmalbaf vividly dramatizes various aspects of the Afghan situation. The first stage depicts Nafas arriving by Red Cross helicopter at the Iran-Afghanistan border to begin her overland journey to Kandahar. We learn that she has already spent one month trying to enter the country; for a journalist reporting women's conditions, a visa has proven hard to obtain. She discovers that she will not be permitted to travel alone, unveiled, or with an unrelated male. A middleman arranges for her to pose as the fourth wife of a refugee taking his family home. Makhmalbaf presents us with two contrasting images of Nafas: the determined Western Muslim woman wearing a head scarf and the submissive Afghan "spouse" obliged, for reasons of self-protection as well as by rules of modesty, to conceal herself beneath a *burqa,* a garment covering head and body, and as such the most complete manifestation of female invisibility in certain Islamic societies. At first Nafas asserts her right to choose her own degree of modesty by revealing her face. The other wives do not have that privilege or self-confidence, but beneath their burqas they surreptitiously apply lipstick and nail polish, while their daughters select gaudy bracelets for their wrists.

Before Nafas lowers her veil at the insistence of her "husband," who wishes to protect his own devout and masculine reputation, the sun reflects the eyelet grille of the burqa over her eyes, the first of several shots suggesting bars imprisoning these women. As her "family" prepares to set out, a series of tracking shots reveals a host of girls also about to return to Afghanistan. We see their luminous beauty accentuated by an array of colorful clothes, but we also see the look of fear and confusion on their faces. A teacher explains to them that in Afghanistan they will no longer receive even the rudimentary schooling of the refugee camp. She also advises them how to avoid land mines, especially small shiny objects easily mistaken for toys or dolls, one of which, Nafas relates, blew off her sister's legs and prevented her escaping Afghanistan with the rest of her family.

An alternative English title of the film is *The Sun Behind the Moon:*

less straightforward or marketable than *Kandahar* but with a resonance in this context of female concealment and disappearance. Given that Nafas's sister intends to kill herself at the "last eclipse of the twentieth century," the opening shot of the film, an image of solar eclipse, symbolizes the fate both of Afghan females and of their entire country in the eyes of the world. Before and during the Soviet occupation, Afghan women had been free to reject the veil and to lead active lives albeit in a traditionally male-dominated society. Even if the idea of female empowerment under Afghan Communism is a myth—the Soviets killed and imprisoned many women and destroyed many homes—40 percent of Afghan women worked under their rule. Even under the stricter eye of the Mujahedin cleric *(mullah)*, "70 percent of the teachers were women, 40 percent of the doctors were women, over half the school students were females, and women were employed in all areas of the workforce" (Ellis 62). Their lot worsened dramatically under the Taliban. While many doctors and nurses retained their jobs—necessary to the preservation of modesty in health care—all other women were ordered into domestic seclusion *(purdah)*, removing their right to outside employment, education, choice of personal appearance, and public mobility.

Nafas records her impressions into a cassette recorder, her use of English increasing the appeal of the film to an international audience. This voice-over narration allows her a measure of discursive authority over the people, places, and events of her journey. Beyond the usefulness of this narration as a dramatic device, it empowers the voice over the look. Nafas may be rendered anonymous beneath her burqa, but her voice cannot be silenced as long as she can commit her thoughts to her "black box." In this way, she maintains her identity as a Western journalist documenting her experience and as an individual addressing her sister—"I'm collecting everything to give you hope"— so as not to lose sight (or sound) of her ultimate preventive goal.

By granting this level of discursive authority to a Westernized female voice, Makhmalbaf also sidesteps representational restrictions in Iranian cinema, where it remains exceptional for female characters to be accorded such a powerful point of view. Another example of this exception is Daryush Mehrju'i's *Leila* (1996), whose leading female character gives voice-over expression to her innermost thoughts and feelings. Exceptional though they are, they indicate the kind of progress made since the 1978–79 Islamic Revolution, when the existence of cinema was under attack on moral grounds, and women vanished from the screen. A representational code was introduced in 1982 to preserve standards of modesty *(hejab)* within the diegesis of Iranian films. In examining the structure and evolution of this code, Hamid Naficy identifies several phases of veiling as cinematic practice, describing how women gradually reentered the diegesis, at first in passive and desexualized ways ("Veiled"). By the late 1980s, women took center screen again as the "restrictive filming grammar which curtailed their diegetic relations with men was liberalized" ("Iranian" 677). With this relaxation of the code, Iranian filmmakers have been able to resexualize the female image by way of subtly nuanced strategies of representation. A growing number of these directors are female, working either within the Iranian commercial sphere—such as Rakhshan Banietemad, Tahmineh Milani, and Mohsen's daughter Samira Makhmalbaf—or abroad, like Shirin Neshat, whose film-video installations, often offering a critique of veiling, have attracted considerable attention in the Western art world.

Bandits rob Nafas's "family" at knifepoint, so the man decides they will return to Iran rather than struggle on perilously without vehicle or possessions. He has few illusions: "Afghanistan is our homeland, we long to return there. But there is nothing there but famine, suffering, and massacre." Undaunted by this early setback, Nafas seeks another guide, who comes in the form of Khak (Sadou Teymouri), a twelve-year-old son of a widow. Many such children were obliged to become family breadwinners, since under the Taliban their mothers could no longer work and so risked destitution. Following Khak's expulsion from a *madrassa* (Islamic theology school) and his consequent loss of subsistence, he must survive by any means, including reciting the Koran at funerals and stealing from dead bodies.

A tracking shot, mirroring that of the schoolgirls, reveals the interior of the madrassa. Under the watchful eye of the mullah who teaches them, rows of boys cross-legged on the floor sway back and forth while reciting verses from the Koran, a rote learning interrupted only by the teacher's occasional questions about a Kalashnikov semiautomatic rifle brandished by one of the novitiates as part of a drilling routine. The combination of God and guns, an idea familiar to some Americans, is shown here in the service of militant Islamism. Unable to recite the Koran correctly, Khak is shown the door, to the anguish of his mother, pleading in vain with the teacher, whose only advice is that he look for work in Iran. As Nafas observes, it is a "dog fights dog" situation, for Khak is quickly replaced by another boy, to the relief of that child's mother, for whom her son's indoctrination seems a small price to pay for the guarantee of food, clothing, and shelter within the relatively comfortable bounds of the school.

Located mainly in Pakistan and in southern Afghanistan, the madrassas responsible for raising the core of the Taliban at one time numbered more than twenty-five hundred, with three hundred to one thousand students in each. Products of a sustained war culture allied to religious revivalism, most of these impressionable and dependent youngsters were Pushtuns from an already conservative and backward region isolated by the vast mountain ranges of the Hindu Kush. Supported by the United Arab Emirates and Saudi Arabia, additional rivals in the Islamic world to Shiite Iran, Pakistan was thus able to play a major part in forging a friendly political force of Sunni Muslims in the form of the Taliban. Their education in the strict Deobandi tradition was based on a fantasy of seventh-century Islam, while their morality was based as much on the Afghan tribal code of honor *(pushtunwali)* as on the Sharia. As Gilles Kepel puts it, under the Taliban, "the mental environment of a madrassa was re-created in the villages and cities of Afghanistan" (230).

Toughened by circumstance, Khak drives a hard bargain. For fifty dollars, plus tips for entertaining her along the way, Khak agrees to guide Nafas on the second stage of her journey toward Kandahar.

Crossing the desert on foot, they stop at a well where women silently wash clothes by hand, their constant movement back and forth mirroring the swaying of the boys in the school. After Nafas falls sick from contaminated well water, Khak leads her to a doctor by the name of Tabib Sahib (Hassan Tantai). He turns out to be an African American convert to Islam who, seeking God in jihadism, fought for and against different Mujahedin factions until, disillusioned by endless war and misery, he turned to humanitarian work. Even though this "doctor" has no qualifications, he justifies his work by the fact that his basic Western medical knowledge far exceeds that of the local populace.

The meeting of Nafas and Tabib Sahib is as strange and moving as any of those extended scenes whereby Makhmalbaf punctuates the monotony of the journey. As an unrelated male, Tabib is not permitted to see the whole of Nafas's body, examining only dissociated parts of it through a peephole in a cloth screen dividing them. Furthermore, he cannot address her directly, using instead as an intermediary her "brother," the ever watchful and importunate Khak. After muttering to himself that perhaps Nafas has malaria, Tabib is startled to hear her contradict him in English, and a clandestine conversation ensues between them. Even before they reveal themselves to one another, the scene has a sexual charge, notably in close-ups of Nafas's eye, mouth, and ear at the peephole. While Tabib observes only these three fragments of her body, their isolated (re)presentation accentuates their erogenous potential. Conversely, via point-of-view shots, we share this temporarily disintegrated, eclipsed woman's freedom to look unrestrictedly at him in his entirety, thereby subverting the presumed dominance of his male gaze.

Another outsider masquerading as an orthodox member of this society, Tabib hides his true self behind a false beard, as he is unable to grow one to the length prescribed by the Taliban. At his request, Nafas emerges from behind the screen, revealing her face. Disclosing his American identity, Tabib removes his "male burqa," the beard—a risky act that under the Taliban was punishable by whipping. He tells Nafas that for the most part, he treats simple conditions such as hunger, cold, and diarrhea that proliferate in the absence of basic food, medicine, and sanitation. Before she arrives at his surgery, we see him dispensing bread to a woman and daughter with chronic stomach-aches, commenting to himself that "these people don't need a doctor, they need a baker." His observation of the backwardness of a country where "weapons are the only modern thing" recalls Doris Lessing's eloquent account of her 1986 visit to the border area between Pakistan and Afghanistan. Lessing describes a village adjacent to a Mujahedin encampment:

> I was sitting in the jeep by myself in the main street of the village, just opposite the little tea house crowded with muhjahidin taking a last meal before journey. [. . .] This "street" was really a lane of hard, rutted mud between mud and straw buildings. Again, this could have been hundreds of years ago, except for the weapons the men were carrying. (129)

Convinced of Khak's unreliability and wary of his potential for informing on them for monetary gain, Tabib persuades Nafas to get rid of him. She does so only after reluctantly accepting as a gift the ring that Khak had taken from a skeleton in the desert and has persistently tried to sell to her. As Tabib needs to visit a Red Cross camp, he proposes that Nafas continue her journey with him in a horse-drawn wagon. On the road, she hears more of his story and views of the Afghan situation. Unsure of the motives of an apparently armed man ahead—"everybody here's a threat or an opportunity"—Tabib tells her to lie down out of clear sight and to pretend they are married. However, the wayfarer proves to be "an opportunity for doing good." On his way to the camp to get new legs for his wife, his "gun" the prostheses he carries, the man is taken aboard.

By highlighting another aspect of the Afghan tragedy, the plight of land mine victims, Makhmalbaf creates in the Red Cross camp scene some of the most memorable and bizarre images in the film. Almost as if in parody of an outlaw band in a Western movie, men hobble as fast as their crutches will carry them from the camp across the desert landscape in pursuit of artificial limbs being dropped by helicopter. Equally surrealistic are shots of parachuted limbs falling to earth, reprising images from the beginning of the film when the helicopter pilot delivers the Red Cross doctor's order of limbs as he conveys Nafas to her overland departure point. By showing locals hustling for new legs—the man Tabib had picked up measuring a pair against his wife's wedding shoes and burqa that he has brought along—Makhmalbaf gives poignant expression to a phenomenon that the outside world has barely registered. During the war against the Soviets, eight hundred thousand land mines were laid in Afghanistan. The toll of death and disablement—more than half a million, including many children—continues unabated today.

After leaving the camp, Nafas and Tabib pick up Hâyat, a land mine victim seen at the camp begging for any limbs he can get, much to the irritation of the Polish medics, who consider him to be an opportunistic liar. When Tabib can go no further, Hâyat is eventually persuaded with enough money to become Nafas's guide on the fourth stage of her journey. Before Nafas and Tabib part company, she asks him to offer some words for her sister. He becomes ill at ease, walking off with the recorder to confess privately that love for other human beings remains his only hope, and that for the Afghan woman, perhaps also with Nafas in mind, "hope is the day she will be seen."

Pretending to be relatives, Nafas and Hâyat join a wedding procession moving slowly across the desert in a phalanx of multicolored burqas. Hâyat disguises himself in one, a gender reversal rendered comical by a shot of him raising his veil to smoke a cigarette. A Taliban patrol halts the procession, interrogating and searching its members. Makhmalbaf again shows with grim irony how a regime whose oppression of women centers on forbidding them to work nonetheless employs black-clad female assistants to carry out "modest" searches. The assistants confiscate a book and a musical instrument, objects emblematic of the aesthetic pleasures proscribed by the Taliban. In another curious shot of role reversal, we see an officially empowered woman discovering a veiled man, Hâyat, who along with Nafas is detained at the checkpoint. In the final shot of the film, Nafas looks at the setting sun through the "prison bar" eyelets of her burqa and comments in voice-over, "Now I'm a captive in every one of those prisons for you, my sister." There is a lack of closure—Nafas has not succeeded in reaching Kandahar or her sister—and Makhmalbaf allows a certain ambiguity to hover over this scene. It remains uncertain whether Nafas will be held or, as a "Westerner," will somehow find a way to negotiate her release.

Kandahar depicts Afghanistan under the Taliban via a chronological story, yet the film may still prove disconcerting to Western viewers unfamiliar with a cinema that locates itself largely beyond Euro-American cultural and ideological spheres. While it is true that some Western viewers, accustomed to a steady diet of Hollywood style and high production values, may resist alternatives to these norms, such resistance often springs less from a conscious rejection of unusual or exotic elements than from an unawareness of their significance. These elements comprise audiovisual details (of architecture, landscape, dress, social customs, rituals and ceremonies, verbal and nonverbal communication acts) that encode a plethora of culturally specific meanings. Informed critical appraisal may here play an enlightening role. While reservations about structure, pace, and technique have surfaced in British and American reviews of *Kandahar,* for most critics, its topicality, emotional power, and visual quality have overridden such doubts. Some perceived flaws of the film include a loose plot, more episodic than causal; a lack of narrative closure, since Nafas fails to reach Kandahar, neither resolving her sister's problems nor gaining any demonstrable victory over evil or repressive forces; shallow character development, even of the protagonist; and awkward dialogue, even in the English used in her narration and her conversations with Tabib.

Yet to denigrate Makhmalbaf's film accordingly is to risk misunderstanding the evolution of his sensibility as filmmaker, intellectual, activist, Iranian, and Muslim. An unfamiliarity with the synthesis of these various identities may obstruct an understanding of how the director conceives and represents his subject. While Iranian auteurist cinema bears the influential marks of a European art film tradition, it equally reflects its own shifting spiritual, political, and industrial contexts. This distinctiveness is one reason why Iranian cinema has drawn such critical attention in the West since the early 1990s. The older generation of directors like Makhmalbaf, Abbas Kiarostami, and Bahram Beiza'i have consistently proposed an immersion in the differences of a culture often misunderstood in the West at the same time as they have relocated a "lost" tradition of Euro-American auteurist film.

The narrative structure of *Kandahar,* for instance, conforms more to our preconceptions if we see it as part of a familiar genre, the road movie—even if this road consists of rough tracks across a desert wilderness. It may be useful here to recall Mikhail Bakhtin's application of the idea of the chronotope to the analysis of literary narratives. Paul Willemen reminds us that "chronotopes are time-space articulations characteristic of particular, historically-determined conceptions of the relations between the human, the social and the natural world" (15–16). Particularly important to Bakhtin is the organizational relationship between roads and human encounters, which is also a structural principle of the road movie. We may identify *Kandahar* as a text that matches this archetypal narrative pattern, yet transforms it in culturally specific ways. In this respect, Willemen agrees with Teshome Gabriel's argument, in his pioneering work on Third (World) cinema, that "a different chronotope determines the narrative images and rhythms of non-Euro-American cinemas" (15).

With this argument in mind, we may relate Makhmalbaf to Kiarostami regarding the chronotope of the road. While much of Kiarostami's articulation of this chronotope reflects his early exposure to Italian neorealism and the French New Wave, it also derives from a non-Western tradition. In his analysis of Kiarostami's *Taste of Cherry* (1996), Devin Orgeron indicates the "critical importance of the narrative structure of the journey to the *form* of Iranian philosophical thought," a conceit originating in the Middle Ages, when an exchange between Eastern and Western ideas brought Persian culture to "its own metaphorical crossroads" (49–50). In another formulation that applies also to *Kandahar,* Orgeron suggests that Kiarostami is fascinated by the literal traffic of the road and by the figurative traffic of images, ideas, and words.

Within this scheme of multifarious exchange, the development of characters may be less important to Makhmalbaf than the journey itself. Apart from Nafas, the characters largely remain figures in a landscape of loss and devastation, her brief encounters with them serving to explore various aspects of the Afghan sorrow. The enormity of place and event eventually overwhelms Nafas, too. Moreover, the film's open ending (as in *Taste of Cherry*) validates her journey as an end in itself in a manner that is theologically consistent with recent interpretations of Mohammed's flight *(hejira)* from Mecca to Medina in 622 A.D. We owe this reworking of the meaning of hejira in contemporary Islamic thought to the Iranian scholar Ali Shariati, who with the cleric (later Ayatollah) Khomeini was the main influence on Makhmalbaf's own ideological formation. In this light, Nafas's journey (and implicitly that of all displaced Muslims) is neither heroic nor foolhardy, whatever its physical outcome. Rather, it is a necessary spiritual trial in each Muslim's endless progress from human clay to God; a way of living Islam, says Edward Said, "as an invigorating existential challenge . . . not as a passive submission to authority, human or divine" (*Covering* 68).

Makhmalbaf's semidocumentary approach to *Kandahar* may also confuse viewers attuned to clearer generic distinctions. In pursuit of his vision, Makhmalbaf weaves documentary techniques and strategies into the fabric of his mise-en-scène. Bouts of "stilted" dialogue become signs of a search to communicate authentic experience. The intrusion of mechanical noise conveys a sense of raw immediacy to the opening moments of Nafas's narration aboard the helicopter. The awkwardness of the later conversation between Nafas, Tabib, and the two Polish medics similarly takes on the unrehearsed spontaneity of an unexpected meeting. But Makhmalbaf equally takes poetic license as a given in his desire to communicate stark realities in unforgettable images. He admits, for instance, that the real parachute drops contained food parcels, but within a dramatization he feels justified in substituting the prostheses as better suiting his purpose. In another instance, Makhmalbaf and his cinematographer Ebraheem Ghafouri "surrealize" a procession of women in multicolored burqas by framing them within the disorienting contours of the vast desert *(registan)* covering the eastern, Afghan end of the Iranian plateau. This brand of poetic realism, exploiting the wide-screen composition of horizontal planes and boundless spaces to create a certain mood for the film, matches Mohammad Reza Darvishi's Indian-themed musical score to produce a hauntingly sensuous yet strangely disquieting texture of image and sound. This lyrical approach attaches Makhmalbaf to an Iranian tradition of the poetic in social and political expression, one that extends backward to early-twentieth-century Persian poetry as the principal oppositional voice in the ideological construction of modern Iran. In the 1930s, Iranian fiction took over this role from poetry, only to be superseded in turn in the 1980s by the emergence of a postrevolutionary cinema in the name of an Islamic state.

Apart from questions of film form and technique, some Western viewers may have one further difficulty: how to locate the viewpoint of *Kandahar* as an Iranian film made within the Islamic world and yet recognizably critical of the Taliban and those who preceded it in power. If, as Said maintains, the dominant images of Islam and its cultures in the Western media have become even more routinely stereotyped and hostile since his original analysis of the problem was published in 1980, then the events of September 2001 have exacerbated this trend. While general knowledge of Afghanistan and the Islamic world has undoubtedly increased in the wake of the attacks, a correspondingly emotive reaction has intensified an already demonized image of the Islamic world at the expense of broader and more balanced perceptions. Said views this negative image as part of a new ideological struggle generated by, in his opinion, an ill-founded and belligerent "clash of civilizations" rhetoric that emerged in American thought in the early post–Cold War period and has influenced greatly the formation of subsequent U.S. foreign policy. Any cultural text, like *Kandahar,* emanating from an Islamic nation now risks falling prey to a circumstantially misguided notion, bolstered by the prevalent rhetoric, that the film must somehow embody an anti-Western view and cannot address the Afghan situation in an open-minded way. The Western viewer must make an effort to accept that Iranian auteurist cinema may be no more ideologically saturated than Hollywood. Naficy preempts certain Western doubts that a critical, open-minded cinema could emerge from an Islamic republic: "Iranian post-revolutionary cinema is not a fully developed 'Islamic' cinema in the sense that it is not by any means a monolithic, propagandistic cinema in support of a ruling ideology" ("Islamizing" 182). This cinema challenges a persistent assumption that since it is ultimately controlled by and accountable to the apparatus of the Iranian state, it must be a mouthpiece of political orthodoxy. This status applies only to a small sector of film production that Naficy characterizes as "propaganda." It exists beside much larger "populist" (mass-produced entertainment films of a conservative nature) and "quality" (auteurist) sectors. While directors like Makhmalbaf regularly feel moved to defend their principles of artistic freedom against governmental interference in the making and content of their films, they operate nonetheless in a paradoxical space. Here they see fit to work against the grain, challenging the norms of Iranian society set by a theocratic establishment that sanctions and oversees their work. In this respect, they belong to a "counterculture," in Said's sense, "an ensemble of practices associated with various kinds of outsiders—the poor, the immigrants, artistic bohemians, workers, rebels, artists." Out of this counterculture comes "the critique of authority and attacks on what is official and orthodox." No culture, Said continues, "is understandable without some sense of this ever-present source of creative provocation from the unofficial to the official; to disregard this sense of restlessness within each culture, and to assume that there is complete homogeneity between culture and identity, is to miss what is vital and fecund" ("Clash" 578).

It becomes clear that if Western views of Afghanistan and the broader Islamic world may differ according to levels of knowledge and to religious or ideological affinities, then so will views from within that world. We must remember that if "official" Islam has reversed the process of Orientalism by constructing the West as an Other, there exist equally complex constructions of otherness and difference within the Islamic world. Given the vast range of diverse perspectives within the all-embracing global community of believers *(Umma),* Said contends that "various *Islamic* attempts to respond to Islamic as well as Western circumstances, in all their variety and contradiction, are no less political, no less to be analyzed in terms of processes, struggles, and strategies of interpretation" *(Covering* 60). An erroneous Western presumption of the Islamic world is that it comprises a monolithic set of social values and religious beliefs. The irony is not lost on Said "that Western views of Islam on the whole prefer to associate 'Islam' with what many Muslims themselves are opposed to in the current scene: punishment, autocracy, medieval modes of logic, theocracy" (68). Such moderate Muslims, not unsympathetic to clerical rule but opposed to fanatics of any persuasion, would include Makhmalbaf among them.

In discussing Western views of Iran, Naficy reinforces "the point . . . made by several theorists that there is no longer a centre but centres, no longer an other but others" ("Mediawork's" 230). In this way, for instance, the Iranian state has found it hard to maintain authority at its margins over a multiethnic population characterized by historically embedded patterns of tribal nomadism and local identity. This centrifugal tension finds expression in general Iranian attitudes to Afghanistan and its peoples. These attitudes are little removed from those of the West in their basic negativity, lack of sympathy, and accumulated misconceptions. Despite their geographical, religious, and linguistic proximities—Dari, spoken by certain tribes in northern and western Afghanistan, is a variant of Farsi, the Iranian national language—little cordiality exists between the two nations, especially as the Islamic Republic of Iran entered into a political pact with the Soviet Union at the time of its invasion of Afghanistan. The majority of Afghan immigrants to Iran have been Dari-speaking Hazaras, the only major tribal group to share with Iranians an allegiance to Shiite Islam. Yet the distinctively Mongol appearance of the Hazaras has contributed to prejudice at even official levels. Pazira has claimed that the Iranian authorities hoped to use *Kandahar* as propaganda against a people widely perceived to be an economic and social problem to Iran. Makhmalbaf has said that he would have been unable to make the film if it had been about forms of repression in Iran instead of Afghanistan. The film nonetheless caused a controversy in Iran over the government's failure to provide proper schooling for refugee children.

Like Makhmalbaf in *The Cyclist,* a number of other Iranian filmmakers have depicted the dilemma of this large Afghan immigrant community in Iran. Its condition is but one local instance contributing to a global debate on the identity, rights, and welfare of uprooted peoples. This subject finds expression in many national cinemas. For instance, coincidentally it seems, the plot of *Baran* (Majid Majidi, 2001), about the plight of Afghan refugees working on construction in Teheran, closely echoes Luc and Jean-Pierre Dardenne's 1996 Belgian film *The Promise.* Other films to deal with Afghans in Iran include *Taste of Cherry, Delbaran* (Abolfazl Jalili, 2001), and *Djomeh* (2000), whose director, Hassan Yektapanah, originally from the Afghan eastern margin of Iran, may lay claim to particular knowledge and insight.

It would be unwise then to categorize *Kandahar* as having a typical "Islamic" or "Iranian" view of its subject. What might constitute such a view is highly problematic in any case. We should also consider the experiences of Makhmalbaf in seeking to place himself within a volatile complex of political, theological, and artistic debate in Iran. A guerilla fighter in the jihadist struggle to overthrow the excessively Westernizing regime of Shah Mohammad Reza Pahlavi, Makhmalbaf was imprisoned in 1974 for stabbing a policeman. This incident and its prelude are the subject of Makhmalbaf's *A Moment of Innocence* (1995). He was tortured by the secret police and released in 1978 by the revolutionary forces that placed Khomeini in power (an experience Makhmalbaf also recreated in *Boycott,* 1985). Recalling his intense dislike of the members of the People's Mujahedin who were imprisoned with him, not least on account of their suspicion of art and culture, Makhmalbaf declares that "even with the worst conditions that I've observed under the ruling clerics, I'd still prefer their rule a thousand times to that of the Mojahedin" (Dabashi 178). After participating in the first government of the Islamic Republic, Makhmalbaf's growing disillusionment with religious and political dogmatism led him to withdraw into radio journalism and screenplay writing before making his first film in 1982. He rapidly established himself as one of Iran's most prominent and provocative filmmakers. His moral conscience and moderate beliefs have combined, as they have often before, with the poetic realism of his camera eye to result in *Kandahar,* his twenty-first film.

Despite formal and cultural differences that may complicate the Western viewer's initial response, *Kandahar* remains a simple, direct, and extremely vivid film that is capable of enhancing our understanding of Afghanistan in the context of the September 11 attacks. The film takes us into an impoverished, ruined, and war-torn country that under the harsh tutelage of the Taliban provided a perfect ideological and physical cover for the al Qaeda faction based there. In 1986 Lessing lamented, "Beautiful parts of Afghanistan have been reduced to desert; ancient towns, full of art treasures bombed flat. One out of three Afghans is now dead or in exile or living in a refugee camp. And the world remains largely indifferent" (34). Disastrous events on the U.S. mainland finally obliged the world to take greater notice of Afghanistan, to send peacekeepers there, and to help start the long, slow process of relieving and reconstructing a country ravaged by more than two decades of war and human suffering. In its courage, compassion, intelligence, and what W. B. Yeats called "terrible beauty," Makhmalbaf's film reveals the extent of that suffering, censures our former indifference, and exhorts us not to forget.

Works Cited

Dabashi, Hamid. *Close Up: Iranian Cinema, Past, Present and Future.* London: Verso, 2001.

Ellis, Deborah. *Women of the Afghan War.* Westport, CT: Praeger, 2000.

Hoberman, J. "Look Homeward, Angel." Rev. of *Kandahar,* dir. Mohsen Makhmalbaf. *Village Voice* Dec. 12–18, 2001. Aug. 25, 2002. <http://www.villagevoice.com/issues/0150/hoberman.php>.

Jones, Kent. "Afghanistan in Focus." *Film Comment* 38.1 (2002): 24–26.

Kepel, Gilles. *Jihad: The Trial of Political Islam.* Trans. Anthony E. Roberts. Cambridge: Belknap–Harvard UP, 2002.

Lessing, Doris. *The Wind Blows Away Our Words: A Firsthand Account of the Afghan Resistance.* New York: Vintage, 1987.

Makhmalbaf, Mohsen. "The Buddha Was Not Demolished in Afghanistan; He Collapsed out of Shame." Interviews and Writings. Makhmalbaf Film House. Aug. 25, 2002. <http://www.kandaharthemovie.com/article/buddha_article.htm>.

———. Interview. "Afghans Are Deserted, Desolate, and Famished People." Interviews and Writings. Makhmalbaf Film House. Aug. 25, 2002. <http://www.kandaharthemovie.com/news_interviews.htm>.

Naficy, Hamid. "Iranian Cinema." *The Oxford History of World Cinema.* New York: Oxford UP, 1996: 672–78.

———. "Islamizing Film Culture in Iran." *Iran: Political Culture in the Islamic Republic.* Ed. Samih K. Farsoun and Mehrdad Mashayekhi. London: Routledge, 1992: 178–213.

———. "Mediawork's Representation of the Other: The Case of Iran." Pines and Willemen 227–39.

———. "Veiled Voice and Vision in Iranian Cinema: The Evolution of Rakhshan Banietemad's Films." *Ladies and Gentlemen, Boys and Girls: Gender in Film at the End of the Twentieth Century.* Ed. Murray Pomerance. Albany: State U of New York P, 2001: 36–52.

Orgeron, Devin. "The Import/Export Business: The Road to Abbas Kiarostami's *Taste of Cherry.*" *CineAction* 58 (2002): 46–51.

Pines, Jim, and Paul Willemen, eds. *Questions of Third Cinema.* London: British Film Inst., 1989.

Said, Edward W. "The Clash of Definitions." *Reflections on Exile and Other Essays.* Cambridge: Harvard UP, 2000: 569–90.

———. *Covering Islam: How the Media and the Experts Determine How We See the Rest of the World.* New York: Vintage, 1997.

Willemen, Paul. "The Third Cinema Question: Notes and Reflections." Pines and Willemen 1–29.

The author thanks Jamsheed Akrami for his suggestions and for enabling him to view his documentary *Friendly Persuasion: Iranian Cinema after the 1979 Revolution,* which was screened by the Sundance Channel in 2000.

11

Reel Terror Post 9/11

Jonathan Markovitz

The September 11 attacks threatened to disrupt virtually every form of American cultural production, as pundits hastened to mourn the death of irony and Hollywood studios frantically began to reshuffle their release schedules. *Collateral Damage* (2002) and *Big Trouble* (2002) were moved to later dates because of a concern that terrorism might have temporarily lost some of its entertainment value, while the releases of *Behind Enemy Lines* (2001) and *Black Hawk Down* (2001) were moved forward, reflecting the fact that highly militaristic displays of patriotism, never entirely out of vogue, suddenly had newfound cachet. (*Black Hawk Down* also benefited from what then seemed like a strong possibility that the Bush administration's "war on terror" would soon expand to Somalia.) Hollywood has a long history of turning widespread fears into cinematic spectacles, but never before has the source of those fears been so singular, so easily isolated, or so thoroughly disseminated to national and international audiences. The box-office receipts for *Behind Enemy Lines* and *Black Hawk Down* suggest that there is still a market for celluloid violence, but now the exploding buildings and dead bodies displayed on screen are likely to be understood in entirely new ways. For audience members comparing these images to those that flickered across their television screens on September 11, suspension of disbelief has become impossible, as the artifice of cinematic terror is now apparent in dramatically new ways. In this context, the popularity of special effects–laden blockbusters may have less to do with their correspondence to real-life events and more to do with playing to an audience desire for revenge. The stark rhetoric of the Bush administration's quest to eradicate "evil" finds a perfect correlate in films that cast A-list Hollywood stars in battles against the calculating and murderous violence of always highly racialized terrorist "others." At the same time, films such as *Panic Room* have taken an introspective (and claustrophobic) turn, finding resonance with audiences whose concerns about personal security and anxieties about the everyday world have been intensified in the current political climate. This essay examines the nature and cultural resonance of cinematic fear and terror in a post-9/11 world and asks whose fears are reflected and reinforced on the silver screen, and at what cost.

For a few months, it appeared that the Arnold Schwarzenegger vehicle *Collateral Damage* might be the first cinematic casualty of the September attacks. Originally scheduled for an October 7, 2001, release date, the film, which follows a firefighter's one-man crusade against terrorism from downtown Los Angeles to the depths of the Colombian jungles and back again, ultimately opened four months later, in February 2002. Once the October release date was canceled, there was speculation (and, for some critics, hope) that the film might be shelved permanently. There was a short period during which the media debated whether big-screen terrorism or indeed any cinematic depictions of violence could ever again be appealing to mass audiences, though Schwarzenegger himself does not appear to have been overly concerned by this question. Indeed, while he explained that the release date had been postponed out of respect for the victims of September 11, as early as October 5 he referenced a long-standing audience fascination with terrorism and a desire to see punishment meted out. Schwarzenegger came close to suggesting that the attacks could actually boost ticket sales, explaining, "People enjoy these movies because they feel it could be real" (Eller). Presumably, that feeling would only be heightened after September 11. By the time *Collateral Damage* was finally released, the film's producers had apparently decided that enough time had passed to demonstrate appropriate respect, and Schwarzenegger declared, "I think people want to get into the minds of people who do this kind of thing. And they want to see Americans kick their butts" (Bowles).

Schwarzenegger's attempt to cater to an audience demand for vengeance fell a bit short, and the film tanked at the box office. Still, there is good reason to suspect that Schwarzenegger's assessment of the national mood was on target and that the reason audiences stayed away in droves can be traced not to distaste for cinematic gore but to the flat and cartoonish delivery of that gore in *Collateral Damage*. The *London Times* suggests that real-life events had raised the stakes of cinematic violence and that in this "strange new world" for Hollywood entertainment, *Collateral Damage* simply couldn't "bear the weight of the extra baggage." With a political sensibility grounded in his own desire for action movies, "Arnie is not the kind of hero one would trust with a tea trolley, let alone the complexities of a war against terror. It wouldn't normally matter a jot. But after 9/11 it does" (Christopher). The devastating effects of the September attacks probably made suspension of disbelief a much more difficult matter for an audience who knew all too well that terrorist violence has physical and emotional consequences and social and political ramifications well beyond what could be captured in a run-of-the-mill Schwarzenegger movie. Now, more than ever, audiences were likely to be acutely aware that very little about this movie "could be real."

Schwarzenegger's reference to "the minds of people who do this kind of thing" provides an important indication of the superficiality of the film's politics. Andrew Davis, the film's director, decided that to avoid what had become a Hollywood cliché, the film should focus on Colombian rebels instead of the Arab terrorists who were initially in the script. But while this might seem like an important move away from Orientalist stereotypes, Schwarzenegger's comment collapses any distinctions between the "minds" of people doing "this kind of thing." Fundamentally, all terrorism is of a piece, and all terrorist motivations are interchangeable. The stock figure of the terrorist remains firmly intact, and the specific racialization of individual characters is probably largely irrelevant, since media saturation of similar imagery over the span of at least two decades means that terrorists are "always already" coded as Arab or, at the very least, Arabs are always already coded as terrorist. Thus, Colombian activists who protested the film, saying that it furthered stereotypical images of Colombians as unthinkingly violent drug dealers, might have been somewhat off the mark. Certainly, those stereotypes are present in the film and are especially troubling as the Bush administration acts to increase military support for the Colombian government. And it is also true that Schwarzenegger has gone out of his way to praise the film's pedagogical functions, saying that "when audiences leave the theater they're not only feeling that they got great entertainment but they also learned something about a specific and complex subject—in this case, the situation in Colombia" (Warner 8). But ultimately, the film is not really about Colombia in any meaningful sense. Instead, we are meant to understand the story in archetypical terms, as a battle between good and evil.

And it is here, in the film's personification of complex forces, that *Collateral Damage* comes across as far too pat. The mass media have a long history of such personification, of course. The 1991 Gulf War was regularly discussed as a battle between Saddam Hussein and George H. W. Bush (at one point, for example, we were told that Bush had "bloodied Saddam's nose.") More recently, Osama bin Laden has become the public face of terror. And the consequences of such personification are dramatic—as long as U.S. foreign policy is seen as targeting specific individuals, there is no need to dwell on the real victims of U.S. actions (for example, the hundreds of thousands of Iraqi children who died as a result of a devastated national infrastructure and brutally harsh sanctions, or the thousands of Afghan civilians killed by U.S. bombing campaigns.) But as simplistic as much of the media coverage of international relations has been, there has always been a solemnity attached to discussions of real warfare that is sorely lacking in a film in which a lone firefighter becomes a substitute for foreign policy and the looming terrorist threat is embodied by a character named "El Lobo" and his wife. In a post-9/11 world, the absence of such solemnity is especially stark, since the popular and political discourse surrounding notions of "evil" and terrorism has shifted so dramatically. While it is true that the press spilled a lot of ink cataloging the crimes and ambitions of Osama bin Laden, the second Bush administration has been at great pains to suggest that bin Laden is only a part of the problem. We are faced not with an isolated monster but with shadowy terrorist networks, an "axis of evil," and a threat diffuse enough to warrant a "war on terror" with no clear targets, objectives, or ending in sight. In this context, the idea that evil can be so neatly contained in one person, or that domestic tranquility can be so easily restored through isolated acts of vigilante violence, is likely to come across as hopelessly naive.

While the film's depiction of foreign policy might seem somewhat dated, there is one area where *Collateral Damage* seems almost prescient, and that is not in its decision to have a firefighter play a lead role on the front lines in the battle against terrorism but in its depiction of political dissent. While the bulk of the film follows Schwarzenegger's efforts to bring El Lobo to justice, his fury is sparked by the spokesperson for the "Latin American Solidarity Committee," who voices support for the Colombian rebels and coldly dismisses the deaths of Schwarzenegger's wife and child by referring to them as "collateral damage." The idea that critics of U.S. foreign policy are also de facto supporters of terrorism fits in well in a political climate in which a series of reporters have been fired for not displaying appropriate levels of patriotic fervor, and White House spokesman Ari Fleischer, reacting to mildly critical comments from talk show host Bill Maher, could declare to a national audience that "Americans . . . need to watch what they say, watch what they do, and . . . this is not a time for remarks like that; there never is" (Reeves).

As troubling as *Collateral Damage* may be, both in its representations of terrorism and for its stance toward political protest, it is so obviously one-dimensional and comically thoughtless that there is little risk anyone would treat it as a serious source of political analysis and information. The same cannot be said of some other recent, high-profile Hollywood films. If *Collateral Damage* can be seen as the quaintly anachronistic opening salvo in Hollywood's own war on terror, its officially sanctioned and far more successful counterpart, *The Sum of All Fears* (2002), turns the charge of naïveté on its head by suggesting that it is not Hollywood but the American public that has barely begun to grasp the kinds of danger present in a world where terrorists have access to weapons of mass destruction.

The press kit for *The Sum of All Fears* trumpets the film's "authenticity and realism," which were enhanced by extensive access to the Pentagon, the White House, and the National Airborne Command Center, not to mention the team of marines who manned three CH-53 helicopters for a rescue scene involving the president of the United States (Paramount 8). Appropriately enough, the film's premier, which was well attended by military brass, was held not in Los Angeles but in Washington D.C. Directed by Phil Robinson and based on a Tom Clancy bestseller, the film is based on the premise that a large number of Cold-War-era nuclear warheads are unaccounted for and that they have tremendous appeal for terrorists. The centerpiece of the film is the detonation of a nuclear bomb in Baltimore, where the president of the United States is attending the Super Bowl. The destruction of Baltimore isn't presented as much of a tragedy in its own right, though the explosion is part of a neo-Nazi attempt to start a full-out nuclear war between Russia and the United States, and we are led to believe that this would be rather unpleasant. (The choice of Baltimore as nuclear target has been the source of much amusement. Joe Queenan, writing from the safe harbor of the *London Guardian* quips that, despite September 11, audiences don't seem particularly put off by the attack "because Baltimore is a complete dump and no one would miss it much if it were leveled by a nuclear weapon," while Baltimore native John Waters has said that he has "no problem blowing up Baltimore in a movie if it's done with joy and style" (Turan).

If the implausibility of *Collateral Damage* helps to account for its dismal showing at the box office, most commentators attribute the success of *The Sum of All Fears* to what is said to be the film's realistic depiction of the dangerous times we live in. But the popularity of a film in which a major east-coast city is *realistically* nuked presents a problem for many critics who seem to suggest that, after September 11, audiences should be too damaged to enjoy this sort of spectacle. David Denby, for example, is "afraid that it's no longer possible to enjoy world-crisis thrillers like 'The Sum of All Fears' as amusingly alarmist entertainment." This statement of course begs the question of why exactly audiences *did* enjoy the film, which occupied the number one slot at the box office for its first two weeks and went on to gross well over $100 million domestically. Kenneth Turan answers this question by offering the faint hope that "maybe, just maybe, in a world where newspapers are running front-page stories about the horrific possibilities of an India-Pakistan nuclear war that could instantly kill as many as twelve million, people are going to see *The Sum of All Fears* because they want to have a sense of what is at stake in a world where nuclear arms show no sign of going away."

The common thread here is that the bulk of the reviews take all of the promotional talk about realism at face value. The military presence surrounding the film's production and reception provided the film with a veneer of credibility that was enhanced by an admittedly stunning simulation of a nuclear explosion, "complete with an ugly mushroom cloud, bewildered casualties and a concussive force that wreaks havoc" (Turan). But while the explosion itself was fairly convincing, the effects of that explosion are ludicrously downplayed. The very fact that Turan can refer to bewildered rather than, for example, incinerated casualties is indicative of the problem. We do see some evidence of the human toll of the bombing, but the camera lingers on few bodies. The *only* casualty of the bombing whom we've come to know at all is CIA director William Cabot (Morgan Freeman). And while his death is presented as tragic, it is not nearly as tragic as it might have been, since he manages to serve his purpose, providing Jack Ryan (the film's hero, played by Ben Affleck) with the military pass he needs to save the day and the gumption to carry on. (Cabot's role all along has been that of enabler—he selects Ryan for a life of espionage and sends him on his way. This role is a depressingly classic one for African American characters in mainstream films.)

Other than Cabot, Ryan, his girlfriend, and President Fowler (James Cromwell) all turn out to be relatively unharmed. Any lingering concern with radioactive fallout dissipates immediately when we learn that the prevailing winds will leave Ryan out of harm's way. (In Hollywood action movies, we always know that the hero will survive, but in this case his fate is exceptionally overdetermined, since an older Jack Ryan is the hero of several earlier Tom Clancy films, and the audience knows that he has to grow up and become Harrison Ford, or at least Alec Baldwin.) Ordinarily, one might want to applaud a Hollywood blockbuster that avoids cheap melodrama and cloying sentimentality, but it would have been nice to see more than token concern expressed for the population of Baltimore (not to mention neighboring cities and states, local and national water supplies, etc.) The film's finale features a blissfully happy Jack Ryan sitting with his fiancée on the lawn of the Washington Mall under remarkably clear skies, basking in his recent glory. The Hollywood happy ending doesn't appear to be even slightly tarnished by the nuclear bomb that has exploded only days ago and a few miles away.

While the film's depiction of a single nuclear explosion is troubling, the heart of *The Sum of All Fears* has to do with much broader questions of U.S. nuclear policy. Affleck has said that the film should be seen as "a cautionary tale" and that "the idea is to make it disturbing, to raise awareness about nuclear proliferation" (Turan). Once the bomb explodes, the race is on to prevent an all-out nuclear war between the United States and Russia. Ryan ultimately convinces the leaders of both countries to back down, but before that happens, we are privy to a series of conversations between President Fowler and his highest advisors. From these discussions, we learn that any nuclear first strike would end badly—Fowler's advisors think that Russia will back down after it is nuked, but the audience knows better, since we've seen government officials at the Kremlin planning for retaliation. A full-out nuclear assault by the United States might leave Russia with only about three hundred relatively minor-yield nuclear weapons, but those three hundred weapons would be launched at American cities.

Thus the film takes a clear, though hardly bold, stance in opposition to U.S. first strikes and is mildly critical of nuclear deterrence strategies. While the presidential advisors believe that a nuclear war can be "winnable" in a meaningful way and are involved in calculations of potential loss of human life that are worthy of *Dr. Strangelove's* General Turgidson, the audience is not encouraged to see their advice as Strangeloveian. While Kubrick's film ridiculed anti-Communist paranoia and suggested that the "Mutually Assured Destruction" policy was truly insane, in this case it is clear that, if not for Ryan's heroism and ingenuity, Fowler would have followed through with a first strike because it was the *reasonable* thing to do. When Fowler gives the launch order (which is soon aborted), he is utterly despondent and laments that this is going to be the mark of "my presidency." Fowler's concern with his legacy hints at an astoundingly unrealistic assessment of a post–World War III social landscape, but again the film does nothing to suggest such a critique. Instead, Fowler's grim determination to do what must be done is presented as appropriately presidential. James Cromwell brings a considerable degree of gravity to the role of Fowler and has discussed the president's predicament with real empathy, saying, "I suppose the ultimate nightmare of any presidency would be to have to make the decision that Fowler is faced with making—whether or not to launch a massive strike. It's an untenable situation. I mean, what would *you* really do if you had to give the order to blow up a city and take the world to the brink of assured destruction? What would go though your mind? The reality of the situation is very sobering" (Paramount 6).

The situation might be sobering, but there is no sense here that the reality of U.S. nuclear policy or relations with Russia need reassessment. Instead, all of the drama in the latter part of the film involves tracking down the terrorists and foiling their plot, and the film's primary message is that the looming terrorist threat is more serious than has been generally recognized. The film's popularity, especially within the military and the Bush administration, surely owes something to the ways that this sort of message complements much of the rhetoric surrounding the ongoing war on terror. The film opened only a week after a widely discussed *New York Times Magazine* article by Bill Keller titled "Nuclear Nightmares" argued that the appropriate question to ask about a nuclear attack on the United States was "not if but when" (22). The film was fueled by a political climate of exacerbated nuclear fears and in turn added fuel to those fears. So much so that U.S. customs officials held a news conference to trumpet their bomb detection capabilities and to argue that they were prepared to prevent the specific terrorist scenario laid out in *Sum* (Hoberman, "Art" 45). The Bush administration may have taken a cue from the film, too, as "Attorney General John Ashcroft timed for the Monday morning that followed *The Sum of All Fears*' second triumphant weekend his proud announcement that the currently beleaguered FBI and CIA had successfully collaborated on the arrest of one Abdullah al-Muhajir, born Jose Padilla in Brooklyn" (Hoberman, "Art"). Padilla, suspected of working with al Qaeda and planning to develop a "dirty bomb," that is, a conventional bomb laced with radioactive materials, had already been in custody for a month by the time of Ashcroft's announcement, which led some to speculate that the administration sought to capitalize on the heightened awareness of nuclear peril fostered by *The Sum of All Fears*.

While *The Sum of All Fears* was perfectly in tune with contemporary social anxieties, that its terrorist scenario was entirely fictional and mostly implausible provided some checks on its political significance. The film could contribute to an overall climate of fear but had very little direct relevance for any particular set of policy discussions. In contrast, *Black Hawk Down* (directed by Ridley Scott and based on a book with the same title by Mark Bowden) addressed the all-too-real U.S. intervention in Somalia and was enlisted in a series of debates about possible directions for the war on terror.

The U.S. military was involved in the production of *Black Hawk Down* to a much greater degree than it was in *The Sum of All Fears*.

The Department of Defense invited the actors in the film to participate in training at assorted military bases and provided Scott with two soldiers who had participated in the actual raid depicted in the film to serve as advisers. Secretary of Defense Donald Rumsfeld's personal intervention ensured that this would be the first time that U.S. troops were sent to a foreign country to aid in the production of a movie (Hoberman, "Art" 45). The Pentagon sent eight helicopters and more than one hundred U.S. Rangers (and "all of the backup military personnel accompanying them") to help out in Morocco, and had U.S. Army pilots man the helicopters during the battle scenes (Columbia 28). The officer in charge of the rangers declared that "what's unique about the military supporting this film . . . is that you actually had the units which participated in the military operation eight years ago, here doing it again. In fact, we have three or four of the actual veterans of that operation flying the helicopters while we film it" (Columbia 29). The resulting production was heartily endorsed by key government officials. Like *The Sum of All Fears*, *Black Hawk Down* premiered in Washington but to an even more prominent audience, whose members included Rumsfeld (who declared that the film was "powerful") and more than "800 other top officials and brass" (Massing). The premier even drew out Vice President Dick Cheney, who was taking a "breather from his undisclosed location" (Hoberman, "Art" 45). Deputy Secretary of Defense Paul Wolfowitz agreed with his boss that it was "a powerful film" and added, "I think it's good for this time. It reminds people what it's all about" (Roberts). As with *The Sum of All Fears*, most critics viewed the tremendous amount of military involvement and government support for the film as evidence of the film's realism rather than of its value as propaganda.

The political value of the film to the Bush administration was, however, all too evident. Originally scheduled for a March 2002 release date, the film was rushed into theaters in December 2001, amid widespread speculation about where the war on terror would lead after the initial bombing campaign in Afghanistan. Somalia was thought to be at the top of the list of possible targets, since it was seen as a likely refuge for Taliban leaders and al Qaeda operatives fleeing Afghanistan. Indeed, by the time the film opened, the Bush administration had already taken significant actions in a stance that suggested Somalia was very much on its agenda. The *London Times* reported the United States had sent agents and special forces to Somalia to identify al Qaeda members and to prevent others from entering the country (Maddox). More damaging, the Bush administration shut down the money transfer offices that Somali emigrants used to send cash to relatives, thereby further destabilizing the country's economy "just as efforts were getting underway to restore civil authority there" (Connell). But before embarking on any new military actions in Somalia, the administration would have to wrestle with the ghosts of earlier excursions into the country. The October 1993 raid in Mogadishu that is the subject of *Black Hawk Down* left nineteen Americans and more than a thousand Somalis dead, and was almost universally condemned as a debacle. Shortly after the raid, in what amounted to a rare admission of defeat, the United States withdrew its forces from Somalia. *Black Hawk Down* is a self-conscious attempt to recuperate the collective memory of this raid—to claim it as a success and as a stunning example of the valor and heroism of U.S. soldiers. In the process, the film works to rejuvenate myths about the benevolence of U.S. foreign policy and to fortify the ideological foundations for future military campaigns, which would not necessarily be limited to Somalia.

While the mainstream media has said stunningly little about the one thousand Somalis killed during the raid, the sheer number of deaths is so high that any effort to rehabilitate the collective memory of the raid would necessitate establishing that the United States had only the best of intentions. *Black Hawk Down* takes this mission seriously. In the opening moments of the film, we see images of emaciated Somali corpses and grieving family members, and the accompanying text informs us,

> Years of warfare among rival clans causes famine on a biblical scale. Three hundred thousand civilians die of starvation. Mohameed Farrah

Aidid, the most powerful of the warlords, rules the capital, Moga-dishu. He seizes international food shipments at the ports. Hunger is his weapon. The world responds. Behind a force of twenty thou-sand U.S. Marines, food is delivered and order is restored.

April 1993. Aidid waits until the marines withdraw and then de-clares war on the remaining U.N. peacekeepers. In June, Aidid's mi-litia ambush and slaughter twenty-four Pakistani soldiers, and begin targeting American personnel. In late August, America's elite soldiers, Delta Force, Army Rangers, and the 160th SOAR are sent to Moga-dishu to remove Aidid and restore order. The mission was to take three weeks, but six weeks later Washington was growing impatient.

The text hints at what will later become an important critique of the political priorities of the Clinton administration, but the primary effect of this opening is to set the stage and provide the cast of char-acters at its most basic level. The narrative suggests that the U.S. in-tervention in Somalia was entirely selfless and had already worked to alleviate the kinds of hunger that we've seen on screen but on a "bib-lical" scale. As important as earlier efforts were, though, they were now threatened by someone who would come across as too unbelievably monstrous in most fictional settings—a man so evil that he would use hunger as a weapon. There is a mild suggestion that U.S. actions were partly defensive, since American personnel were targeted, but the overall implication is that the welfare of the Somali population was our chief concern. Clearly, this was a necessary mission.

This is about as much detail as we're given about the factors that led to the raid depicted in the rest of the film, though we do see a U.S. helicopter crew outraged by the atrocities committed by Aidid's men at a Red Cross food distribution center. The crew requests permission to intervene and is frustrated when their request is denied by their su-periors. Thus, from the outset, the film presents the American soldiers as highly empathetic and concerned with the victimization of ordinary Somalis, though hamstrung by problematic bureaucratic restrictions.

Once the film has established that the American military values Somali lives, any concern with Somali victimization quickly drops away as the narrative begins to focus on the raid, which soon goes spectacularly awry. The point of the raid was to capture two of Aidid's top officers, who had been spotted at a building in downtown Mogadishu. In the film's portrayal, some of the soldiers become uneasy early on when they're informed that "Washington, in all its wisdom" had turned down a request for light armor and air support from Specter gunships because they were "too high profile" and that they would instead have to rely on the far less powerful Black Hawk and Little Bird helicopters. Sure enough, while the Americans are able to accomplish their objective, things go badly almost from the outset, as one ranger fails in his attempt to climb down a rope dangling out of a helicopter and falls sixty feet to the street. From then on, things only get worse, as armed groups of Somalis attack the Americans, and manage to shoot down two of the Black Hawk helicopters. The remainder of the film follows American efforts to protect and rescue the crews of the two helicopters, who are under constant assault.

At this point, the earlier images of Somali suffering are replaced by scene after scene of Somalis as an absolutely undifferentiated and unthinkingly brutal threat. The Americans, forced to fight for their lives, are faced with never-ending hordes of Somalis intent on their deaths. Whenever one Somali is shot down, another rushes in to take his (or her) place without a moment's pause. (In contrast, the camera lingers on every American injury or death. One American injury is presented as so startling that the pounding soundtrack momentarily comes to a sudden and complete stop so as to allow the significance to sink in.) The film allows for no distinctions to be made between armed members of Aidid's militias and ordinary Somalis, as one officer announces, "Hostiles advancing. . . . Be advised women and children among them. . . . We're fighting the whole city." The wholesale slaughter of Somalis by the Americans is thus presented as utterly justifiable. Indeed, in interviews about the film, Mark Bowden suggests that the Somali deaths should actually be seen as evidence of American heroism, saying for example, "It goes to show you how context is everything. . . . If tomorrow you read that we captured two of Osama bin Laden's key advisers and killed and wounded 1,000 of Al Qaeda, and in the process lost 18 men, you'd think they'd done a helluva job" (Malanowski 13). This sentiment is echoed in many of the mainstream press's reviews of the film, including an essay in *Time* declaring that "under fire. . . [the soldiers] were, indeed, all that they could be" and noting that the leader of the mission considers the raid a success, since the soldiers captured the men they were after and, "killed at least 300 of the enemy" (Schickel 75). Insofar as *Black Hawk Down* works to highlight American valor, the extent of the killing is presented as an accomplishment worth celebrating.

The dehumanization of Somalis is so complete as to be casual and automatic. It is even reflected in the language of the soldiers, who consistently refer to them as "skinnies." There is one moment in the opening minutes of the film where a key character seems to regard this term as slightly distasteful, but once the fighting starts, it is uttered repeatedly and without hesitation. This particular epithet is especially shocking given that the expressed goal of the U.S. intervention was to eliminate starvation. That the term is never seriously critiqued in the film, despite the Pentagon having vetted the script and presumably being concerned with ensuring that the film presented the military in a favorable light, suggests an underlying racism so deeply ingrained and unquestionably accepted as to have been unrecognizable.

And, for the most part, the racism was unrecognizable to mainstream critics. There were important exceptions, most notably Elvis Mitchell in the *New York Times,* who decried the film's "jingoism" and wrote that the film's "lack of characterization converts the Somalis into a pack of snarling dark-skinned beasts." But, by and large, the media offered nothing but praise for the film's realism. The reviews often include capsule historical summaries, clearly taken from the film's press kit or Bowden's book but presented as straightforward and uncontroversial accounts of what happened. A typical example is Richard Schickel's portrayal of "armed clansmen" who often advanced "behind human shields of women and children" (75). Schickel emphasizes the raw numbers of American casualties, noting, "Eighteen Americans would die, 73 more would be wounded," but suggests that the numbers tell only part of the story, encouraging us to attempt to comprehend the full extent of the horror in his declaration that "you cannot imagine the hot chaos those chilling figures contain" (75). While an informed reader might ask how much more chaotic the situation must have been for the residents of Mogadishu, having to deal with the deaths of more than a thousand of their family members, friends, and neighbors, to say nothing of the countless number of Somali wounded, there is nothing in Schickel's review to encourage any empathy for the people he refers to simply as "the enemy." In fact, most mainstream reviewers seemed utterly incapable of discussing Somali deaths at all, and when they did, the tendency was, as noted above, to present those deaths as a testament to American bravery.

A key part of the film's process of dehumanization rests in its failure to ask why the Somalis were so angry at the United States. After all, if U.S. motivations and policies were as pure as we've been led to believe, then the only logical reaction on the part of the Somalis would have been to display gratitude. Any hostility, much less expression of rage, comes across as completely irrational. The film's status as the most dominant, even "official," version of the raid (a status secured not only by the size of its audience but also by the government sponsorship discussed above) is therefore made even more problematic not because of what is presented on screen but because of what is left out.

Aside from the opening text, the film presents absolutely no context for the raid and therefore leaves the impression that the United States decided to intervene in Somalia only when faced with a humanitarian crisis of nightmarish proportions. Missing is any discussion of the role played by the United States and the international community in fostering that crisis. There is, for example, no hint of IMF austerity measures in the 1980s that had the effect of dismantling the local agricultural economy and exacerbating poverty (Urbina) or of the $50 million in annual arms shipments that were used to prop up Somali dictator Siad Barre, "whose destructive policies helped create the vacuum that the warlords rushed to fill" (Massing). More immediately relevant, the film ignores the fact that, before leaving the United Nations to administer Somalia, the United States had backed Aidid and Ali Mahdi in a conflict with another clan chief, "shoring up their power just as it had started to collapse" (Monbiot). In the days that led up to the raid depicted in the film, U.S. special forces, who were "over-confident and hopelessly ill-informed," led a series of comically inept raids against the "headquarters of the UN development programme, the charity World Concern, and the offices of Médecins sans Frontières," but this was only the prelude to a truly disastrous mission during which the U.S. forces destroyed a building in Mogadishu where members of Aidid's clan were meeting to discuss a peace agreement with the United Nations. The U.S. military killed fifty-four people in that attack, and then, when faced with retaliatory gunfire, the special forces fired missiles at residential areas, thus succeeding "in making enemies of all the Somalis" (Monbiot). Had this information been presented in *Black Hawk Down,* the Somali rage depicted in the film would have taken on a very different character, and the narrative of U.S. benevolence would have been severely compromised. Even the much vaunted American bravery under fire during the October raid would have appeared somewhat dubious had the film included scenes of the U.S. Special Forces taking refuge in a Koranic school and putting terrified children and teachers in harm's way (Clayton), or if it had focused on the U.S. soldiers who "with an understandable but ruthless regard for their own safety, locked Somali women and children into the house in which they were besieged" (Monbiot).

As problematic as the film's presentation of the U.S. role in Somalia is, ultimately there is good reason to suspect that Somalia is actually largely beside the point. The dearth of social and historical context presented in the film works to erase any real sense of specificity. The film demands to be read metaphorically, as a generalized statement about war or, more accurately, about the ways that the United States should wage war. As Mark Bowden says, "Ultimately, *Black Hawk Down* is about soldiers at war, any war, anywhere, anytime" ("First"). *Time* suggests that Scott wanted "to create an anatomy of a war that could be any war" and that "to that end he stripped away all talk, all thought, of this fight's larger geopolitical implications" (Schickel 74). These statements are a bit misleading, since the opening text does address the political stakes of this particular battle and because the generic references to "soldiers" and "any war" obscure the fact that the audience is meant to root for only one particular set of soldiers here. Certainly, though, the film would be of relatively minor significance, and would not have merited the kind of attention that it received, had its message been limited to one particular battle waged nearly a decade before its release. Instead, the film's importance rests in the lessons it proposes for future actions by the United States.

There is some ambiguity about the nature of those lessons. For example, the *New York Times* expresses concern that *Black Hawk Down* and the battle it depicts have been responsible for sending the message that casualties "are completely unacceptable in American military operations. At the first sign of blood, politicians abandon missions and generals are retired" (Kristof). This interpretation is somewhat off the mark, however, since the *Times* inadvertently conflates press coverage of the actual battle in 1993 with the representation of that battle in the film. As noted above, *Black Hawk Down* was intended as a reclamation project, and it works to refute and reconfigure earlier representations and collective memories of the Mogadishu raid. Bowden agrees that "the Somali episode sent the message that, you know, we'll fight them on the beaches and we'll fight them on the cliffs but if they kill a few of our soldiers, we'll give up and go away" (Goffe). But he has not been content to leave it at that. Instead, in a series of interviews, Bowden is always careful to argue that there is a more appropriate lesson to be drawn from the raid and from the more recent military campaign in Afghanistan, which is that "success depends on enlisting the active support of the local population, and on using the full complement of weapons in the U.S. arsenal" (Bowden, "Inside"). Bowden might be overstating the case here, since the "full complement of weapons in the U.S. arsenal" includes nuclear weapons, and there is no indication in the bulk of his writing that he would have advocated a nuclear strike in Somalia or elsewhere. Still, the general sentiment rings true to the film. The intended lesson is not that the United States should flee when the going gets tough, but that, once the United States decides to get involved in a military conflict, it is necessary to protect U.S. lives at any cost, with any and all available military options, no matter how many of the "enemy" are killed. Far from advocating a stance of noninvolvement, as the *Times* fears, the film thus presents a profoundly hawkish critique of elected officials who lack the political will to see that military operations are carried out in an appropriately thorough manner.

Bowden makes this position explicit in his claim that the Mogadishu raid prompted "a withdrawal of American military force from the world," and that "even the Sept. 11 attacks were connected, in that the Clinton administration had not forcefully enough gone after Osama Bin Laden and Al Qaeda after the 1999 bombings of U.S. embassies in Kenya and Tanzania" ("First"). The filmmakers considered adding text to the end of *Black Hawk Down* that would make this argument directly but finally decided that "it was better to leave such connections to the viewers' imaginations" ("First"). This decision has not stopped Bowden from drawing those connections in virtually every interview he has given since the film's release. While President Clinton is the direct target of Bowden's comment, his arguments have clear implications for contemporary political debates.

The decision to omit any direct reference to September 11 in the final cut of the film might have less to do with trusting the audience to come to its own conclusions, and more to do with a sense that attaching such an openly partisan political message would have diluted the film's metaphorical significance, for the real power and resonance of the film lie in its articulation of a new sense of American identity. The Hollywood film that comes closest to *Black Hawk Down* in terms of its reliance on racist stereotypes of unthinking brutality is D. W. Griffith's *Birth of a Nation* (1915), and like *Birth, Black Hawk Down* plays off highly racialized fears in shaping and disseminating a new national mythology of victimization. And, as in the Reconstruction-

era South, this mythology is likely to be mobilized for the retrenchment and aggressive pursuit of political power, though this time on a
world stage. Somali fears (the film was boycotted by the Somali Justice Advocacy Center in Minnesota because of a concern that it could
lead to anti-Somali violence in the United States) are one important
indication of the film's power, and like African Americans watching
Birth, Somalis have good reason to fear that the violence displayed on
screen might be enacted on the streets, whether of Mogadishu or St.
Paul. But more broadly, by heightening a national sense of "aggrieved
injury" (Hoberman, "Bully") and suggesting that military power can
provide a salve for that injury, the film helps pave the way for the global
extension of U.S. hegemony—in places like Iraq, for example—under the guise of the war on terror.

The three films addressed thus far feed into debates about the nature of terrorism in fairly direct ways and have clear relevance to discussions of the aftermath of the September attacks. Additionally, the
nearly unprecedented level of government involvement in *Sum of All
Fears* and *Black Hawk Down* make these films truly noteworthy. In
the end, though, the recent film that most speaks to post-9/11 social
anxieties may well be a much more modest movie with a minuscule
cast, and a scale limited to the events that occur in one Manhattan
brownstone in a span of less than twenty-four hours. David Fincher's
Panic Room (2002), which was filmed with a budget of less than $50
million, went on to gross in excess of $100 million worldwide, and
its suggestion that there is no such thing as a safe haven clearly struck
a chord with audiences.

The plot of *Panic Room* is quite simple. Meg Altman (Jodie Foster)
and her daughter Sarah (Kristen Stewart), who have been shopping for
a house after Meg's recent divorce, buy a brownstone with a unique
feature—a "panic room," or a specially built, hidden, high-tech bun-
ker intended as the final line of defense from anyone who might break
into the house. The Altmans' timing is unfortunate, since a band of
intruders (played by Forest Whitaker, Dwight Yoakam, and Jared Leto)
force their way into the house the very first night that they move in.

The Altmans manage to make it to the panic room but not to safety, since the intruders have come for a fortune hidden in that very room by the previous owner of the house. Whitaker's character designed the panic room and has ideas about how to get into it. The rest of the movie charts the Altmans' heroic efforts to fend off the intruders.

The film's concern with personal safety had obvious appeal after September 11 and the subsequent anthrax attacks. In the months immediately after the attacks, there was a dramatic increase in sales of virtually every type of personal safety device, ranging from parachutes specially designed to be used for escapes from skyscrapers, to home anthrax-detection kits. When *Panic Room* was released in March 2002, virtually every major English-language newspaper, from the *New York Times* and the *Boston Globe* to the *London Times,* ran articles about the dramatic rise in construction of panic (or "safe") rooms after September 11. The *Washington Post* explains the appeal of a panic room by referring to it as "a perfect encasement of safety in a world that's so suddenly turned hostile" (Hunter). *Panic Room* was in production well before the attacks, but the *New Yorker* nevertheless credits the director with an impeccable sense of timing, declaring that "Fincher must know that if he was ever going to make a film about security the moment to do it was now, when insecurity has become as common as migraine, with its paralyzing throb" (Lane 95). Indeed, the film's producers appear to have decided to aggressively market the film by highlighting the ways in which it resonates with post-9/11 security concerns within a new culture of fear. The film's press kit, for example, includes information about "staggering" levels of "paranoia" and the boom in personal security devices (Sony 2).

But all of the attention to personal safety equipment provides a bit of a red herring. After all, the film rests on the premise that panic rooms cannot be counted on and provide only a false sense of security. Foster herself appears to reject the need for panic rooms. When asked about whether her experiences with John Hinckley Jr. have affected her views about safety, she responded, "I feel safe. I'm not a particularly paranoid person. Burglars are a little different than stalker assassins" (Calvo). She sums up the message of the film by saying that "if you get a panic room and you get paranoid, bad things will happen to you. The time to be vigilant is before the bad things happen" (Hemblade 18). The panic room does provide temporary refuge to the Altmans, but ultimately their survival is due to an extraordinary degree of ingenuity and bravery, along with a decision by Forest Whitaker's character to help them out. As a practical matter, this combination of resources is likely to be unavailable to most of the people in the market for survivalist gear. (A British critic finds the Altmans' resourcefulness particularly intriguing, remarking, "personally I know very few people who could rig up a phone line from the mains to a mobile, or even send an SOS signal via torchlight. Is this the kind of thing they're teaching them in American high schools today?" [Quinn]). Thus, while the film has certainly capitalized on the growth of the personal safety industry after the September attacks, it finally rejects an approach to security that relies on consumerist impulses or individual heroics.

By suggesting that true safety cannot be found in panic rooms nor be secured through personal acts of bravery, the film raises the question of how to develop a reasonable response to troubling times. This question takes on added significance as the film ends—the Altmans have made it through their ordeal and have decided to sell the house. They appear a bit more confident and somewhat emboldened by what they've gone through, but there is no hint of triumph here. Instead, as Anthony Lane notes in the *New Yorker*, "there is something horribly apt in the way Fincher closes the drama in joyless exhaustion, leaving you certain that there will be a sequel to these events, not onscreen but in someone's home tonight." There may not be a need to panic any longer, but as the Altmans walk through the streets of Manhattan and merge into the city crowds, it becomes clear that the potential sources of terror are unending. Foster's emphasis on the need for continuous vigilance therefore turns out to be the closest the film can come to offering any sense of closure. The critic for the *New Yorker* claims that there "isn't a line in *Panic Room* that encourages a political reading." But as the Bush administration advocates the expansion of trial by secret tribunal, encourages us to keep a watchful eye on our neighbors, and sets its sites on Iraq and possibly other unknown locations in what has the potential to become a never-ending "war on terror," *Panic Room*'s final moments seem remarkably in tune with the dominant political discourse of our times.

Works Cited

Bowden, Mark. "First Person: More Than the Heat of Battle." *Los Angeles Times* Dec. 18, 2001, Calendar sec.: 1.

———. "Inside Story: Back to Hell." *Guardian* Jan. 24, 2002, Features sec.: 6.

Bowles, Scott. "Studios Invest 'Collateral' with Post-9/11 Hopes." *USA Today* Feb. 5, 2002: 1D.

Calvo, Davin. "Opening a Door to Panic Rooms." *Los Angeles Times* Mar. 27, 2002, Calendar sec., part 6: 1.

Christopher, James. "Brawn of a New Age." *Times (London)* Apr. 4, 2002. Nexis. Aug. 15, 2002.

Clayton, Jonathan. "Somali Warlords Await US Rematch." *Times (London)* Feb. 20, 2002. Nexis. Aug. 15, 2002.

Columbia Pictures. *Black Hawk Down* press kit. Los Angeles. 2001.

Connell, Dan. "War Clouds over Somalia." Mar. 2002. Middle East Research and Information Project. Aug. 15, 2002 <http://www.merip.org/newspaper_opeds/Dan_Con_war_clouds_somalia.html>

Denby, David. "Men in Trouble." *New Yorker* June 6, 2002. Nexis. Aug. 15, 2002.

Eller, Claudia. "Studios in Quandary over Timing." *Los Angeles Times* Oct. 5, 2001: C1.

Goffe, Leslie. *"Black Hawk Down." New African* Apr. 2002: 36.

Hemblade, Christopher. "Jodie Foster Says." *Time Out* Apr. 3, 2002: 18–20.

Hoberman, J. "The Art of War: How Hollywood Learned to Stop Worrying and Love the Bomb." *Village Voice* June 6, 2002: 45.

———. "Bully Pulpit." *Village Voice* Feb. 8, 2002: 1.

Hunter, Stephen. "*Panic Room:* If Walls Could Stalk: No Exit from Tension in Jodie Foster Film." *Washington Post* Mar. 29, 2002: C1.

Keller, Bill. "Nuclear Nightmares." *New York Times* May 26, 2002: sec. 6: 22+.

Kristof, Nicolas D. "The Wrong Lessons of the Somalia Debacle." *New York Times* Feb. 5, 2002: A25.

Lane, Anthony. "Home Fires: David Fincher's *Panic Room.*" *New Yorker* Apr. 8, 2002: 95.

Maddox, Bronwen. "A Cautionary Tale for America's Hawks." *Times (London)* Jan. 17, 2002. Nexis. Aug. 15, 2002.

Malanowski, Jamie. "War, Without Any Answers." *New York Times* Jan. 16, 2002: B13.

Massing, Michael. "Black Hawk Downer." *Nation* Feb. 25, 2002: 5.

Mitchell, Elvis. "Film Review: Mission of Mercy Goes Bad in Africa." *New York Times* Dec. 28, 2001.: 1E.

Monbiot, George. "Comment and Analysis: Both Saviour and Victim: Black Hawk Down Creates a New and Dangerous Myth of American Nationhood." *Guardian (London)* Jan. 29, 2002: 15.

Paramount Pictures. *The Sum of All Fears* press kit. Los Angeles. 2002.

Queenan, Joe. "The Guide: Better Red Than Dead." *Guardian* Aug. 17, 2002: 12.

Quinn, Anthony. "Film: They Know Where You Live." *Independent* May 3, 2002, Features sec.: 10.

Reeves, Richard. "Patriotism Calls Out the Censor." *New York Times* Oct. 1, 2001: A23.

Roberts, Roxanne. "Hollywood's 21-Gun Salute, Washington Brass Help Trumpet 'Black Hawk Down.'" *Washington Post* Jan. 16, 2002: C1.

Schickel, Richard. "Soldiers on the Screen: An Unsparing Portrait of Men under Fire." *Time* Dec. 17, 2001: 74+.

Sony Pictures. *Panic Room: Production Information.* Press kit. Los Angeles. 2002.

Turan, Kenneth. "Perspective: A Fearful Sum Recalculated." June 23, 2002. Calendarlive on latimes.com. Aug. 15, 2002 <http://events.calendarlive.com/top/1,1419,L-LATimes-Movies-X!ArticleDetail-63577,00.html>.

Urbina, Ian. "Why Black Hawks Go Down." Feb. 2002. Middle East Research and Information Project. Aug. 15, 2002 <http://www.merip.org/newspaper_opeds/IA-Black_Hawks_Go_Down.html>

Warner Brothers. *Collateral Damage: Production Information.* Press kit. Los Angeles. 2002.

12

Survivors in *The West Wing*
9/11 and the United States of Emergency

Isabelle Freda

> Ours is indeed an age of extremity. For we live under continual threat of two equally fearful, but seemingly opposed, destinies: unremitting banality and inconceivable terror.
> —*Susan Sontag, "The Imagination of Disaster"*

Visual culture, the cinema in particular, has always served as a template on which collective experience and its invariably distorted representation are inscribed. Screen memories, however fantastic, continue to speak to our present predicament, that posture which Susan Sontag has called "the imagination of disaster": Sontag's insights into the interplay of cinema, politics, and the spectator in the face of terror are of great interest today, almost forty years later, as we consider what "terror" is.

The effects arising from the terror of 9/11 reverberated across multiple and overlapping realms of cultural and political memory in film, politics, and the news media. This chapter pursues one aspect of this interplay of visual and political culture by investigating the cinematic outlines of political narration, particularly the thematic and structural intersection of spectatorship and presidential leadership as it was constituted through the narration of the post-9/11 war on terrorism, or the "state of emergency." Slavoj Zizek, with characteristic speed and precision, observed only days after the attacks that they had punctured a *Truman Show*–like sphere of American irreality. In this

1998 film, Jim Carrey stars as Truman Burbank, a man living his entire life in a small California town called Seahaven. His life is as idyllic as campaign advertisements and commercials are: picket fences, friendly neighbors, a decent but boring job. Unbeknownst to Truman, however, his entire life is actually a television show, and outside the painted horizon lies the "real" world of the television studio. The story entails his eventual realization that his entire world is what, in *The Matrix* (2000), was so aptly called "the desert of the real." Nine-eleven was, in part, such a shock because of the force with which it brought death—*American* mortality—into the carefully guarded world of American irreality, one policed by a commodified news media.[1] The attacks seemed to invert outside and inside, "them" and "us," or fiction and reality, providing a potent site of (potential and actual) destabilization of what we might call "American spectatorship."

The world turned upside down by 9/11 had its political parallel in the near-hallucinatory transformation of the president into a popular, decisive, wartime leader. This essay examines representative moments of this interplay between the "new" reality of death that emerged suddenly from 'off-screen space'—that space outside the norm—and its mass-cultural and political context. One way to contextualize this off-screen space is to examine the manner in which the terror of 9/11 reverberates with that *other* crisis of mortality, that other death that had the power to reach American shores: the nuclear bomb exploded over the city of Hiroshima in 1945. This "event" has been repressed, but it has never stopped unfolding, as the amnesia that elides or displaces its referent testifies to the extremity of its traumatic truth.

"Nine-eleven" is not merely a date, nor is it an event with stable parameters; it is, rather, fully mediated through experiential frames of mass culture and politics, and carries with it a history even as it is framed as absolutely unique—a framing that is itself historically and ideologically intelligible. Its "origin" and visual center are the destruction of the World Trade Center towers in Manhattan and its massive, and immediate human toll, an event that seemed to be absolutely singular in its horror—"nothing like this had ever happened before"—

and uncannily familiar: it was, many also said, "like a movie." It was not only like the disaster movies of recent memory in the "American" cinema but also like those of the 1950s. This genealogical proximity exceeds the thematic parallels that connect them—both groups of films convey disaster—to include their role in comprising a part of the broader spectacular horizon, one that functioned to mask the terror that was their referent, with political consequences and effects. As Sontag found a positive complicity between the films and the abhorrent truth they masked, so also the clichéd and reductive narration of 9/11 reproduced a defensive jettisoning of terror to an absolute outside along with its resulting emotional and identificatory effect of political paralysis.

Nine-eleven also names the spectacular memorialization that emerged in the wake of the day's horrors, a narration of unity that appeared to address the traumatic rupture in the horizon of the American "norm" but actually extended its effects in a refoundation and expansion of the "state of emergency" that has characterized the nation's military and political posture in the postwar period. The centrality of the president within this scenario is superficially one of reassurance, a generic presidential posture that is exacerbated in times of crisis and grounded in a hyperbolic delineation of psychological and geographical boundaries. The paternal-patriarchal resonance of this stance and its enfeebling consequences were central components of the spectacle of national unity, the effort to sustain and extend what Zizek calls American "irreality." This fiction of protection and safety is perfectly literalized in the fantasy of a workable space shield that will form an umbrella over American soil, protecting it from nuclear danger, as well as the president's repeated belief that the attacks of 9/11 proved the viability and the need for this system. We see here the power of this image and the related power of the president to deploy it effectively.

Nine-eleven first emerged in a stutter of repetition across the nation's television sets, images in search of a coherent narrative arc. The framing devices that were quickly brought to bear on this event brought it into alignment with well-worn paths of historical narration: patriotism, unity, a wartime president—or "commander in chief"—leading the nation in a just cause, invocations of past wars, particularly World War II, so thoroughly embalmed by official and unofficial narratives. The special broadcast of *The West Wing* on October 3, 2001, revealed the breadth and speed of the radical new political-media orientation after 9/11 and is an exemplary guide to the production of political spectacle in its aftermath.

Beginning with its most narrow referential scope, this episode nicely literalized the spin that had been put out in response to questions regarding the president's whereabouts during the day of the attacks. Bush was in Florida on that morning and had been immediately flown across the country from air base to air base before finally returning to Washington in the evening. The public was assured that the president had been a "viable target" and that the White House had been the actual destination of the plane that crashed into the Pentagon. While we must ignore the obvious weakness of this claim in light of the president's actual whereabouts, it is nonetheless worth notice for the manner in which the president was constructed as a "survivor" himself. This episode of *The West Wing* superbly conveys this construction and, with it, the contours of the extratextual identificatory interplay operative between the president and the spectator in this process, an interplay of proximity and blindness in the careful transformation of the citizen to the position of survivor. As a survivor, the individual is well positioned to be solicited emotionally; as a survivor, she is assured but not shown the logic and details of the government's actions undertaken to protect her. The liminality of this position of "survivor" is a complex and vital location, a boundary governing psychic, emotional, and political identificatory stances.

Alan Sorkin's special episode was inserted into the prerecorded season lineup and so constituted a powerful and immediate expression of the impact of 9/11 as we might read it within the narrative framework of the more or less Clintonesque NBC White House. Indeed, this episode established the definitive closure to the Clinton era both on- and off-screen, as the previously liberal corridors of presidential power were transformed into a highly charged state of emergency in response to a threat on the president's life by terrorists. The show's narrative strategies encourage audience identification with the story's surrogate citizens, a multiethnic group of bright but docile honor students from around the country, caught in the middle of their tour by the Secret Service lockdown of the White House. They sit together as a literal audience in the White House kitchen and are subjected to a string of lectures about the delicate balance between civil liberties and the need to reduce their scope in the fight against terrorism, capped by a visit from the president himself. Crucially, they have no idea what is happening but understand that not knowing is in their best interest. While the television spectator identifies with these good-looking and smart students, they *also* enjoy the usual pleasures of spectatorial omniscience that *West Wing* uniquely provides, the intimate "access" to the Oval Office, not to mention the presidential bedroom. This essential identificatory structure is accomplished through editing, as it releases the spectator from the claustrophobic mise-en-scène through regular cutaways to the potential terrorist's interrogation and, crucially, to the president himself. The spectator, then, maintains a close identification with the president as well as the diegetic citizen-spectators. This episode allows us to ask, within its modest but dense textual frame, some of the larger questions that comprise the 9/11 problematic: for example, what dangers lie in this style of identification with power, and how is entrapment translated into "access" within it? How is ignorance translated into a kind of knowledge? How is isolation produced as "safety"?

The enlargement and transformation of presidential power and the passivity of the governmental and nongovernmental system of "checks and balances" were all striking effects of the attacks. About the time the special episode of *West Wing* aired, Senator Robert C. Byrd, the West Virginia Democrat and Constitutional expert who stands constant guard over Congressional prerogatives, stood in a nearly empty Senate chamber and observed that the Senate had too hastily dropped, without debate, a provision that would have limited President Bush's authority to conduct missile tests and then passed, again without debate, a use-of-force resolution giving him unfettered power to wage war. Noting that the rush by members of Congress to display unity in the face of terrorist aggression was understandable but mistaken, Senator Byrd warned that "a speedy response should not be used as an excuse to trample full and free debate" (Clymer). We might observe that Congress had adopted the posture of the docile high school students, cowed by the sense that the president had become invulnerable, even as their actions served to produce this. The elimination of political debate in Congress, now "united" behind the president, occurred in tandem with the same alignment in the public sphere and news media. What Toby Miller has described as the "emotionalization" of 9/11 disallowed analysis of foreign policy, religion, history, or the law in favor of stark apolitical oppositions and emotional reportage of the attacks and their effects (4). This was matched by a similarly apolitical, personal framing of George Bush and more talented surrogates such as Secretary of Defense Donald Rumsfeld, each of whom gained a largely emotional relation between his leadership and individual citizen-spectators.

The crisis here, the attacks of 9/11, functioned much like the fast-paced suspense narrative, and this dramatic spine on which action takes place enables what Arthur Schlesinger Jr. has diagnosed as the "imperial presidency," the broad expansion of presidential power because of the (perceived or actual) need for speedy and decisive action in the nation's defense. Civil liberties are the first to fall before this rush to relinquish responsibility to the chief executive and the military-security apparatus. The expansion of executive power after 9/11 repeated and intensified the pattern inaugurated during the Cold War, a war that, much like the one against terrorism, had no discernable spatial or temporal limits. Congressman Abraham Lincoln eloquently summarized the threat of presidential power in this regard: "to allow the president to invade a neighboring nation whenever *he* shall deem it necessary to repel an invasion . . . and you allow him to make war at pleasure. Study to see if you can fix *any limit* to his power in this respect." (qtd. in Schlesinger 42).

Wars—both hot and cold—are favored means through which crisis is extended. To perpetuate crisis is to sustain power. A brief consideration of *Leviathan* by seventeenth-century philosopher Thomas Hobbes is valuable in better understanding the interplay between the state of emergency and political leadership. The social contract described by Hobbes is one in which society elevates one entity above all others to provide for their common safety, and obedience to this ruler is ensured, in part, because the citizens' right to exercise power over life and death is relinquished at the same time. To confer such power on one individual—such as, in Hobbes's historical context, the absolute monarch—was meant to solve the threat of violence from within society (being murdered by one's fellow citizens for religious or other reasons) or from attack by forces without. Hobbes writes,

> The only way to erect such a common power as may be able to defend them from the invasion of foreigners and the injuries of one another . . . is to confer all their power and strength upon one man, or upon one assembly of men . . . which is as much to say, to appoint one man or assembly of men to bear their person. (Hobbes 132)

The metaphor of the nation-person has long been applied across diverse political and cultural systems. It indicates the manner in which the leader, in times of war—or internal crisis—may more easily take action outside the law as civic society defines it. It is okay to kill the enemy in times of war. It is also acceptable to kill one's citizens by sending them to battle. This logic must be extremely persuasive, and the viability of the political leader as a source of agency is crucial. "Though the modern democratic nation-state is not a monarchy, we have seen that we still metaphorically understand a nation as one person and this understanding structures much of our thought" (Rohrer 132). *Leviathan*—and its durability within the context of emergency—has interested thinkers of modern political history for the way it describes a shift *within* democratic regimes toward an increasing reliance on one sovereign figure to govern, or more precisely, on the concentration of power among a small elite. "The tradition of the oppressed," wrote Walter Benjamin sixty years ago, "teaches us that 'the state of emergency' in which we live is not the exception but the rule," an observation that remains compelling today (Benjamin 257). The postwar American president, beginning with Dwight D. Eisenhower, utilized both legs of Hobbes's contract in the institutionalization of the state of emergency: internally, subversives had to be guarded against, and thus a massive security apparatus was imposed; externally, the nuclear standoff paralyzed political agency except as conducted within the context of superpower relations. The violence of the Cold War, exported in the name of a global state of emergency, is what many outside the U.S. believed was "returned" during 9/11, rupturing the sphere of irreality that comprised its norm and sustained its sense of innocence. Yet this violence always *already* had a powerful distorting effect on the American polity, as democracy was increasingly staged as spectacle, and the national security state rendered the temporary conditions of wartime permanent. The Leviathan had come to stay, and did so astride the atomic Bomb.

Writing in the early 1950s, with World War II's political and aesthetic dimensions still fresh in mind, Philip Rieff cast a steady, critical eye across the sociopolitical landscape of Eisenhower's America and diagnosed a critical illness in the American polity, what he described as a loss of an end beyond the political. In Rieff's terms, the "visual-aesthetic realm" overtook the "discursive realm," with grave consequence to the health of the nation. The decimation of the political sphere took place along intersecting pathways of advertising, television, and the ideological conformity that characterized Cold War culture. Of particular interest to this discussion is Rieff's critique of the insidious effect of the demand for national unity, which he describes as an empty call to conformity. Unity, which might be necessary during moments of crisis as a call for short-term collective action, should never be institutionalized. This institutionalization of crisis became the Cold War, and its politics was that of enforced consensus through political persecution and governmental-military secrecy—and an aestheticized, spectacularized politics. The state of emergency was conveyed in its disaster films by mutating insects and monsters, loss of agency and emotion, and impending global destruction. Its identificatory political locus, the benign patriarch Dwight Eisenhower, was transformed into a commodity emptied of content: "I Like Ike." It is a profound interpenetration of the commodity and the spectacle that has marked American political identity, not an incidental one, as it colonizes language and communicability itself. "It is precisely the emptying of discursive values and their replacement by aesthetic that is one of the chief problems of our time," Rieff wrote. "The aesthetics of rhetoric is largely displaced by the aesthetics of spectacle as a general device of political unification" (Rieff 480).

The spectacle of national unity quickly congealed the linguistic-visual frame of reference that comprised the 9/11 horizon, accomplished through the unprecedented coherence of official and unofficial discourse and imagery. Thousands of American flags appeared in the streets, store windows, and cars; the television networks quickly hardened the tag lines promoting their news programs, as "America under Attack" changed to "America's New War" and "America Rising," and television anchors abandoned any attempt to appear objective, fearful of being attacked as unpatriotic. In a remarkable interview given by Dan Rather in April 2002 to the progressive, anti-Bush British newspaper the *Guardian,* he condemned the American censorship of information about the "war on terrorism" and the military attack on Afghanistan, describing the post-9/11 national spectacle as "patriotism run amok." Rather warned that the freedom of American journalists to ask tough questions was in jeopardy and admitted that he had shrunk from taking on the Bush administration in the war against Afghanistan, wearing his flag pin in "total solidarity with the American cause" (Engel).

Although the media's lock-step alignment with official discourse after 9/11 was, as Rather so strikingly indicates, unprecedented in its depth and breadth, its role as passive conduit of official discourse does have precedent, most notably in what Mark Hertzgaard has described as the "palace court press" that capitulated to the demands of the photo-op during the Reagan administration in the 1980s, and the decline has only accelerated since then. Reporters have noted that the Bush administration was more obsessed with controlling information than any other, and this situation became even more extreme after 9/11. Like those classic Hollywood film stars protected by a tight public relations apparatus seamlessly linked to the media, the leading figures in the Bush administration offered constant "access" within a very tightly controlled environment. After 9/11, Bush emerged from the half-light of his carefully sheltered presidency to a regime of full exposure, attending innumerable events commemorating 9/11 and the war that had been declared in its name. Exactly one month after the attacks, he held his first prime-time press conference, an event discussed with much excitement but little substance in the press. David Jackson of CNN told his audience, for example, that the press conference was held in prime time because "aides felt like Mr. Bush was ready to go on prime time, that he was ready for his first prime time news conference." When asked how he thought the president had changed since Sept. 11, he noted that the president's hair had gotten grayer, that he had become more somber and serious, that he was "almost single-mindedly focused on a nearly incomprehensible terrorist attack." The audience presumably sympathized with the weight of this task, which nicely complemented the graying hair. In Hollywood, this strategy protected stars from scrutiny by offering a convincing simulation of "straight" domestic life; in Washington, the strategy offers a convincing simulation of a working democracy. The staging of the Leviathan through a centralized and commodified media can be usefully understood as the design of modern spectacle within the context of American postwar culture and the state of emergency that undergirds it.

Donald Pease has analyzed what he terms "post-national spectacles" in a way that sheds additional light on this dialectical movement of aesthetics and politics in the construction of political spectacle within a world forever on the edge of nuclear devastation. Pease explains that the "end of the world" Cold War scenario enabled U.S. citizens to reexperience everyday doubts, confusions, conflicts, and contradictions as the Cold War's power to convert indeterminacy into an overdetermined opposition, a kind of knowledge, but of the crudest dimensions: them-us; patriot-subversive; American-commie, and so on. When this paradigm failed, that is, when the individual experienced doubt, it then manifested the Cold War spectacle, in which doubt itself was a threat to national security. Once doubt—political discourse and dialogue—is eliminated from the public sphere, it becomes irreparably depoliticized (Pease 566). This depoliticization occurs through the language of inclusion and exclusion, the inscription of an absolute outside for the Other. Yet the postnational spectacle is precisely the troubling of the clarity of this opposition, as the individual is forced to shift borders within her- or himself to sustain the link to national identity and thus, presumably, safety. The border, as Etienne Balibar has elaborated in his analysis of the impact of globalization on the traditional nation-state, is a sign of both internal and external division (Balibar 76). The potential inversion of identificatory stability produces a danger that one might, at any moment, end up "outside" the community of patriots. The crucial function of spectacle in this sense is to maintain a misalignment to real conditions; here, in the deflection of political engagement to a depoliticized identificatory stance *as* patriotism and as national identity.

If we again consider the spectator who was addressed in the aftermath of 9/11, it is notable that visual drama was invoked as an experiential frame of reference in initial efforts to contextualize 9/11's meaning. Neil Gabler in the *New York Times,* for example, observed that the hijackers were "not only creating terror" but "were [also] creating images" (Johnson). The American spectator was, it appeared, on the wrong side of the camera, as images of violence no longer seemed to be contained within a recognizable narrative frame and therefore had an unusually strong (and potentially destabilizing) impact. Cinematic analogies emerged in the mass media as commentators struggled to find a way to describe what had occurred, often focusing on its similarity to disaster blockbusters such as *Independence Day* (1996) and *Deep Impact* (1998), films awash in large-scale spectacular—and digitized—destruction of buildings, cities, and the earth itself. As a group, they conveyed an eerie mixture of messages and themes: first, that of strong leadership—the combat president of *Independence Day* standing in "victory" amidst the smoldering ruins of what *was* the United States or, at the other end of the spectrum, the nihilistic passivity of *Deep Impact,* as the world waits to be destroyed by forces outside any human intervention. The films conveyed disaster with an uncanny combination of distance and proximity, unimaginable yet also somehow deeply familiar.

The uncanny effect is, Freud tells us, produced by "effacing the distinction between imagination and reality, such as when something that we had hitherto regarded as imaginary appears before us in reality" (Freud 398). The World Trade Center's destruction powerfully recalled images of a cinematic disaster and devastation that had, however, always happened "elsewhere," in and through the multivalent imaginary of the cinema or in the news framed by the television screen; it was always in another place, another country, or another time. It was as if something—something terrible—lay just on the other side of the image of the World Trade Center's destruction, a troubling of reference, a destabilization of official histories. The ill-fitting analogy of Pearl Harbor becomes intelligible as a response to this interpretive destabilization and rupture, as World War II has been successfully memorialized as the "good war," a triumph of historical narration as amnesia. One history of the uncanny oscillation evident in the 1990s disaster film extends back along a generic arc to the science fiction disaster film of the 1950s. This interplay between the Cold War and the "war on terrorism" is also evident in the arc of presidential power as it hyperbolically developed in the nuclear age, and the corresponding numbness of society to its true dimensions. The disaster films that splashed their digitized destruction across cinema screens in the 1990s are, in this light, productively set alongside those disaster films described by Sontag. Sontag's analysis of the disaster film illuminated the manner in which the spectator withdrew in numbness from the yawning abyss of the crisis that lay at the very heart of the Cold War, the nuclear bomb. The explosion of the atomic bomb above the city of Hiroshima in 1945 was, Sontag writes,

> the trauma suffered by everyone in the middle of the twentieth century when it became clear that, from now on to the end of human history, every person would spend his individual life under the threat not only of individual death, which is certain, but of something almost insupportable psychologically—collective incineration and extinction which could come at any time, virtually without warning. (Sontag 224)

This referent, and its political frame, is still with us, comprising the underbelly to 9/11, its flip side, its off-screen resonance. While everywhere people felt that "everything had changed," this sense of a break was far in excess of the attacks, as horrible and deadly as they were. The nuclear referent threatens the well-patrolled boundaries of official discourse: between citizen and enemy, war and peace, danger and safety, inside and outside, and, of course, across all of this, competence and incompetence in the political leader assigned the responsibility of wielding weapons of mass destruction. The unleashing of this referent by the attacks of 9/11 was evidenced, in part, in its redeployment by the administration, as they warned of new nuclear attacks by terrorists or, in the summer of 2002, by Iraq.

The disaster films of the 1950s were, in Sontag's words, "above all the emblem of an *inadequate* response," normalizing what was psychologically unbearable (Sontag 224–25). Cliché and naïveté together served to dampen the sense of otherness—of radical fear—with a spurious familiarity, thereby eliciting passivity and withdrawal rather than (fearful) resistance and demands for change. This *other* meaning of the 1990s disaster film—still accomplishing the same effect as its Cold War generic predecessors—must be read in tandem with this *other* meaning of 9/11, part of a profound continuum whereby the spectacular state, like the films analyzed by Sontag, sustains an attitude of amnesia-driven paralysis in the face of the nuclear threat it actively controls.

Borders are important in the analysis of 9/11's impact, particularly the intersection of concrete and symbolic boundaries, representation and its referential stability. The ease with which the terrorists crossed the physical border of the country was inversely matched by the density of the symbolic-political boundary erected by official discourse in response. The massive rhetorical reinscription of the national border, of a coherent and localized national identity (as solid and as simulated as that horizon that comprised Jim Carey's universe) can be considered as a recognizable and preexisting symptom of globalization, dramatically intensified in the aftermath of 9/11. This reinscription occurred through various devices: the omnipresent flags with inarticulate but forceful slogans such as "United We Stand;" the invocation of World War II paradigms for the attack (and the response); and, finally, the starkly drawn centrality of the president in all of this.

The legitimization of the president was one of the spectacular effects of 9/11, as his approval rating rose by 35 percent within the first month (Dunham). Bush's new persona was as artificial as his old one, not only because of the self-consciously Reaganesque management and control of his public exposure but also because of the generic sense in which presidential agency is *always* a construct. In general, the term *leader* evokes an ideal type that presidents try to construct themselves to fit, and in this sense leadership is dramaturgy; it is also in this sense that we can understand how the Leviathan exceeds the individual occupant's strengths or weaknesses. Murray Edelman has superbly analyzed the tendency by the public to confuse incumbency with leadership, which is particularly the case with the president in times of war. It is difficult in modern politics to discern the relation between an incumbent's actions and their effects, an observation even more potent in the face of official efforts to keep information secret. "The clue to what is politically effective is to be found not so much in verifiable good or bad effects flowing from political acts," he writes, "as in whether the incumbent can continue indefinitely to convey an impression of knowing what is to be done" (Edelman 76–77). This is different, notes Edelman, from Max Weber's famous distinction between bureaucratic and charismatic leadership. What is involved in this "leadership" is dependent not on determinable results but on mass assurance; nor does it rely, as with the charismatic leader, on extraordinary personal qualities, demonstrable successes, or the dramatic smashing routines in order to display genius. "It depends rather upon the impossibility of demonstrating success or failure, a disinclination to rock the boat, and the disposition of alienated masses to project their psychic needs upon incumbents of high office" (Edelman 77). The desire to attach trust in a leader is partly informed by the sense of despair over changing conditions of existence, what Erich Fromm so perfectly called the "escape from freedom." This is also an escape from the difficult, and necessary, task of exercising one's franchise within a democracy.

Bush's status was transformed by and through the crisis he was now called upon to respond to. On December 26, 2001, ABC's *Good Morning America* featured a "hard" news segment reviewing the president's first year in office. In a strikingly representative echo of the 9/11 *West Wing* episode, the president's transformation is authorized by former Clinton press secretary George Stephanopoulos during a conversation with Claire Shipman:

> *Stephanopoulos:* Claire, so many people have said the president seems a changed man. You have spoken to the president. Does he feel he's changed?
>
> *Shipman:* Interesting question. George W. Bush, as you know, is not a man or a president prone to much self-analysis. But friends say that he does believe 9/11 changed not only the country but him, and it's handed him his life's calling. So what we see on the outside is a more serious leader, and aides describe behind the scenes a remarkable certainty with almost a religious tone in his belief that fighting terrorism is his life's work. (ABC)

Bush's new stature after 9/11 was enabled by the "state of emergency" produced by the attacks, and the border between inside and outside became that much more porous at precisely the same moment that it seemed to be reinforced: the deeply inscribed outline of Bush's identity was interlaced with that of the spectator, now given privileged "access" as an American, united with, yet radically excluded from, the workings of power. We learn of personal beliefs and appearance but nothing of the working of government.

Michael Rogin's concept of the "covert spectacle" provides one final perspective of the spectacular interplay of spectatorship and political knowledge. "The spectacular relation to political life," writes Rogin, "has implications for democratic governance. Spectators gain vicarious participation in a narrative that, in the name of national security, justifies their exclusion from information and decision making" (519). The series of actions taken by the U.S. government after 9/11 testify to the intensification of the mutually supportive interrelation of secrecy and spectacle in American politics. Analyzing the systematic lying that formed the core of the Reagan administration's illegal covert operations and subsequent cover-up in "Contragate," Rogin delineates an important dimension of spectatorial identification that has become part of the displacement of politics in the postwar period, especially after 9/11. He argues that if the spectator accepts *not* having access to the truth of their government's actions, then she will be drawn that much more strongly to an emotional identification with the state, which has "become the single anchor in the midst of the shifting realities it displayed." A case in point is the secretary of defense, the most visible member of the administration after the president. Donald Rumsfeld has been described by CNN as a "rock star," and the conservative Fox network called him the "babe-magnet for the seventy-year-old set" (Kalb par. 13). Rumsfeld's frequent press briefings are a central component in the maintenance of a high wall of secrecy regarding the government's actions: the war in Afghanistan, the development (and anticipated use) of nuclear weapons, planned attacks on other states (Iraq)—all of these things are inaccessible to the citizen-spectator, even as they are given "access" to the star players. As Walter Cronkite so devastatingly observed in a C-Span interview in April 2002, we have no war reporters and we have no independent record of the war in Afghanistan (nor did we in the Gulf War). As a consequence, we have lost our ability to exercise our democratic franchise intelligently: the American people, he said, are operating in the dark.

"Political infantilization" has as its corollary "presidential intimacy," the strategies that replace the political with the personal (Rogin 519–20). If this process is successful (and it usually is, particularly the more dangerous the crisis is), then the citizen-spectator identifies with the state as trustworthy in a *general sense* (and without, significantly, any alternative sources of information in the media) and through an emotional bond with the president. It is in this way that the violence he authorizes is rendered benign and the citizen ignorant but complicit. The spectator, then, "knows" that she is on "the right side," that she can trust the actors in a drama that is always only given through carefully calibrated photo opportunities and star discourse: "access" as withdrawal, a star-based official aesthetics. Thus the border between the outside and the inside is perforated or torn as a founding distortion of the Cold War, as it institutionalized temporary and ad hoc strategies of disinformation and secrecy.

In this perspective, the manner in which the U.S. citizen-spectator is "protected" from violence—and, well, unpleasantness—is *also* part of the same process through which she is prevented from apprehending the actions of her own government and their effects on others and on herself. That is, the state, claiming the necessity of secrecy, also, of course, must lie. The lie, in the interests of "national security" and particularly during war, is in the first instance directed toward the enemy. Yet there is no *other* place where reality is stabilized for the domestic citizen-spectator without, that is, an aggressive media to provide a contestatory and investigative role in democratic governance; there is, then, no "outside" to the spectacle designed for the enemy. One holds a position "inside" only through an identificatory desire that is emotionally solicited and maintained by official discourse centered on the figure of the president. The opaque divide displayed in *The Truman Show* is not necessarily, or not only, a powerful image of the blindness of the American populace to the outside world. It is *also* between the populace and its representatives.

Note

1. See also Borjesson; Gitlin.

Works Cited

ABC. *Good Morning America*. "Looking Back at George W. Bush's First Year in Office." George Stephanopoulos and Claire Shipman, coanchors. 12/26/01.

Balibar, Etienne. "World Borders, Political Borders." *PMLA* 117.1 (2002): 71–78.

Benjamin, Walter. "Theses on the Philosophy of History." *Illuminations.* Ed. Hannah Arendt. Trans. Harry Zohn. New York: Schocken, 1989: 253–64.

Borjesson, Krina, ed. *Into the Buzzsaw: Leading Journalists Expose the Myth of a Free Press.* New York: Prometheus, 2002.

Clymer, Adam. "Senator Byrd Scolds Colleagues for Lack of Debate after Attack." *New York Times* Oct. 2, 2001: A16.

Cronkite, Walter. *Interview with Walter Cronkite: Ernie Pyle and War Reporting.* C-Span. Apr. 10, 2002.

Dunham, Richard S. "The Tricky Business of Being Mr. Popularity." *Business Week* Dec. 10, 2001: 34.

Edelman, Murray. *Constructing the Political Spectacle.* Chicago: Chicago UP, 1988.

Engel, Mathew. "US Media Cowed by Patriotic Fever, Says CBS Star." *Guardian.* May 17, 2002. May 18, 2002 <http://www.guardian.co.uk>.

Freud, Sigmund. "The Uncanny." *Collected Papers.* Vol. 4. Trans. Joan Riviere. New York: Basic, 1959: 368–406.

Fromm, Erich. *Escape from Freedom.* New York: Holt, 1995.

Gitlin, Todd. *Media Unlimited: How the Torrent of Images and Sounds Overwhelms Our Lives.* New York: Metropolitan, 2002.

Hertzgaard, Mark. *On Bended Knee: The Press and the Reagan Presidency.* New York: Farrar, 1988.

Hobbes, Thomas. *Leviathan.* 1651. New York: Collier, 1962.

Jackson, David. *President Bush's Prime-Time Press Conference.* CNN. Oct. 12, 2001. May 14, 2002 <http://www.cnn.com/2001/community/12/12/02.gen.jackson>.

Johnson, Brian D. "In the Wake of Sept. 11, Hollywood Steps Away from Apocalyptic Porn." *Maclean's* Oct. 1, 2001: 80.

Kalb, Marvin. "Interview with Donald Rumsfeld." *The Kalb Report: Journalism at the Crossroads.* Apr. 10, 2002. May 15, 2002 <http://www.defenselink.mil/news/Apr2002/t04102002.t0410sd.html>.

Miller, Toby. "September 2001." *Television and New Media* 3.1 (2002): 3–5.

Pease, Donald E. "Hiroshima, the Vietnam Veterans War Memorial, and the Gulf War." *Cultures of United States Imperialism.* Ed. Amy Kaplan and Donald E. Pease. Durham, NC: Duke UP, 1993: 557–80.

Rieff, Philip. "Aesthetic Functions in Modern Politics." *World Politics* 5.4 (1953): 478–502.

Rogin, Michael. "Make My Day! Spectacle as Amnesia in Imperial Politics [and] The Sequel." *Cultures of United States Imperialism.* Ed. Amy Kaplan and Donald E. Pease. Durham, NC: Duke UP, 1993. 499–534.

Rohrer, Tim. "The Metaphorical Logic of (Political) Rape: The New Wor(l)d Order." *Metaphor and Symbolic Activity* 10.2 (1995): 115–37.

Schlesinger, Arthur, Jr. *The Imperial Presidency.* Boston: Houghton, 1974.

Sontag, Susan. "The Imagination of Disaster." *Against Interpretation.* New York: Dell, 1966. 209–25.

Zizek, Slavoj. "Welcome to the Desert of the Real." Sept. 15, 2001. Sept. 21, 2001 <web.mit.edu/cms/reconstructions/interpretations/desertreal.html>.

CONTRIBUTORS
INDEX

Contributors

Rebecca Bell-Metereau teaches film at Southwest Texas State University and directs the interdisciplinary media studies program. She was the recipient of a Fulbright scholarship to study media in Senegal (1999–2000). Her publications include *Hollywood Androgyny* (2nd ed.), *Simone Weil on Politics, Religion, and Society,* and articles in *College English, Journal of Popular Film and Television,* and *Cinema Journal.*

Mikita Brottman is the author of a number of books on the horror film and is the editor of *Car Crash Culture* (2001). She is a professor of literature at Maryland Institute College of Art and has published essays in *New Literary History, Film Quarterly, Cineaction, Biography, Chronicle of Higher Education,* and elsewhere.

Wheeler Winston Dixon is the James Ryan Endowed Professor of Film Studies and a professor of English at the University of Nebraska, Lincoln; the editor for the Cultural Studies in Cinema/Video series published by the State University of New York Press; and the editor in chief of the *Quarterly Review of Film and Video.* His latest books are *The Second Century of Cinema: The Past and Future of the Moving Image* (2000), *Film Genre 2000: New Critical Essays* (2000), *Collected Interviews: Voices from Twentieth-Century Cinema* (2001), *Straight: Constructions of Heterosexuality in the Cinema,* and *The Experimental Film Reader,* coedited with Gwendolyn Foster.

Isabelle Freda received her Ph.D. from New York University and is currently researching the international political and social reception of George W. Bush, especially in Germany. She has taught film history and criticism at Middlebury College and NYU in Berlin, among other institutions.

Ina Rae Hark is a professor of English and the director of the film studies program at the University of South Carolina. She has edited *Screening the Male, The Road Movie Book,* and *Exhibition, the Film Reader.* Her most recent work has appeared in *Film History, Quarterly Review of Film and Video,* and the collections *Adaptations, Hitchcock Centenary Essays, Key Frames,* and *Sugar and Spice: Cinemas of Girlhood.*

Marcia Landy is a distinguished service professor with a secondary appointment in French and Italian at the University of Pittsburgh. Her latest books are *Italian Cinema* (2000) and *The Historical Film History and Memory in Media* (2000).

Jonathan Markovitz is a lecturer in the Department of Sociology at the University of California, San Diego, where he received his Ph.D. in 1999. He has published articles on film, race relations in the United States, collective memory, gender, and popular culture. His forthcoming book is entitled *Legacies of Lynching: Collective Memory, Metaphor, and Racial Formation.*

Philip Mosley is the author of *Split Screen: Belgian Cinema and Cultural Identity* (2001). He teaches literature and film studies at Penn State University–Worthington Scranton.

Murray Pomerance is the chair and a professor in the Department of Sociology at Ryerson University. He is the author, editor, or coeditor of numerous volumes, including *Enfant Terrible! Jerry Lewis in American Film* (forthcoming) and *Ladies and Gentlemen, Boys and Girls: Gender in Film at the End of the Twentieth Century.* He is at work on an anthology about evil in cinema, entitled "Bad: Infamy, Darkness, Evil, and Slime on Screen."

Steven Jay Schneider is a Ph.D. candidate in philosophy at Harvard University and in cinema studies at New York University's Tisch School of the Arts. His essays appear or are forthcoming in such journals as *Cineaction, Film and Philosophy, Post Script, Journal of Popular Film and Television, Kinema, Scope,* and *Hitchcock Annual* and in such anthologies as *British Horror Cinema* and *Car Crash Culture.* He is the coeditor of forthcoming collections: *Horror International* and *Understanding Film Genres.*

David Sterritt is a film critic for the *Christian Science Monitor* and a professor of theater and film at Long Island University. He also teaches at Columbia University and is the author or editor of books about Jean-Luc Godard, Alfred Hitchcock, Robert Altman, and the Beat Generation.

Juan A. Suárez teaches American studies at the University of Murcia, Spain. He is the author of *Bike Boys, Drag Queens, and Superstars: Avant-Garde, Mass Culture, and Gay Identities in the 1960s Underground Cinema* (1996). His most recent articles have appeared in *New Literary History* and *Journal of American Studies*.

Index